Mrs. Freddie Lamb
152 Clarendon Circle
Danville, Va.

IN RESPONSE TO GOD

IN
RESPONSE
TO GOD

HOW CHRISTIANS
MAKE ETHICAL DECISIONS

BY ISABEL ROGERS

THE COVENANT LIFE CURRICULUM

PUBLISHED BY THE CLC PRESS • RICHMOND, VIRGINIA

THE COVENANT LIFE CURRICULUM

the authorized curriculum
of the following denominations

ASSOCIATE REFORMED PRESBYTERIAN CHURCH
CUMBERLAND PRESBYTERIAN CHURCH
MORAVIAN CHURCH IN AMERICA
PRESBYTERIAN CHURCH IN THE UNITED STATES
REFORMED CHURCH IN AMERICA

affiliated denomination

THE EVANGELICAL COVENANT CHURCH OF AMERICA

© M. E. Bratcher 1969
Printed in the United States of America
First Printing 1969
51—8080

Preface

THE COVENANT LIFE CURRICULUM starts with the fact of revelation. It is based on the conviction that God has made himself known to man in Jesus Christ. It has its roots in the Presbyterian and Reformed tradition with strong emphasis on the centrality of Jesus Christ as the source of the life of the church. It offers the Bible, the Church, and the Christian Life as three areas of study through which the living Lord may continue to confront men today. It is made available to the church in the hope that God will bless it, and in the prayer that through it the faith of our fathers will come alive in the life of each succeeding generation.

Contents

How does a Christian make ethical decisions?
How does he decide what is right for him to do?
There is no way to avoid acting
and acting requires

in response to God

making multitudinous decisions every day.

Making ethical decisions is not always simple.
We face conflicting obligations and responsibilities.
We face problems for which there is no clear-cut rule
and no completely satisfactory answer.
Sometimes the making of moral choices seems to us

like threading an obscure way through
a labyrinth.

We must act in response to what is going on,
to what is happening at this juncture of history,
to what God is doing in our lives and in our day.

God
is always
at work
in our midst,
creating sparrows
and clothing lilies,
giving sight to the blind
and hearing to the deaf,
and healing the sick.

We do not make ethical decisions
in an isolation booth
but in the midst of the swirling
interactions of group life.

We are free and responsible selves—
free not to do just any old thing we
but free to act within the situation where
There will be consequences of what we do,
and we must take responsibility for

please

we find ourselves.

those consequences.

God addresses
his people,
and
they
must reply,
in trust or
distrust,
in
obedience
or rebellion.

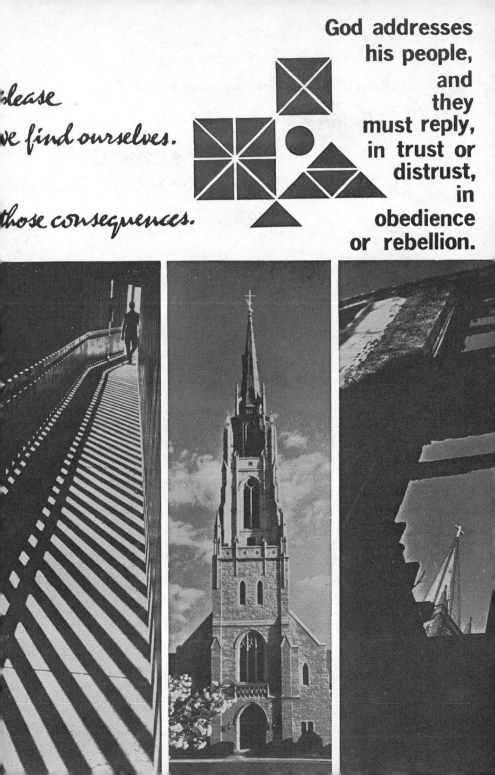

Decision-making is never ended—
there are always new situations,
new problems.
It is rare that we can face today's situation
with yesterday's decision.

We live our lives in the midst of action
and interaction.
We must be constantly seeking to make
the fitting response.

in response to God

PROLOGUE

CHAPTER 1

The Complexity of Ethical Decisions

How does a Christian make ethical decisions? How does he decide what is *right* for him to do? There is no way to avoid acting, and acting requires making multitudinous decisions every day. From regulating the children's TV-watching to casting a ballot for President, we are constantly making decisions, trying to do what we believe to be right and to avoid doing what seems to us wrong.

We who are called by the name of Christian seek to be obedient to God, but how are we to know the will of God in the particular circumstances of our lives? The laws of the Bible, we say; but those laws must be applied, and situations differ. Pray for guidance, we say; but how can we be sure that this insight which has come to us in prayer is really *God* speaking, and not just our own desires?

The disturbing thing about deciding what is the right thing to do is that two sincere, devout Christians can read the Bible, can pray earnestly, yet come out with opposite conclusions! Take, for instance, our nation's efforts to eradicate poverty. Some honest Christians, after prayerful study, have come to believe that in compassion our society ought to try to lift the poor out of their poverty: train them for jobs, help them to find jobs, provide them with opportunities to attain a place of dignity in society. Other Christians, equally honest, after equally prayerful study, conclude that compassion *precludes* lifting the poor out of their poverty; it is better in the long run for them to lift themselves. God intends for us to be responsible and mature; to do things *for* people is an invasion of their dignity and selfhood.

What shall we say to each other where we thus disagree? Can both be right? On what grounds shall we make our moral choices?

In the study on which we are embarking this year we will be tackling just such questions as those. None of us has a perfect understanding of the will of God, but how can we sharpen our understanding and deepen it?

TO GET US STARTED: TWO FAMILY DECISIONS

Here are two situations which Christian adults sometimes have to face. The first is not an earthshaking crisis; it is doubtful that family relationships will be permanently shattered, whatever Jim and Sue decide about their vacation. The second is far more serious, for the whole life of a young boy and girl—and of an unborn child—will be determined by what they do now. In both situations, however, a decision has to be made, an action taken.

Think through these problems for yourself and be prepared to discuss them with your study group when you meet. What sort of decision would you make if *you* were in that situation? How would being a Christian affect your decision?

Note that these situations are presented here simply to start your thinking about the decision-making process. As you work through these two particular problems, you may become aware of the complexity so often involved in making choices, whether those choices are great turning points or simply the routine decisions of every day.

If you were Jim or Sue, or Ed or Jane, what would you do?

Little League and a Family Vacation

Jim shrugged his shoulders. "We can't do it. Not time enough."

"But we don't do much together, as a family, Jim. It would be so great to hike around in the mountains, and George and Susan could wade in the creeks, and. . . ."

"George would sulk the whole time; he'd want to be home with his team, Sue."

His wife made a face. "Why do they have to schedule little league playoffs right when families want to take vacations? Why do they even have to *have* playoffs?"

"Well, it's hard on us, but if George is going to make the all-star team, he has to play with the Wolves all the way through." He paused. "And the kids need to learn about competition. They'll be facing it soon enough in the world."

"OK, but doesn't he have to learn to adjust to other people, too? His family, for instance? Does he own our family calendar? Is it good for *everything* to revolve around him?"

"Well, golly, I wonder what we ought to do. . . ."

What should these parents do?

Ask yourself these questions:

1. Assuming that all-star status means a great deal to George, would his parents be selfish if they insisted on the family trip? Won't there be other summers for trips to the mountains?

2. On the other hand, are they encouraging him in selfishness if he comes to assume that he can manipulate the calendar of the rest of the family to adjust to *his* wants? Is this the occasion for teaching him to give up something for the pleasure of others?

3. Assuming that Jim and Sue are committed Christians, what difference will their faith make as they face this decision?

Christian Families and an Unwanted Pregnancy

Jane Johnson's heart was clutched when she asked Ed about his talk with young Ted. An hour they'd been closeted, after dinner, and since then Ed's face had been grave. Now, in the privacy of bedtime, they could talk.

"Ted's in trouble. Bad trouble."

Jane's heart clutched tighter. "What's happened?"

Ed could not look at his wife. "It's Louise. She's pregnant."

"*Pregnant.* Not—you mean—not *Ted?* I mean, that's—and just 12th-grade kids. Pregnant?"

"Pregnant."

"But—not Ted. I mean—Ted's not interested in Louise."

"May not be. I guess Louise is more interested than he is. But there it is, Jane."

"What happened?"

"It was the night of the prom." Ed had trouble framing his words. "They'd necked some on dates, but nothing serious. That's the . . . that's the pattern, he says; everybody does it. All the gang. The night of the prom, back in April. They double-dated, you remember; the all-night party. . . . Did we do wrong, letting him go to that? But he's 17—we couldn't have stopped him. Well, the other couple left 'em, and on the way back to The Cave for breakfast, they stopped, and—and—parked. And—well—that's it."

"We should never have let Ted go to that party."

"But he's 17."

"It was Louise's fault, Ed, I know it was. Ted wouldn't . . . well, Ted just *wouldn't.*"

"Well, he's man enough to say it was his fault, too. Poor fellow. I guess—I guess we should have realized he was depressed when he didn't get his first choice in college. He's only a boy, and . . ."

"Ed, maybe some of it's our fault. Have we pushed? I mean, Tom and Elsie are so great, and we thought it would be *perfect* if Ted got together with their Louise. Did we push?"

"Well, growing up together and all, and with all of us in the same church, it *did* seem right natural. . . . I know I'd sort of assumed . . ."

"Ed, how could this happen to—us—*Christians?*"

"I don't know, Jane, I don't know. But it *has.* What'll we do? What'll we do?"

What Should These Parents Do?

Ask yourself these questions:

1. What are the possibilities open to these parents?
   a. Insist that Ted marry Louise
   b. Advise that Louise go off somewhere to have the illegitimate child and:
      put the child up for adoption (note that chances are less and less promising for this)
      have the child placed in an orphanage
      keep the child herself
   c. Advise Louise to seek a legal abortion:
      in this country on grounds of health
      in another country: Puerto Rico? Japan? Switzerland?
   d. Other possibilities

2. What are some of the problems involved in each course of action?
   a. What chances does a marriage have if it is forced by this kind of situation? Could this create tensions later? A sense of having been "trapped" into something?
   b. What chance does a child have in life if he grows up in an institution? or with an unmarried mother?
   c. Should Louise's parents go into debt to raise money to send her to Japan or wherever? What share should the Johnsons take in whatever financial burden is involved?
   d. How can the young people be required to take responsibility for the consequences without making them suffer a lifetime for what they have done?

3. Where can these parents find help in their decision?
   a. How would the Bible help them in making their decision? the Golden Rule? the Sermon on the Mount? the Ten Commandments?
   b. What help can they find in the understandings of God and man in Christian theology?
   c. On what grounds should they make their decision? Which decision would be best?

CHAPTER 2

Decisions
in Response to God

Making ethical decisions is not always simple. Jim and Sue must consider not only the welfare of the family as a group, but also George's individuality within the family. When those obligations conflict, how do you choose between them? Jane and Ed must help their children face possible options, each of which involves risk and hurt. When no course of action is really satisfactory, how do you choose among them?

Our choices are often like that. We, too, face conflicting obligations and responsibilities. We, too, face problems for which there is no clear-cut rule and no completely satisfactory answer. How do we decide which candidate to vote for, how severely to discipline our children, whether or not to move to another job—when no candidate, no parent, no job is perfect? Sometimes the making of moral choices seems to us like threading an obscure way through a labyrinth.

What shall we do? H. Richard Niebuhr has observed that our forefathers and contemporaries have approached this question in three different ways.

Some Christians have approached the question in terms of the ends, the objectives, the purposes for which we exist. Why are we here? these people ask. What is the purpose for which we live? What is the ideal we are called upon to realize? What is the chief end of man?

Those who raise the question in this way often speak of the Christian responsibility as that of "bringing in the kingdom" or of "furthering the work of the kingdom" or of "realizing the fatherhood of God and the brotherhood of man." They begin with some ideal, some vision of the way things ought to be, some great objective which they have in mind, and they see their responsibility as realizing this ideal, fulfilling this vision, achieving this objective. Thus, they pray, "Thy kingdom come" and look forward to and work for the time when the kingdoms of this world shall become the kingdom of our Lord Jesus Christ. They hear the Sermon on the Mount as a description of the good and faithful life, and try to shape their existence in light of this ideal. Or they catch a vision of the unity of mankind in Jesus Christ and try to realize, make concrete, this vision in living out their life with others.

A second group of Christians approach the question, What shall we do? not in terms of the ends or purposes for which we exist, but in terms of the laws, the commandments, the mandates under which we live. What is our duty? It is not to realize some future goal. It is to obey the commandments of God. "He has showed you, O man, what is good," these people say, quoting Micah, "and what does the LORD require of you but to do justice, and to love kindness, and to walk humbly with your God?" (Micah 6:8)

There is, in this second group of Christians, a profound sense of the immediacy and inescapable clarity of God's claims. What does God want us to do? The word has been given: "You shall love the Lord your God with all your heart, and with all your soul, and with all your mind." This is the great and first commandment. And a second is like it, "You shall love your neighbor as yourself." Or again this: "Let him deny himself and take up his cross and follow me." Or again: "Go therefore and make disciples of all nations." In whatever way obedience to these commandments may take shape in any particular situation, the ultimate responsibility of the Christian is clear: he is to obey the law of the Lord to whom he belongs.

There is yet a third approach to the question, What shall we do? Here we begin not with great ideals to be realized nor with basic commandments to be obeyed, but with the living situation in which we find ourselves and the active Lord who confronts us here and now. What we are called upon to do, in any situation in which we find ourselves, is to make the appropriate response to what is going on. And because we, as Christians, believe that God is active in everything that happens, our basic responsibility is to respond faithfully in every situation to what God is doing in our midst.

Now, I have no desire to try to prove the superiority of one approach over the other, but I do want to confess my own preference for this third way of arriving at ethical decisions. And I believe that this third approach provides a more complete, if not wholly adequate, key to understanding the Biblical approach itself. Look, for example, at the prophet Amos.

Amos is speaking, of course, to a whole nation, not just to individual Jims and Sues or Janes and Eds who face decisions related to their own particular families. Yet what he says to a whole covenant people holds true for us as individual Christians: the decisions we make and the actions we take should be in response to the God at work among us—to what he has done and is doing in our midst.

We will study three passages in which Amos proclaims to Israel God's ways of working among men. Then, looking toward a way of making our own ethical decisions, we will see what conclusions we might draw from these things Amos has said.

Study this thoroughly for yourself, and be prepared to discuss it with your Covenant Life Curriculum class.

A PROPHET'S APPROACH TO ETHICS

The Message of Amos

Recall the situation in the Northern Kingdom of Israel when Amos comes to them warning of disaster. All seems peaceful and

secure under the rule of Jeroboam II—in the middle of the eighth
century B.C. The nation knows the satisfactions of military triumph,
and the whole country basks in the warm glow of prosperity. They
are God's chosen people: their God will protect them, will vindicate
them against all their enemies in that great day of the Lord which
is coming soon. They've got it made!

To these complacent people comes the meddling shepherd
from Judah. "The LORD roars from Zion," Amos says (1:2), and
any shepherd knows what that means: when the lion roars he is
about to leap on his prey. God is about to act in judgment; and it
is Israel who is to be punished—punished for their callous indifference to the poor in their midst; punished for the bribery which has
perverted their justice. Behind that facade of prosperity and peace
lurks the ugly reality of corruption and injustice, and their God
cannot let this go unpunished.

Amos must warn these people of impending doom, whether
they like it or not, for he knows this God he's talking about. He is
a God of active love, of love at work in history. He cares—cares
deeply—how men treat each other, and he acts in events to call
them to the righteousness he intends for them. When men respond
in unrighteousness rather than in righteousness, God's love must
act in punishment. This is what is about to happen to Israel.

So Amos warns, "The LORD roars from Zion." A desert man,
who is accustomed to looking behind a shadow or a noise to discover its cause, Amos looks at the ominous shadow on Israel's
horizon and discerns what is happening. The imperial power of
Assyria is moving in the east; this will be God's instrument for dis-
ciplining his people. There is rottenness beneath the prosperous
surface of Israelite society, and punishment will come through the
armies of Assyria. The lion is about to spring.

That is the burden of Amos's message. God is here in our
midst, he is saying, working out his purposes through the things
that are happening, calling us to the response of obedience. God is
speaking through events, for those who have ears to hear. If the
people will repent, suggests Amos, the approaching disaster may
be averted (5:14–15). "The Lion has roared; who will not fear?"
(3:8)

What the Shepherd Heard: A Study of Amos 2:6—3:15

Read 3:1–2; 2:9–11—God's goodness to Israel.
Note what God has done for the Israelites.

1. They are "known" by God.
   For the Hebrews, "knowing" involves more than the intellectual process, "knowing about." It refers to intimate association, to being in close personal relationship with another person. Amos is saying here that God has chosen to bind himself to Israel in a special way, a way in which he is not related to other peoples.

   Why the "therefore" here? What is the connection between being intimately related to God and being punished by him? What would the Israelites perhaps have *expected* Amos to say following the "therefore"? What conclusions might they have drawn from the idea of chosen-ness? What conclusions does Amos draw? Read Luke 12:41–48. How does 48b relate to what Amos is saying here? What does all this say about the severity of Judgment upon the lives of us who know—and are "known" by—God in Jesus Christ?

2. They are *cared for* by God.
   What has God done for the Israelites? Why is the deliverance from Egypt so important in their history? What does it reveal about God's relationship to Israel?

   Note the use of the pronoun "I": "*I* destroyed the Amorite," "*I* brought you up out of the land of Egypt." This is not just the mechanical operating of blind law; God is directly and personally involved in what is happening to his people. Amos is pointing out what God *has* done for his people in the past, suggesting indirectly what he *can* and *will* do for them now if they will be loyal and obedient.

Read 2:6–8, 12. Israel's response to God's goodness.
Note how Israel has fallen short of God's intention for them.

1. God's intention—holiness. Read Leviticus 19:2; 20:7.

2. Israel's failure in responsibility
   In what ways has Israel failed to embody God's holiness in her
   society? What kinds of things are the Israelites doing? How
   have the people received the Nazirites and the prophets? What
   is the significance of offering wine to Nazirites? What attitude
   toward the prophets do you find here and elsewhere? (compare Amos 7:12–13; Jeremiah 26:23–24; Matthew 5:12; 23:
   30–35)

Read Amos 3:9–15; 2:13–15. God's punishment of Israel.

1. God's use of pagan nations
   What connection does the God of Israel have with Assyria and
   Egypt? (compare Amos 1:3—2:3)

2. Destruction by Assyria
   What does Amos mean in his figure of speech in 3:12? What
   does he mean by "a cart full of sheaves," in 2:13? Will anyone be able to escape the coming disaster?

Amos Could Hear Because He Listened

Amos could not help being a prophet of doom, for he preached
a God who is both righteous and sovereign. He is the God who
holds all history in his hands and can work through the things that
happen to call men to justice and mercy. He is the "I" who is there
in events: "I brought you up out of the land of Egypt," "I destroyed the Amorite before them."

But when men refuse to be just and merciful, then the "I" who
is there in events is there in judgment and discipline. The people
of Israel have rebelled against God; "therefore I will punish you
for all your iniquities." And in his judgments he is free to use any
nation.

In Isaiah 10 God says, "Ah, Assyria, the rod of my anger, the
staff of my fury! Against a godless nation I send him, and against
the people of my wrath I command him." And in Jeremiah 27: "It

is I who by my great power and my outstretched arm have made
the earth . . . and I give it to whomever it seems right to me. Now
I have given all these lands into the hand of Nebuchadnezzar, the
king of Babylon, my servant." The prophets all agreed: the Assyrian or the Babylonian, caring not at all for the Hebrew God
Yahweh, could become the very instrument of Yahweh's will, for
Yahweh is Lord of history.

In the ominous advance of Assyria Amos could hear the Lord
roaring from Zion—could hear because he was on the alert, attuned
to God's presence in events. "Listen," he was saying in 3:3–8, "listen attentively and you will discern what is happening." When two
men are walking together in the desert, it cannot be by chance;
there must have been an appointment. When a lion roars, he must
be leaping on his prey. When the trumpet sounds, a city is being
attacked. When Assyrian armies march, God is moving in judgment. Listen, for God is at work in our day. "The lion has roared;
who will not fear?"

OUR RESPONSE TO GOD

Response in the Situation

What was Amos doing? Well, he was not primarily trying to
convince the Israelites that they ought to follow certain laws and
principles of behavior. Rather, he was urgently pointing out to them
what God was doing and how they ought to respond to him. Yahweh was a God who *had done* things in Israel's past and *was doing*
things in Amos' time. And the people had answered his actions
with actions of their own—sometimes with loyalty and obedience,
more often with distrust and rebellion. When they acted in rebellion against Yahweh's will, then he in turn replied to *their* action
with further action: judgment and discipline, or mercy and redemption—or both; for God's judgment has always been discipline
for the sake of redemption. Amos was urging these people to answer God not with rebellion but with the kind of actions that fulfill
his intention for their human life together.

What Amos was describing was a sort of *dialogue with God:*
God acts, man replies to God's action, God replies to man's reply,

and so on, in the kind of constant interaction that characterizes any personal relationship. Amos and all the prophets proclaimed a God who was doing things, and through the things that happened called men to do things in reply, to live every day in obedience and righteousness.

Turn to the New Testament and you hear Jesus saying the same sort of thing. God is always at work in our midst, creating sparrows and clothing lilies, giving sight to the blind and hearing to the deaf, and healing the sick. Our task is to respond in every situation as unto him. To the God who sends rain on just and unjust—a God of overflowing generosity—we are to respond by being generous and loving ourselves, to just and to unjust, to outcasts and prostitutes as well as to "good" people.

You can see in Jesus' own life this kind of response. As he acted in reply to what human beings did, he was at the same time acting always in reply to God's action. The Judas who betrayed him, the Pilate who sentenced him—in these Jesus could see the God who wills the salvation of all mankind; he "reads these signs . . . as words in a divine sentence."[1] God was working even through betrayal and death to bring healing and redemption to men, and Jesus responded with the utter surrender of himself.

The fact is that the whole of Biblical ethics can be interpreted as a call to respond to what God is doing, and this can be a helpful pattern for us as we ask about our own decision-making. It is the ethical approach associated with the name of the late H. Richard Niebuhr, one of the great teachers of ethics in our day, and it will be the approach followed in this book.[2] For this writer believes that as we make ethical decisions, it is not so much that we sit down quietly by a fork in the road and ponder by what law or by what principle we shall decide which road to take. Rather, it is that we act in response to what is going on, to what someone else has done, to what is happening at this juncture of history, to what God is doing in our lives and in our day.

The life we live is a life of constant interaction with other persons, and our moral decisions are to a great extent responsive actions. This means for one thing that we cannot always work out rigidly in advance just what we ought to do in every conceivable situation; there is a quality of newness and of uniqueness in each situation which means that many decisions cannot be completely worked out beforehand. It means also that the process of decision-making is never ended; we cannot settle down complacently with this decision we have made, for life moves on: new situations develop, new problems present themselves, and it is rare that we can face today's situation with yesterday's decision. We live our lives in the midst of action and interaction, and we must be constantly seeking to make the fitting response.

It is the firm conviction of the Biblical writers, however, that we are never dealing with human beings only; God is in every situation, and he calls us to respond to *him*. Our dialogue is with men, but not with men alone; most importantly, the dialogue of our lives must be with God.

As Christians, the privilege is ours to learn with Amos to listen, to hear what God is saying through the events of our day, and so to discover what the proper response should be. We can surely hear him, for instance, in the racial revolution of our time, speaking in judgment upon us for our past sins and speaking redemptively in new opportunities for genuine brotherhood. We can hear him in the family tensions of our homes, judging our selfishnesses and providing new opportunities for forgiving love.

"Listen," said Amos, "listen attentively, for God is at work in our day. The lion has roared; who will not fear?"

The Elements in Response

God speaks through the things that happen and calls us to response. Fundamentally, then, our actions are *answering* actions; they are responses to what has been and is being done. For the Christian, to do the right thing is to respond in the right way to what God is doing. Making ethical decisions is not so much a matter of comtemplating ideals in some abstract sense as it is *acting*— acting in the midst of the things that are happening. It is seeking to give the fitting response to what is happening around us, and especially to what *God* is doing. As Richard Niebuhr puts it, "God is acting in all actions upon you. So respond to all actions upon you as to respond to his action."[3]

There are three significant dimensions of this answering action. First, it is response to the meaning of what has been done. Our response depends on the way we *interpret* what is happening. Amos in 3:3–8 is talking about the *interpretation* of what is going on. The lion roars; the shepherd understands that the flock is in danger and acts to defend them. The trumpet blows; the people understand that the city is being attacked, and they spring to their posts. Use your discernment and see God at work, demands Amos. Understand what God has done and is doing, for only so can you respond fitly to his presence in your midst. It has been said that the Christian makes decisions with the Bible in one hand and the newspaper in the other. He must know and understand what is happening in order to reply properly to the God who is there in the situation before him.

The first major section of this year's study of ethics will deal with this matter of interpreting what is happening around us. We will be asking in Section I, How can we discern what God is doing, so that we can respond fittingly? We will talk about how God has acted in the past, in Jesus Christ; this will help us to recognize God at work in our times—a God who is the same yesterday, today, and forever. We will talk about the ways in which we directly seek his will for us in our day: through prayer, through the study of the Bible, through the worship and community life of the church. And we will inquire about how we can sharpen our understanding of the great public events of our time, in order to better understand what God is achieving through those events. We can respond appropriately to God's actions in our midst only if we have an understanding both of how God works and of what is actually happening. We must know how to interpret God's acts among us.

There is a second aspect of this answering action: we reply to God within a social context. It is in groups that God often confronts us. Amos addresses his sermons to *the people*. "For three transgressions *of Israel,* and for four," God will punish. "Hear this word . . . against the *whole family* which I brought up out of the land of Egypt." The nation is a family, and all are involved together in what happens. They know the joys of shared life and mutual help; they know also the sorrow of suffering for each other's

sins. And this is perennially true of human life. We help to form
each other's consciences, we suffer for the sins of others. We do
not make our ethical decisions in an isolation booth but in the
midst of the swirling interactions that constitute group life. And
though we must always act as persons, we never can act as isolated
individuals. *Christian ethics is personal but not individualistic.*

In Section II of our study, then, we will be talking about the
social context of our ethical decisions. We will talk about the way
we make decisions in church life, the give-and-take of it, the richness of continuing tensions and disagreements. We will study the
process of making decisions in our families, in the organized life of
work and business, in our political life. We will talk about the decisions forced on us by the population explosion and the increasing
urbanization of our life. We can respond fittingly to God's actions
in our midst only if we realize that we are never *merely* individuals;
only if we can learn the joy and responsibility of answering to God
in the midst of the groups in which it is our privilege to live.

*Acting in response to God has a third aspect: answering action
is accountable action.* There will be consequences of what we do,
and we must take responsibility for those consequences. We are
accountable on the human level, of course, but most importantly,
God holds us accountable to himself. "You only have I known,"
says Yahweh in Amos 3; "therefore I will punish you."

In Section III of our study—the final section—we will be dealing with some difficult questions regarding the extent of our accountability. We know that our freedom to respond to God is
somewhat limited; the molding power of social influences and the
continuing influence of our own self-centeredness hold us back from
making the fitting response to God. How free *are* we, then, to join
God in his work? And how can he really hold us accountable for
what we do?

We will be affirming in this last section that we are, indeed,
free and responsible selves—free not to do just any old thing we
please, but free to act *within the situation* where we find ourselves.
And as we decide and act in the midst of a sinful society, we cannot escape the reality of suffering, large or small—"the fellowship
of Christ's suffering," as Paul puts it. But through that very suffer-

ing we come to know more deeply than ever the power of the God who raised Christ from the dead and who raises us, too, to newness of life in our own day. Then we can know what it means as responsible selves to serve God, whom to serve is perfect freedom.

One of the bewildering problems of Christians in our day—or in any day—is the question of determining what we *ought* to do. How do Jane and Ed Johnson decide what they as Ted's parents must do? We have already seen that there are different approaches to ethics and that ethical thinkers do not agree on which is the best. How do any of us decide what is right to do in our own situation? In this study on which we are embarked we will be exploring one way in which Christians can make ethical decisions, seing how an understanding of the meaning of response to God can help us to know what we must do in obedience.

"Hear, O Israel!" This is one of the most characteristic phrases of the Old Testament. God addresses his people, and they must reply, in trust or distrust, obedience or rebellion. We must learn to listen to God in our time, that we may make the fitting response.

SECTION I

HOW CAN WE DISCERN WHAT GOD IS DOING?

This book is about how Christians determine right from wrong. We have said that our ethical decisions constitute a sort of dialogue with God; we act in response to what he has done and is doing. Out of the complexities of our concrete situation, whoever we may be—the perplexed parent, the confused businessman, the concerned teacher—we attempt to respond to the work God is doing in our midst: this is the Christian ethics of response. To do the right thing is to respond rightly to what God is doing.

Our response, however, is always to the *meaning* of what is happening, as we understand it. The way we will reply to God depends on how we interpret the signs of the times. And how shall we discern God's action? We Christians have not been handed some precise calendar of events, telling us what God will do on November 5, 1969. Nor have we been given a precise rule book, telling us what *we* must do on November 5, 1969. God does not deliver us from the complexities and ambiguities of our particular situations. We have to face up to the responsibility of real decision.

We are not, however, left without guidance. There are some clues to what God is up to, and in this section we will be studying some of these clues and pointers. Our response is to *interpreted* action; how, then, can we properly discern and interpret God's acts among us? We find the key to understanding what God is doing today by looking at what he did in Jesus Christ. God has given us such helps in knowing right from wrong as the Bible, the church, and prayer. The next few chapters of this book are about how these help us know what God is doing and what we ought to do.

CHAPTER 3

God's Mighty Acts in Jesus Christ

We will not respond fittingly unless we can interpret rightly. And we will not interpret rightly unless we understand God's overarching purposes in history. The man who knows something of what God is *always* doing will have a good indication of what he is doing *now*.

The Christian church has always believed that the great climactic clue to what God is doing in history can be found in Jesus Christ. In Christ—his life, his death, his resurrection—we meet the one decisive moment which illuminates the whole sweep of God's work in human life. In the light of what God did in Christ we can look at what is happening in any period and know something of what to expect of God.

How shall we respond to God? Let us look at God's mighty acts in Jesus Christ—*incarnation, crucifixion,* and *resurrection*—to see how these help us to understand the direction and content of our own response. The Christian is called to join God as he acts in these three ways.

I. INCARNATION

The God Who Reveals Himself in a Human Life

The early Christians did not sit in comfortable armchairs and idly think up a doctrine of the incarnation as a parlor game for intellectuals. They were *driven* to affirm the fact of the incarnation by what had happened in their midst. A man had lived a life among them, a life of such dazzling purity and love that they had no choice but to say, "Surely this was God himself."

They knew full well that he was a man like themselves; they had been with him, had seen him tired and hungry and sleepy. The truth of his humanity was too plain to be doubted. But there was more to this life; there was a divine quality here. Moreover, they knew that through him they had come to know release from the power of sin and a new power to be God's children in the fullest sense. This was clearly something no human being could do; only God could reconcile men to himself.

What else, then, were they to say? This was man *and* God, they said. *"Incarnatus est,"* the church was to say it later, in the Nicene Creed; God was incarnate in Jesus Christ.

In the study of *Christian Doctrine,* many of us explored what the church means by that affirmation. Dr. Guthrie suggested to us that the doctrine of the incarnation points to the "exaltation" of man and the "humiliation" of God. First, God exalts humanity. The story of Christmas tells us that God made himself known as a *man.* and thus manifested his approval of human life. What God wills is not that we men escape from our human existence into some sort of "spiritual" realm, but that we live our humanity fully and thankfully, that we be authentic human beings. Thus God supports every movement, religious or secular, which is helping to make human life more fully human. "For in Jesus God took up the cause of men in order to judge, help and renew *human* beings."[1]

Second, the doctrine of the incarnation points to the "humiliation" of God. God is not too holy or too good to involve himself in human affairs. As a matter of fact, the very way in which he *expresses* his goodness and holiness is by identifying himself with sinful men in a sinful world. This means that he does not remain aloof in heaven, calling us to come apart from our human existence if we would serve him; rather he is at work in our world, calling us to join him.

> Whoever will have God only in heaven, or in church, or in religious affairs, or where there is success and happiness, whoever will not look for him or accept him in the everyday world, among ordinary men, participating in secular human affairs, present also in human struggle and failure—that man will never know God at all.[2]

This means for us in the church that if we would discern what God is doing, we must look for him in the world, wherever men are being made human. God is not limited to some "spiritual" realm; he works through the material and the mundane to achieve his purposes. God stoops, says Paul in Philippians 2. Christ washes his disciples' feet, says the writer of John 13. God "is not afraid of getting His hands dirty if dirty hands are the way to salvation for His people."[3]

Our Response to the Incarnate God

If we are to respond to God, it is to *that* kind of God we must respond—a God who affirms human life and identifies himself with it.

First, for us, as Christians, this means that *we can affirm life and celebrate its goodness.* "All things were made through him, and without him was not anything made that was made." (John 1:3) An ancient churchman put it this way: "Whatever is, is good." He did not mean that whatever is, is right—for the natural goodness of the created order is distorted and corrupted by sin. He did mean that because "all things were made through him" we can rejoice in this created world and appreciate its rich diversity. The incarnation teaches us to love the world without worshiping it and to enjoy the goodness of life without making it our final goal.

It means for us, also, that *there can be no final division between "sacred" and "secular."* When we draw that kind of distinction, we are often assuming that our response to God can be limited to the sacred part of life and that reasonable service to him means working in the church, and only that—teaching a class, singing in the choir, serving on committees, or whatever. But this would be to deny the incarnate God whom we seek to serve. The God who condescended to share the fullness of human life does not call men *out* of that life into a spiritual otherworldliness; he calls them, rather, to serve him in the world where they are—and to find God himself beside them in their service.

". . . there are few more dangerous words than 'Spiritual' "[4] once observed George MacLeod, of the Iona Community in Scotland. For we can let ourselves become so absorbed in the spiritual things that we forget about our responsibilities among men in the world, and the spiritual can become an escape. But if we are acting in response to God, we can know that he is an *incarnate* God, and that there is nothing so humble or dirty that it is outside the pale of his concern. There can be no final distinction between sacred and secular, and we must respond to God with concern for *all* of life.

Thirdly, the fact of the incarnation means for us Christians that *God is a seeking God, who comes where men are* to call them to fellowship with himself. God does not sit back and wait for men to come to him, to "discover" him in mystic vision or philosophical speculation. He goes out actively to find men and to bring them into his family. In like manner, Jesus lived his life, not withdrawn in the sanctuary of a religious organization, but right in the midst of the world, where men were—men who needed forgiveness and healing and love.

In response to that kind of God, we too must go seeking, where men are. Too many of us in the church have lost this awareness of the meaning of the incarnation. Too often we have been content to stay within our church buildings and minister only to those who came our way, content to focus on the private world of the saints—leisure time, family problems, the ups and downs of prices. What we have done, one writer suggests, is to make religion

tion" of God. God is not too holy or too good to involve himself in human affairs. As a matter of fact, the very way in which he *expresses* his goodness and holiness is by identifying himself with sinful men in a sinful world. This means that he does not remain aloof in heaven, calling us to come apart from our human existence if we would serve him; rather he is at work in our world, calling us to join him.

> Whoever will have God only in heaven, or in church, or in religious affairs, or where there is success and happiness, whoever will not look for him or accept him in the everyday world, among ordinary men, participating in secular human affairs, present also in human struggle and failure—that man will never know God at all.[2]

This means for us in the church that if we would discern what God is doing, we must look for him in the world, wherever men are being made human. God is not limited to some "spiritual" realm; he works through the material and the mundane to achieve his purposes. God stoops, says Paul in Philippians 2. Christ washes his disciples' feet, says the writer of John 13. God "is not afraid of getting His hands dirty if dirty hands are the way to salvation for His people."[3]

Our Response to the Incarnate God

If we are to respond to God, it is to *that* kind of God we must respond—a God who affirms human life and identifies himself with it.

First, for us, as Christians, this means that *we can affirm life and celebrate its goodness.* "All things were made through him, and without him was not anything made that was made." (John 1:3) An ancient churchman put it this way: "Whatever is, is good." He did not mean that whatever is, is right—for the natural goodness of the created order is distorted and corrupted by sin. He did mean that because "all things were made through him" we can rejoice in this created world and appreciate its rich diversity. The incarnation teaches us to love the world without worshiping it and to enjoy the goodness of life without making it our final goal.

It means for us, also, that *there can be no final division between "sacred" and "secular."* When we draw that kind of distinction, we are often assuming that our response to God can be limited to the sacred part of life and that reasonable service to him means working in the church, and only that—teaching a class, singing in the choir, serving on committees, or whatever. But this would be to deny the incarnate God whom we seek to serve. The God who condescended to share the fullness of human life does not call men *out* of that life into a spiritual otherworldliness; he calls them, rather, to serve him in the world where they are—and to find God himself beside them in their service.

". . . there are few more dangerous words than 'Spiritual' "[4] once observed George MacLeod, of the Iona Community in Scotland. For we can let ourselves become so absorbed in the spiritual things that we forget about our responsibilities among men in the world, and the spiritual can become an escape. But if we are acting in response to God, we can know that he is an *incarnate* God, and that there is nothing so humble or dirty that it is outside the pale of his concern. There can be no final distinction between sacred and secular, and we must respond to God with concern for *all* of life.

Thirdly, the fact of the incarnation means for us Christians that *God is a seeking God, who comes where men are* to call them to fellowship with himself. God does not sit back and wait for men to come to him, to "discover" him in mystic vision or philosophical speculation. He goes out actively to find men and to bring them into his family. In like manner, Jesus lived his life, not withdrawn in the sanctuary of a religious organization, but right in the midst of the world, where men were—men who needed forgiveness and healing and love.

In response to that kind of God, we too must go seeking, where men are. Too many of us in the church have lost this awareness of the meaning of the incarnation. Too often we have been content to stay within our church buildings and minister only to those who came our way, content to focus on the private world of the saints—leisure time, family problems, the ups and downs of prices. What we have done, one writer suggests, is to make religion "into one of the twenty-two sections of *Time* magazine and generally unrelated to the most vital areas of human life."[5] We have not allowed our faith in God to send us out seeking, out into life where the people are.

If, however, we are to respond to an incarnate God, we must do it by living in the midst of the world and fully sharing its life. Faith in this God who gets his hands dirty cannot be a completely mystical and other-worldly faith; it is a down-to-earth faith, concerned with the mundane realities of every day. We serve a God who himself lives and works and speaks in the world; in response to that kind of God, we Christians are to give ourselves to that world, which Christ came to save.

2. CRUCIFIXION

The God Who Gives Himself in Suffering Love

"I decided to know nothing among you except Jesus Christ and him crucified" (1 Cor. 2:2), said Paul, for in Christ crucified we know the fullness of the power of God and the wisdom of God. Paul believed that the cross is absolutely central to our faith and that without it we would have a woefully twisted notion of God's relation to men. So if we are concerned to understand the way God works in history, in order fitly to respond to him, we must look to the cross for what it says to us about God and about the love to which he calls us.

We ought to note that the cross does not stand by itself in our faith, for in a sense it was the inevitable outcome of the incarnation. Having involved himself in human life, God was willing to submit to whatever that involvement would bring in its train, including the suffering inflicted by men who could not bear his presence among them. In the crucifixion of Christ God showed his willingness to go to any lengths, pay any price, for the salvation of men.

Quite evident here in the cross is the incarnate character of God's work—the way in which divine and human, eternal and temporal, are inseparably intertwined. The crucifixion happened in history; real men hammered in the nails, a real man hung there and died. Yet God was also in that event. He was acting there as he always does, taking up what men do and weaving it into the pattern of his purpose. And this is why the church has never been willing to talk about the cross as merely a noble expression of human self-sacrifice. It *is* the utter self-giving of a man, yes; but beyond that it is the supreme vehicle of God's own self-giving.

Again we can look back to *Christian Doctrine* to recall what was said there about the cross (chapter 13). Dr. Guthrie suggested that in the cross we can see the *love* of God and the *wrath* which is an expression of that love. We see the love of God in that "while we were yet sinners Christ died for us." (Rom. 5:8) It is not that God waited for *us* to break down the barriers of rebellion we had erected against him; God cared so much for us that he himself did what was necessary to bring us back into fellowship with him. And he did this at great cost. His reconciling love, far from being a good-natured indulgence which winks at our rebellion with all its consequences in our lives, is, rather, the costly love which, while enacting his judgment, shares with us in the hurt of it.

It is costly love because the "wrath of God" is part of it; he will not let us get by with our sin. Dr. Guthrie pointed out that God cares enough to be hurt by what we do. He cannot bear to see us denying our own humanity—refusing to live the truly human life to which he calls us. So in the cross he stamps his divine No on our rebellion. In the cross he labels faithlessness as the folly it amounts to, exposes pride as the highway to destruction. And this awesome judgment is an expression of God's love. Not *in spite of* his love for us, but precisely *because of* his love for us, God judges, and his judgment is always a judgment for our good. "The cross of Christ 'for us' means that he judges and punishes *in order to help,* to put an end to the inhuman, self-destructive road we have chosen, and to set us on the right road again."[6]

Moreover, it is costly love because God takes upon himself and bears with and for us the consequences of our sin. We are speaking here of the deepest mystery of the Christian faith. The church has never been able to develop a universally acceptable interpretation of the meaning of this mystery. Nevertheless, the church has traditionally affirmed that at the very moment when sin was at its worst, God took that sin upon himself; at the precise instant when sin was ultimately judged, the Judge himself endured the judgment; at that exact time when our separation from God was greatest, God crossed over the gulf.

"God was in Christ, reconciling," said Paul. God was there in Christ's suffering on the cross, taking upon himself the consequences of our rebellion against him. And very early in the history of the church, Christians came to realize that they were called to share in this costly love, and called to be willing to suffer for their neighbors as God had suffered for *them*. "For to this you have been called," Peter wrote, "because Christ also suffered for you, leaving you an example, that you should follow in his steps." (1 Peter 2:21) The God who calls us to respond to him is a God of suffering love, and we are to be involved with him in that suffering.

Our Response to the God of the Cross

The cross was more than just a human event, we have said; it was at the same time an act of God. This means that in it we can discern something of what God is like and what he is up to in human history. As we seek to respond to this God in our own day, then, we can look to the cross for some clues to what he is doing among us.

One thing we see when we look at the cross is that this God of costly love is *a God who both judges and forgives.* Part of our response to that kind of God must be repentance, which is both a painful awareness of our own sin and a profound determination to "turn around." Had Jesus been crucified by "bad guys" those of us who are "good guys" could escape the judgment of the crucifixion. But it was precisely the "good guys" who put Jesus to death. It is a sobering thought—and one we should never forget—that the religious leaders who engineered the crucifixion thought that they were doing the will of God. The cross compels us to realize that at any time, on any issue, even when we act with the very best of motives, we may well be dead wrong—and in our wrongness, help to crucify the sons of men.

Response to this judging and forgiving God also means acceptance—acceptance of his forgiveness and of ourselves as "forgiven." The ultimate word of the cross is not, "You are a sinner," but "You are forgiven." The cross stands in history as God's demonstration, to those with eyes of faith, that nothing we do can ever separate us from his love. He accepts even the unacceptable. He forgives even those who nailed his son to the tree. Now, to be forgiven is not to be spared all the consequences of our sin. Whatever a man—or nation—sows, that will he reap. The God who forgives remains the judge. But God's judgment is seen by the forgiven man as the chastisement of one who loves him. Out of the hurt of judgment God brings the healing of reconciliation.

Secondly, when we look at the cross we see that *God, who is love, identifies himself with those he cares for*. This is characteristic of love. Love refuses any privilege which would separate it from those loved; it bears any hardships which they have to bear. Moses asked to share his people's doom if they could not be forgiven. God gave himself freely in Christ to share the life of men. "There can be no doubt of a love which is willing to sit where others sit, and to suffer what others suffer, *yes, to offer itself* to do so."[7] It is this kind of love which we see on the cross. It is a God of this kind of love to whom we must respond in our own day.

This means that we are called to love and care for people in need, not in a distant and condescending way, but in genuine identification with them, sitting where they sit, suffering what they suffer.

During World War II a French girl took seriously the call to identify with suffering countrymen. In 1940 Madeleine Barot visited a Nazi concentration camp in France and was appalled at what she saw there. The prisoners desperately needed encouragement and support in their suffering, but it was obvious that only from inside the camp could this be effectively given. So she persuaded two other French girls to join her in voluntary imprisonment, the only avenue she could see for making direct contact with the prisoners who so desperately needed help. They lived there among the prisoners, sharing their tragic lot, helping to catch and to cook the rats they all ate, and trying to communicate to their wretched countrymen the love of a Christ who is Lord of both life and death.[8]

To respond to the God of the cross means to have the kind of love we can see in Madeleine Barot—love which identifies with those loved, identifies without holding anything back. We must be willing to share fully in the lives of other men, whatever suffering this may bring with it.

That points to the third thing we see in the cross: the God who suffered there in Jesus Christ is a God who continues to suffer because he identifies himself with men; *and he calls us to share in his suffering.* Christ has left us an example, Peter tells us (2:21), that we "should follow in his steps."

We often think of "following Christ" in terms of hearing his teachings, trying to live in his spirit, with his attitudes. This is part of it. But for the early disciples, to follow Christ meant more than that; it meant to keep company with him, to share in his lot. Luke tells us that Jesus invited his disciples to follow him by taking up a cross, and shortly thereafter "he set his face to go to Jerusalem." (Luke 9:23, 51) Those who would follow Jesus had to follow him to Calvary.

In Christ's sacrifice is the pattern for our own discipleship. This is what Peter is saying to suffering Christians in his first letter. This suffering is part of their Christian calling in the world. What else can one expect if he undertakes to follow Christ? "For to this you have been called," he says (2:21); so "rejoice in so far as you share Christ's sufferings, that you may also rejoice and be glad when his glory is revealed." (4:13) To share Christ's sufferings— that is the Christian's response to a suffering God.

But we are comfortable Christians, most of us; should we rush out deliberately to suffer? Not necessarily—though it may be true that we have not suffered because we have not been deeply obedient. The narrator in Hermann Hagedorn's poem "The Bomb That Fell on America" is confronted in the desert by a man on a cross. The man asks him, "You have never been crucified. Do you know why?" And the narrator replies, "I have never made people angry enough."[9]

Be that as it may, we can surely expect that our love for people will many times be rejected, and this is a part of the experience of the cross. George Webber, who has worked for years as a Protestant minister in Harlem, tells about the kind of suspicion and mistrust he often encounters. He seeks to minister to, say, a Puerto Rican in the slums, but he has to overcome that man's previous experience with white men. The Puerto Rican is an orderly in a hospital, where every day he is ordered around by white doctors and nurses and treated as though he were not a person but a thing. So when Webber offers him friendship and love, he meets only hostility and bitter rebuff. The Puerto Rican is calling the white man's bluff. "I must learn to expect that the way of the Cross will involve testing," comments Webber, "and seek in it whatever meaning God will grant."[10] Webber is speaking there of the experience of us all.

When in love I identify myself with the person in need—whether it be hunger or loneliness or anxiety or whatever—I have to face the possibility of rejection of my love. But love takes those consequences upon itself, making the guilt of the other its own.

It is perhaps something like this that Paul had in mind in his strange words to the Colossians. "I rejoice in my sufferings for your sake, and in my flesh I complete what is lacking in Christ's afflictions for the sake of his body." (Col. 1:24) He does not mean to suggest that Christ's passion is not final and perfect, as though there were something *we* could add to it or subtract from it. What he is saying is that Christ and the Christian are connected; we are incorporated into his life by faith and become his organs for working out his purpose in the world. He lives in us, and we share in his ministry of suffering for others. "It is one of the great principles of Christianity," said the great Frenchman, Pascal, "that all that happened to Jesus Christ must fulfil itself *in the spirit and body* of every Christian."[11]

> I listen to the agony of God—
>   I who am fed,
>   Who never yet went hungry for a day.
>   I see the dead—
>   The children starved for lack of bread—
>   I see, and try to pray.
>
> I listen to the agony of God—

I who am warm,
Who never yet have lacked a sheltering home.
In dull alarm
The dispossessed of hut and farm,
Aimless and "transient" roam.

.   .   .

I listen to the agony of God—
But know full well
That not until I share their bitter cry—
Earth's pain and hell—
Can God within my spirit dwell
To bring His kingdom nigh.[12]

3. RESURRECTION

The God Who Raises Christ from the Dead

For the New Testament, the crucifixion was not the last word; it was the resurrection that made the cross into victory, not defeat. Yet Christian thinking often stops with the cross. There are theologians who focus on the crucifixion, the atonement, as the payment of our debt, the revelation of God's love—and stop there. The danger is that they will let us assume that since the debt is paid, no more need happen. We will fail to move on to the newness of life which is ours in Christ. And even among Christians who emphasize the resurrection, it is often simply one fact among others in the story of Jesus, one article of belief among many—"the third day He rose again from the dead." It is important because it certifies the validity of the rest of the faith, and that's the extent of it.

For the early Christians, however, the resurrection was the most tremendous event of their lives. And it was an event of which they were not just spectators; they entered into it, they participated in it. At first they did not grasp the full theological import of what had happened, of course. They only knew at the time that he was alive and with them, and that his mission had not failed after all.

As they reflected on the fact of the resurrection, however, they were guided to understand something of what had happened. The word the New Testament writers used was not "rose" but "raised";

this was the greatest of all of God's mighty acts. The giving of life is quite clearly an act of creation; only the Creator, God, can do this. The church came to see the resurrection as an act of God's creative energy and—the joy of it!—an act in which the believer can become a participant. For the God who gave life anew to Jesus Christ can give life anew to the Christian who shares Christ's life. As Paul put it, "if any one is in Christ, he is a new creation." (2 Cor. 5:17) To come to know Christ—to be closely related to him, to be "in Christ"—is to be caught up in the great tide of God's creating power. It is to become a new creature, made anew.

It is this being caught up in the creating and re-creating energy of God which Paul has in mind when he talks about knowing Christ and the "power of his resurrection." (Phil. 3:10) In the risen Christ is the power to make us into new people—less intent on having our own way in the family, more willing to seek to give pleasure to the others; less intent on making the other fellow at work look small (so that we can look big), more eager to see that his morale is raised along with our own. And note that along with the "power of his resurrection" Paul hopes to know the fellowship of his suffering, for the two are inextricably linked together. The man who would be raised with Christ to newness of life must first be crucified with Christ. The old self must be put to death if the new self is to be raised up (Rom. 6:5–11).

Our Response to the Re-Creating God

The new life is Christ's risen life, made available to us by God through the Holy Spirit. To respond to that God, then, first of all is *to know Christ as alive and present in our midst today*—to know him and be changed by him, as were those first disciples in Galilee.

Those men who lived and worked closely with Jesus felt the tremendous impact of his life on theirs, changing them into new men. People came to see that they were different, for "they had been with Jesus." It was not overnight transformation—far from it. It took a while for the vacillating Peter to become The Rock. And it was not all sweetness and light, either—far from it. Jesus' demands were frightening: "If any man would come after me, let him deny himself and take up his cross and follow me." (Mark

8:34) Yet these men could not be with Jesus without being changed. They could not help coming to know in their own lives something of what it meant to love others as he had loved them.

Then came the ascension, which to all outward appearance was a "going away"; yet the disciples came to see it not as *losing* Christ but as the gateway to knowing him in a new way. Henceforth the relationship with Christ would not be limited to the small group with whom he could be physically present; the knowledge of God in Christ would be available to as many as would receive him. "It is better for you that I go away," Jesus said to them, "for I will return as the Counselor, the Holy Spirt. Henceforth I will dwell *within* your lives, and you will know me in a deeper, more vivid way than ever before. Your knowing me will no longer depend on my being physically present with you. Wherever you go, I will be with you." (See John 14:3, 16–17, 18–20; 15:26; 16:6–15, 16, 22.)

Christians down through the ages have testified that the living Christ has kept his promise. From Paul, who affirmed that "Christ lives in me," and Ignatius, who claimed to have Christ within his breast, to Dietrich Bonhoeffer in our own day—who knew the warmth of Christ's presence in a Nazi concentration camp—countless believers have confessed their faith in a living Christ at work in their lives. And not just famous martyrs, but plain people who have known the power of the risen Christ for living in the daily routine, bearing the frustrations and disappointments and failures that make up so many of our days.

Christ had promised that the grave could not hold him, that in the Counselor he would come back to live with his disciples. Today we can have that same assurance of his presence with us. And this is at least part of what we mean by the doctrine of the Holy Spirit. We can use all sorts of different words to express it—"the living Christ," "the Holy Spirit," "the inward presence of God." All these phrases point to the same reality: God in Christ is present and at work in our lives. As Rachel Henderlite has put it, "The Christian belief in the Holy Spirit is the belief that when we give ourselves to Christ, the divine life which was incarnate in Jesus of Nazareth becomes incarnate in ourselves."[13]

To respond to a re-creating God means, secondly, *to draw upon a new source of moral power*. Paul calls Christ "the last Adam," who became a "life-giving spirit" (1 Cor. 15:45). In Christ, he says to the Colossians, you "are sharing the miracle of rising again to new life—and all this because you have faith in the tremendous power of God, who raised Christ from the dead." (Col. 2:12)[14] Because of the presence of the living Christ, the Holy Spirit, we are enabled to rise to heights of loving obedience which we would never have thought possible.

Now, no one would contend that we are overnight made perfect, any more than Peter and Andrew and Matthew were. Impudent teen-agers will continue to aggravate even parents who know Christ; inconsiderate bosses will continue to make even Christian businessmen bite their tongues; swaggering bureaucrats will use their power to put plain citizens on the irritated defensive—even Christian citizens who are being made new creatures. "Not that I have already obtained this or am already perfect," said Paul, "but I press on." (See Phil. 3:12.) This is a *process* we are talking about, not a state of perfection.

The fact remains, however, that the Spirit of Christ can enable us not only to bear the irritations and aggravations but also to be concerned about the people who cause them. Christ can make parents more sensitive to what is happening in the lives of those aggravating teen-agers—the fact that they are trying to become unique persons in an age when people are often treated as just numbers in a computer's memory. Christ can make a businessman more sensitive to the boss's needs as a person—a person whose wife may be gravely ill and his own heart sick with dread. Christ can make us citizens more sensitive to the bureaucrat as a person with problems —a person who perhaps was pushed around as a child and now salves his ego by pushing other people around. There *is* power in the presence of Christ, not to remove the daily problems that are ours but to enable us to face them and live with them and genuinely care for the people who cause them.

The injunctions of the Sermon on the Mount are far beyond our power to obey. "If any one strikes you on the right cheek, turn to him the other also." "Love your enemies and pray for those who persecute you." Who of us can claim to have *that* kind of love for our neighbors? Dr. A. M. Hunter reminds us, however, that the Sermon on the Mount is addressed to believers, who can be presumed to have in their lives the empowering presence of the Holy Spirit. We must never forget, he says,

> . . . that the Sermon is an ethic for those who call Christ Lord and Saviour . . . we are not asked to scale the heights of the Sermon in our own unaided strength; we are offered the continuing presence, through the Spirit, of him who promised, 'Lo, I am with you alway.'[15]

The person who shares in Christ's crucifixion can be raised up a new creature; God gives him the power for living a new and different kind of life. "Praise God" cries out Paul—and we cry out with him—"who by the power at work within us is able to do far more abundantly than all that we ask or think." (Eph. 3:20) No wonder he exults as he prays for his friends, "that according to the riches of his glory he may grant you to be strengthened with might through his Spirit in the inner man, and that Christ may dwell in your hearts through faith." (Eph. 3:16–17) How can we who have at our disposal the infinite resources of the power of God do other than exult with Paul, and go off confidently to face the problems of every day?

Finally, to respond to the God of the resurrection is *to live in hope.* We serve God in an incredibly complex world, a world in which our efforts often meet with failure and frustration. We work for equality for black and white, but we face the intransigence of Black Power and White Backlash. We work to raise living standards in India or Chile, but population increases nullify all our efforts. We work to bring our children to chronological maturity, only to discover that spiritual maturity is as far away as ever.

Such frustrations are of the very fabric of the lives we live. But if we know the presence and power of the living Christ, we can live confidently, even joyously, in the midst of defeat and discouragement. For we have hope in the future consummation of God's kingdom, the expectation that God will fulfill in the future the promises he has made in the past. And we have hope in the present kingship of the Christ who is risen. He has been raised, says Paul, "far above all rule and authority and power and dominion, and above every name that is named, not only in this age but also in that which is to come." (Eph. 1:21) He is sovereign Lord, and he can use our work even when it seems to us to be bearing no fruit whatsoever. We can persevere in our service, leaving the results to him who is Lord of all.

George Webber testifies to the glow of hope in his own ministry:

> To keep on ministering as best one can to drug addicts, even when no names are added to the church rolls and only a handful are in any sense healed—that is possible only in the confidence that Christ has called you to that task, and whether you succeed or fail, the issue is in his hands.[16]

That is the kind of trust we can have as we serve the reigning Lord.

In an early Anabaptist Confession of Faith (1527) it is required that a candidate for baptism be one who "desires to walk in the resurrection of Jesus Christ."[17] One who does so walk will know assuredly the presence of a living Lord, enabling him to serve and love in joy.

*   *   *

The New Testament witnesses to a God who is with us—Immanuel, a God who gives himself in a close, warm relationship to man. He is a God who has incarnated himself in human life, who has been willing to go the full length in identifying himself with sinful human beings, even unto death on a cross. And he is a God who raised Christ from the dead and calls us to share in Christ's risen power.

We look at these acts of God in Christ, and we know what kind of God this is to whom we must respond in our daily lives. And we know something of what that response to him must involve. "If any man is in Christ, he is a new creation." Let us "walk in the resurrection of Jesus Christ." It is to this that we are called.

Questions for Thought and Discussion

1. Incarnation
   a. What does it mean to be "made human"? Does this term suggest that we are *less* than we ought to be—less than human? In what ways?
   b. In what ways can our daily work be worship? What kind of thinking originally led Christians to divide life into sacred and secular?
   c. List some activities we think of as sacred; show how they are also secular. List some activities we think of as secular; show how they are also sacred.
   d. In what ways would an understanding of the inseparability of sacred and secular free us for a more effective witness?

2. Crucifixion
   a. Who are some of the persons or groups with whom we must identify if we are to be able to care genuinely for them?
   b. When we are called to identify with, to understand, a group or a person we dislike or disagree with, how is this a part of our suffering as Christians?
   c. How can we learn to sit where another person (or group) sits when he is quite different in culture and attitudes, yet maintain our own integrity and our own "ideas about life"? For example: how is this accomplished with—

others from your own class	John Birch member
Negro	Red Chinese
white	mental patient
Ph.D	

   d. What is your reaction to Pascal's statement: "that all that happened to Jesus Christ must fulfill itself *in the spirit and body* of every Christian"?

3. Resurrection
   a. Is it possible to "follow Christ" and remain unchanged? What kind of changes occur? What causes these changes?
   b. In what ways do you think suffering paves the way for God to bring about new life?

CHAPTER 4

The Bible and Christian Decisions

We will not respond fittingly to God unless we can interpret rightly what he is doing, for our response is always to the *meaning* of what is happening, as we understand it. The way we will reply to God depends on how we interpret the signs of the times.

But how do we read the signs of the times? How can we discern God's action among us? Well, God has given us some clues. In chapter 3 we talked about Jesus Christ and what we learn through him about how God works and what our response should be. But we can look behind Jesus Christ to the whole Bible, the witness to what God has done in many generations leading up to Christ. The church has always believed that the Bible is absolutely essential to the Christian as he makes his ethical decisions. In this present chapter we will be inquiring into what this means. How does the Bible point us to our proper response to God?

THE INFALLIBLE RULE

To the Presbyterian Church, U.S. General Assembly of 1966 the president of Louisville Seminary made a notable address. Directing the Assembly's attention to ethics and the Christian life, the autumn emphasis of the Covenant Life Curriculum, Dr. Winn said:

> Years ago, a minister friend of mine asked me a riddle: "Do you know what the Southern Presbyterians really believe?" And I replied, as one always should to a riddle: "I give up. What do Southern Presbyterians really believe?" His answer was: "They believe that the Bible is the Word of God, the only infallible rule of faith [whisper] and practice." Now, as I understand it, in Year Three of CLC we are trying to say AND PRACTICE loud and clear.[1]

Historically, we in the Reformed tradition have made that or a similar affirmation: the Bible provides for us our rule of faith and practice. And yet this bothers many of us. "Is it an infallible rule for practice?" we ask. How can this be, when so much of the Bible is outdated? The Bible speaks to the first century A.D. or the eighth century B.C.; it cannot tell us what to do in the twentieth century. Let us first face this problem honestly, and then we can see how we might answer it.

The Problem of Relating Scripture to Life Today

Let us raise this whole question of the Bible's ethical relevance by looking at a specific passage from the New Testament, a passage in which Paul is giving ethical guidance to the Corinthian Christians. We will use this passage as an example, to illustrate the problems we may encounter as we turn to the Bible to guide us about right and wrong.

Recall that Paul devotes a large proportion of these two letters to Corinth to discussion of Christian living. He is trying to deepen these people's understanding of how Christians should work and live together and worship. Our question is, to what extent does Paul speak also to us?

Chapter 11 of First Corinthians begins a section in which Paul is talking about Christian worship: what is appropriate in the worship of God and what is not. He is concerned with two specific problems here: the matter of women's worshiping with heads veiled and the question of the proper observance of the Lord's Supper. Study this passage on your own, and be prepared to discuss it with the group. Let us ask ourselves in what ways this chapter provides us with infallible rules for our practice today.

Read 11:3–16.

Note by way of background that in the Near Eastern culture of Paul's day, the veil symbolized a woman's protection by and subordination to a man—husband, father, brother. Only prostitutes appeared in public without it, and thus the veil constituted a badge of respectability. The problem here is that Christian women were celebrating their new status as fully *persons* in Christ and were asserting their equality with men by coming to worship without the traditional veil on their heads. (Consult a commentary for further details.)

Consider these questions:

1. With which of the following evaluations would you agree?

    John Short, in "The Interpreter's Bible": "The section should be ranked as among the least permanently valuable of Paul's writings."[2]

    Charles R. Erdman: ". . . it is the principle on which Paul bases his instructions to which his opponents object, and which . . . makes his statement of present importance and of abiding value."[3]

2. Does this passage provide an infallible rule for our conduct in our day? How would you state that rule?

Read 11:23–32.

Paul is discussing here the celebration of the Lord's Supper. He passes on to the Corinthians the apostolic tradition about what had happened on that night before the crucifixion. In telling the story of what Jesus said and did, he is leading up to his instructions in verses 27–32. There his deep concern shows itself, concern lest the Corinthians celebrate the Supper in complacency and carelessness.

Consider these questions:

1. How does Paul interpret the significance of this ceremony?

2. In what sense did Jesus' sacrifice ratify the new covenant?

3. V. 27: "to eat and drink unworthily" Would this not shut out all of us sinners from the Lord's Supper? Is anyone worthy?

4. What does it mean to eat and drink "without discerning the body"? Compare v. 22.

Compare the two passages.

Many people would say that those two passages differ in their authority for our lives today. They suggest that 23–32 has *direct* relevance to our church life and worship, while 3–16 relates to our day much more remotely.

1. Would you make this kind of distinction? On what grounds?

2. Can you draw from this study a general rule about the ethical application of the Bible to our lives?

"The Bible Says"—But Does God Say It?

When the Bible is read in our services of worship, the reading is often prefaced by "Let us hear the Word of God." The revivalist preacher vindicates what he has to say with "The Bible says"— the assumption being that what the Bible says, God says. Many churchmen today, however, would balk at a simple, unqualified identification between the actual words of the Bible—all of them— and the direct Word of God. They are far too aware of the human and the historical in the Bible.

We have real problems with the Old Testament. For one thing, we find much there that has no relevance for our day at all. Leaf through the book of Leviticus and note some of the laws there—

laws that were vital and necessary in pastoral and agricultural Hebrew society but which have no direct meaning for us at all. Look
at these few:

> If [a man's] offering is a burnt offering from the herd, he shall
> offer a male without blemish (1:3).
> If any one touches an unclean thing, whether the carcass of an
> unclean beast or . . . unclean cattle . . ., and he has become
> unclean, he shall be guilty (5:2).
> Every animal which parts the hoof but is not cloven-footed or
> does not chew the cud is unclean to you; every one who
> touches them shall be unclean (11:26).

As a matter of fact, many Christians would say that all these
laws have been done away with in Christ; they are no longer binding upon those who know Christian freedom. We are not always
sure, however, in just what sense the Old Testament law *has* been
set aside. Often we assume that we need not offer burnt offerings
but that we *are* required to give tithes and observe the Sabbath.

There are considerable portions of the Old Testament, then,
which we are not likely to accept as infallible rules for our living;
we do not consider them relevant for us. Moreover, there are parts
of the Old Testament that are not just irrelevant; they are morally
objectionable, quite sub-Christian from our point of view. We read
about Joshua's military campaigns against the Canaanites, dispos-
sessing from their land the people who rightfully inhabited it. We
read about the brutal custom of *herem*—complete destruction of
the enemy and all his possessions. The Biblical writers claim God's
approval for these things, but shall we consider them the pattern
for our lives?

The answer seems clear. The Presbyterian scholar John Bright
puts it bluntly and well: ". . . the Bible cannot be flattened out and
used indiscriminately . . . by the prooftext method, for the simple
reason that there is much in the Bible that is not authoritative over
the Christian at all."[4] We simply have to recognize that not all
parts of the Bible are of equal authority for the believer. Jesus
clearly puts his own commands on a higher plane than those of the

Old Testament. "You have heard that it was said, 'An eye for an eye and a tooth for a tooth. But I say . . .' " (Matt. 5:38–39) Paul could affirm that we are no longer under the Old Testament law (Gal. 3:24–25; Rom. 7:4–6). John speaks more authentically of what it means to obey God than does Judges; Luke is clearer on the matter than Leviticus. We have to see each part of the Bible in its proper historical perspective.

Even the New Testament, however, causes us problems. We find much there that hardly seems the standard for our ethical decisions. Shall we treat Paul as an infallible oracle? Well, he never claimed infallibility for himself. Sometimes, speaking on disputed questions, he would say, "Now, this is just my own opinion on the matter." (See, for example, 1 Cor. 7:12; 2 Cor. 11:17.) Once he even corrected himself as he was writing (1 Cor. 1:14–16). What Paul had to say in advice to those early congregations was inevitably colored by his environment, his training, his prejudices, the culture of his time. We have to think carefully and honestly, therefore, about how we shall apply Paul's ethical counsel to our day.

Jesus himself did not tell us all we need to know for making our own ethical decisions. He was the Son of God, but he was also a man of his time, living and teaching amid conditions quite unlike the affluent society of the U.S.A., 1969. So we find many of our crucial ethical questions simply not touched in what Jesus taught. What shall we think of wars of national liberation or of our struggle against worldwide Communism? What shall we do about strikes which cripple the nation's transportation system? Jesus does not speak directly to these problems, but we must decide about them.

All of this means that we cannot simply equate "the Bible says" with "God says" without considerable qualification. The Bible was written by fallible men, not by angels. They were men who were immersed in and affected by the culture and the thought-forms of their day. As we ask about the Bible's authority for our lives, we have to take these things into account.

So we get to feeling all hemmed in and we throw up our hands in bewilderment. Does the Bible really speak to our decisions *at all?* Then it is that we need to hear again the "[Thus] says the LORD" in Isaiah 55:10–11.

"For as the rain and the snow come down from heaven,
   and return not thither but water the earth,
making it bring forth and sprout,
   giving seed to the sower and bread to the eater,
so shall my word be that goes forth from my mouth;
   it shall not return unto me empty,
but it shall accomplish that which I purpose,
   and prosper in the thing for which I sent it."

What we have to ask, then, is, What is "the thing for which I sent it"?

THE BIBLE'S AUTHORITY FOR OUR LIVES

Two Important Reminders

How is the Bible authoritative for us in ethics? As we come to grips with this question, we ought to keep two things in mind. *One,* we need to recall what we said in chapter 3 about our incarnate God: *in the Bible as elsewhere the divine works in and through the human.* "We have this treasure in earthen vessels," said Paul. God speaks to real men in the midst of real history, and that history is a complex of selfishness and nobility, heroism and brutality, the best and the worst.

As God has spoken to men where they were, so men have responded to that revelation where they were, and not in a vacuum, cut off from the influences of their culture. People in the days of the Judges and of Samuel tried to obey God's will as they understood it, but their understanding was colored by the patterns of their culture. (It might be interesting to compare the attitude toward Israel's enemies reflected in Psalm 137:7, 9 with that found in Isaiah 53. Consult a commentary to find out about the historical setting of each. What events and social situations might have helped lead Deutero-Isaiah to his rich understanding of God's saving purpose and of Israel's part in that purpose?)

This is to say that the Old Testament is not an anthology of infallible oracles, to be consulted for magical guidance; its writers never intended it as such. It is the inspired record of God's redemptive dealings with Israel, a group of sinful men and women (like us!) who misunderstood what God said and distorted his will for their lives (just as we do!). God was constantly pressing these people toward righteousness, and development of ethical understanding in the Bible reflects the development in men's response to that pressure.

As we come to the Bible and ask about its authority, then, we need to keep in mind that it records men's response to God's revelation where they were, amid all the limitations of their culture. We need to remember, *secondly,* the very nature and purpose of revelation itself. *It is not primarily information about God that is given in revelation, but God himself and personal relationship with him.* God was giving *himself* in these Biblical events more than propositional truth *about* himself, and he was calling men into fellowship with their God. So the Biblical writers aimed to give us not a precise catalog of doctrinal truths about God or a listing of ethical rules, but rather a record of God's saving activity and with it, a picture of what a trusting response to him involves. And as we read their testimony, we are called by God to that same trusting response which they knew—acceptance of God's gift, obedience to his demand.

Always that was the pattern of the relationship—gift and demand, grace and obligation, Gospel and Law. As these people were enabled to see God in action and to hear his call to fellowship, they came to know his gracious offer of mercy and along with it the obligation of obedience. "I am the LORD your God, who brought you out of the land of Egypt, out of the house of bondage. You shall have no other gods before me." God had rescued Israel from Egypt; therefore Israel was to obey God's commandments. "I appeal to you therefore, brethren, by the mercies of God, to present your bodies as a living sacrifice, holy and acceptable to God." God has given us salvation through Christ (Rom. 1—11); therefore we are to seek to do his will (Rom. 12—16). The relationship was one of trust and obedience.

Out of this pattern of revelation and response the Bible developed, and as we read the transcript of *their* encounters with God, he calls *us* to response. The thrill of those people's encounters with

God is preserved for us in their writings. As we read, we can enter
—if we are willing—into the same kind of experience. The Bible is
the means through which God confronts us, calling us to receive
the gift of salvation and to respond to him in glad obedience. Thus
it is that we rightly call it the Word of God himself to us.

This is what the Bible is all about. It is not a compendium of
information about God or of oracles for our guidance (though
there is both information and guidance there); it is primarily an
instrument which God uses to call us into fellowship with himself.

This is borne out in the Bible's witness to Jesus Christ. As the
New Testament pictures him, Jesus was not concerned so much
with delivering "doctrine" as he was with leading men to new life,
enabling them to be open to God's communication of himself. For
Jesus knew that the ability to see and to understand the things of
God, including his will for our lives, is not a special human faculty
which simply awaits information; it is, rather, a dimension of man's
relationship to God, dependent upon reconciliation. Jesus' work
was basically this reconciliation; if men could be released from
their twisted affections and the falsehood of their thinking, they
would be open to God's gift of himself in fellowship, both in mercy
and in judgment, in grace and in obligation. Jesus' task was to re-
deem us from those things which serve to wall God out of our lives.

It is here that we find the authority of the Bible: not that it
gives us infallible answers to our ethical questions, but that through
this book God lays his claim upon us and calls us into fellowship
with himself. To the fact that God does thus give himself through
the Bible, we have the witness of the saints through the ages. Augustine testifies that God spoke clearly to him in Ambrose's garden,
through the words of Romans 13:13–14. Martin Luther tells us
that his long struggle for peace of soul ended when God spoke
through Romans 1:17. And John Wesley's heart was warmed when
the preacher expounded from Luther's commentary on Romans.

God keeps his promises. His word accomplishes that which he
purposes, and prospers in the things for which he sends it.

The Bible as a Source of Guidance

More needs to be said, however. Though the Bible is not a
source of infallible oracles, it *does* give us guidance for the living

of these days of ours. In the next chapter we will be examining
two specific places in the Bible where most of us expect to find
light for our decisions—the Ten Commandments and the Sermon
on the Mount. To these passages we often turn to learn something
of the general pattern our response to God will follow even as we
answer him in quite specific situations. For right now, let us look
at one way in which the testimony of the whole Bible speaks to
our ethical decisions today. The Bible witnesses to the sovereignty
of God, and this says important things to us about the living of the
Christian life.

God is the one source of all reality, say the Biblical writers.
He is in control of all that happens. As Deutero-Isaiah puts it:

> I am the LORD, and there is no other,
>   besides me there is no God;
>   I gird you [Cyrus], though you do not know me,
> that men may know, from the rising of the sun
>   and from the west, that there is none besides me;
> I am the LORD, and there is no other. (Isa. 45:5–6)

Even the Persian military leader who has never heard the name of
Yahweh is girded by him for the battle and used in the working
out of his redemptive purpose.

This says to us, for one thing, that *God's concern is universal.*
He has created and sustains all men; none is beyond his care. And
our concern must be universal if we are to respond to that sovereign God. To focus our final loyalty on any one part of mankind,
to treat any group as "outsiders" and therefore beyond the pale of
our trust and concern is to settle our worship on less than the One
God who cares for all. But it is so easy for us to do just that! How
many of us Americans are really willing to *hear* what the Russians
might be saying to us? We can't really believe they are worth our
attention. How willing are many of us middle-class folks to *hear*
what is said from the slums? Surely those people can give nothing
to us!

It is easy for all of us to narrow our loyalties to our own kind
—our families, our race, our nation—and to suspect the outsiders
who are different. But if God is sovereign, there *are* no outsiders.

We are all his creatures, all one in our dependence on him for every breath we breathe, every bite we eat.

The Bible's testimony to God's sovereignty says something else to us, too: *there is no sphere of life which is outside his concern.* He claims all realms for himself, and we cannot serve him in the ecclesiastical while shutting him out from the political. So we cannot split ourselves up, obeying God when we are at home or at church, but living by other allegiances when we are in the voting booth, or at the bowling alley, or behind the counter or desk. The one sovereign God calls us to wholeness and integrity in life; he means for us to live our lives under him *as a whole.* The office worker caught in the 8:15 traffic, the housewife chauffering the children to Scout meetings or music lessons, the school teacher coping with young primitives at recess time—if these people would respond to God, they must do it where they are, in the routines of every day. God is a sovereign God: "I am the LORD and there is no other." Our responses to him must be one and whole.

Thirdly, when the Biblical writers affirm the sovereignty of God, they are saying that *God's claim on our lives is absolute.* We live under all sorts of rules, orders, claims, commands. From our earliest years people about us say, "This you must do." "That you must not do." "Eat your spinach." "Don't pull sister's hair." "Sit up straight." "Quit talking in class." "Pay your taxes." "Don't drive over 60." What so often becomes apparent to us, however, is that many of the claims made upon us are quite relative: they are binding on us only at particular times, in particular places, in particular circumstances. What is right in one culture is wrong in another; what is forbidden in one society is encouraged in another. It becomes apparent to us, moreover, that many of the claims made on us are contradictory or incompatible with each other; to accept one claim is to reject another. It becomes apparent, finally, that some of the claims made on us are morally invalid; oftentimes we find ourselves having to "unlearn" things we learned as children. All of these demands and counter-demands are confusing, and we find ourselves wondering whether in the midst of all this relativity there is any absolute.

The Bible affirms that there is. It tells us that there is one claim laid upon us that is not relative but absolute, not finite but infinite, not conditional but unconditional. This is the claim laid on our lives by the sovereign God, who calls us to love, serve, and obey him with all that we are in all that we do. God's claim of love applies no matter where you are or what situation you are in. "You shall love the Lord your God with all your heart, and with all your soul, and with all your strength, and with all your mind," said Jesus, for God is our sovereign Lord, and his claim is absolute.

The fact that God is sovereign means, finally, that *our response to him has drastic consequences for us.* It is not customary for American preachers these days to preach "hell fire and damnation" sermons, and this is well, since many such sermons preached by our forefathers were only caricatures of the authentic Biblical theme. Yet the Bible surely makes clear that one does not ignore, neglect, or violate God's claim with impunity. Whatever else the Biblical word about the wrath of God, the wages of sin, or the agony of hell means, it surely means this: one cannot go against the grain of the universe without getting splinters. One cannot defy the claim of the sovereign God without getting hurt. One cannot put himself, his nation, his race, his church, or anything else in God's unique place without being broken. This is a hard truth, an awesome truth, a condemning truth; but this is an ultimate truth, God's truth. And for our salvation and well-being, we had better hear and believe.

We have been saying here that there is guidance in the Bible. Not infallible oracles, no; but considerable light to help us—more light, indeed, than most of us really want to walk by!

But we've been talking about the *general* Biblical witness, the testimony of the *whole* Bible. How about some specific ethical teachings? The Ten Commandments? The Sermon on the Mount? Do these ethical portions of the Bible—from 1400 B.C. or A.D. 30—give us light on how we are to respond to God in our own day? To that question we turn in the next chapter.

Questions for Thought and Discussion

1. What are some of the problems we face if we accept all parts of the Bible as equally authoritative? On the other hand, what

problems do we face if we begin to discern differing degrees of authority in the Bible?

2. *Who God is* lies behind the words of the Bible as the total personality of a person lies behind his words. Explain this.

3. We have said that the men of Biblical times responded to God's revelation *where they were* and that their understanding was colored by the pattern of their culture. How do our own understandings of and responses to that revelation reflect our involvement in *our* culture?

4. In what ways do new developments in transportation and communication help us to understand that God's concern is universal? In what ways do they lead *us* to a universal concern? In what ways do they hinder that kind of concern?

5. In what way do the forces of nationalism hinder our concern for all men? The force of racial prejudice? Of class differences? How can we learn genuinely to identify with those who are culturally different from ourselves?

CHAPTER 5

Ethical Teachings of the Bible

In response to God—but what is God doing? How can we rightly interpret God's action among us so as to respond fittingly? Chapter 3 suggested that we have some clues to what God does now in his *past action* in Jesus Christ; he is a God whose work follows the pattern of *incarnation, crucifixion, resurrection.* In chapter 4 we found a clue to what God does now in the Biblical testimony to *what he is like:* he is sovereign over all men and all of life. Now we want to look at some explicit ethical teachings of the Bible which tell us something about God's concerns, *what he cares about.* This will give us still another clue to the pattern our response to God ought to take. For our response is response to a Person, and part of that response is to share in the concerns of that Person.

NOT TO ABOLISH BUT TO FULFILL

In this chapter we will be facing a worrisome question which many of us are probably asking at this point. We have been talking about the authority of the Bible—well and good. Authority residing not in specific, infallible teachings *within* the Bible, but in the whole Bible as God's instrument for giving himself to us—this we can understand. But does all that we've been saying mean that we just throw out the explicit ethical content of the Bible? Does the Bible give us no *instruction* for our ethical decisions?

The question makes sense. All through this book we've been saying that we make ethical decisions in response to God, not in obedience to laws. We've said that if we assumed there were laws laid out in the Bible to cover all our decisions, we might not be open to the newness and uniqueness in every situation. We might focus so much on obedience to laws that we would not have the flexibility to respond to what is happening *now*. To make decisions, then, does not mean simply to apply a law or a principle. It is rather to act in the midst of and in response to what is happening around us, especially to what God is doing in these events.

But, you ask, and rightly, does this mean that we are left all alone in the situation, without any guidance whatsoever? Do the great ethical teachings of the Bible—like the Ten Commandments, or the Sermon on the Mount—not give us any help as we attempt to decide what to do?

Jesus spoke reassuringly about this question: "I have come," he said, "not to abolish the law, but to fulfill it." The religious people of Jesus' time were quite sure that he was subverting the Mosaic Law. And indeed he *was* quite casual about those traditional laws around which Jewish life revolved—the Sabbath laws, for instance. "The sabbath was made for man, not man for the sabbath." (Mark 2:27) So, he reasoned, why should not my disciples pluck grain on the Sabbath if they are hungry? Why should a man not be healed on the Sabbath? The needs of persons were far more important to Jesus than obedience to traditional laws. So he looked like a dangerous revolutionary to the religious leaders of that day; he was subverting the very foundations of their faith.

Not so, was Jesus' reply. He had no intention of abolishing the law. His concern was to *fulfill* it—to *fill it full,* to enable people to see the full, rich meaning of the law for their lives. Jesus was trying to help his disciples to see that the Scriptural laws point beyond themselves to God and his concerns. What God cares about is *persons*. His intention is that we live together in responsible love for each other, that we act out of deep concern for the welfare and the human dignity of the people we encounter. The laws guide us not as legislation to be obeyed blindly, but as light on what God cares about and therefore what *we* ought to care about.

Not to abolish, but to fulfill. The laws still hold, insofar as they point us to God's concern for persons and call us to share in that concern.

Using the word "Law" in a broad sense—to refer to the content of the Bible's ethical teachings and not just to specific "laws" —let us look at two portions of that teaching and ask how they help us to respond fittingly to God. In the distillation of moral law which we know as the Ten Commandments (Exod. 20 and Deut. 6), and in the compilation of Jesus' teaching which we call the Sermon on the Mount (Matt. 5—7 and Luke 6), we can find something of the general pattern in which responsible love will live and act. These teachings are saying to us that we respond to God by seeking the welfare of our neighbors; this is to share in his concern for them.

In these passages let us look for light on what God cares about and therefore what *we* ought to care about. Study them for yourself and be ready to discuss them with your class.

LAWS FROM MT. SINAI

The Place of the Law for the Christian

In some congregations we begin the Communion service by reading together the Ten Commandments. Why? Well, in a sense, we're holding up this statement of the Law as a mirror. In its reflection we see ourselves as we are, recognizing how far short we fall of God's intention for our lives and how much we need forgiveness in Christ. The ritual of the Ten Commandments read in unison by the congregation still holds a secure place in the church.

But in the Christian life? Here the place of the Decalogue is not so clear. Most books on the Ten Commandments start out with a chapter entitled "Are the Commandments Obsolete?" or "Has the Decalogue Been Abolished?" Now, the writers always answer this question "No" (otherwise there would obviously be no point in writing the book they're writing!), but at least they recognize that the question needs answering.

Such a problem nags at us a bit, for we are quite aware that the Commandments did not come down out of heaven written by a finger of fire, Hollywood to the contrary notwithstanding. We recognize that these laws were not something spectacularly new, which nobody had ever heard of before, but that they grew out of the life of the people. Produced in their present form by priestly editing late in the period of the exile, they likely represent an earlier formulation of some basic moral understandings of the Hebrew people. What we have, then, is a selection out of a whole mass of moral and religious precepts, put together by Moses and other leaders to embody the people's covenant obedience to God. But these were *their* laws; do they also apply to us? We who know Jesus Christ and his commandment of love—do these Commandments any longer say anything to us?

There is debate of all sorts on that question. Many would answer it "Yes, absolutely!" These commandments are still absolutes for us. God has so created us that certain kinds of behavior are always right, certain kinds always wrong—and the Commandments tell us the difference between them. To break one of these commandments is to sin against God and the moral order of the universe.

Others would answer the question with a flat No. Joseph Fletcher in his *Situation Ethics* asserts that ". . . Christian situation ethics has only one norm or principle or law . . . that is binding and unexceptionable, always good and right regardless of the circumstances. That is 'love'—the *agape* of the summary commandment to love God and the neighbor. The situationist follows a moral law or violates it according to love's need."[1] Many would agree with Fletcher that no law, including the Ten Commandments, can tell us in advance what we are to do or not to do in a particular situation. Rather, we are to do in that situation what love requires us to do. The law of love is the only absolute.

This writer is convinced that the Ten Commandments *do* speak to us today, *do* guide us in our ethical decisions, in that these laws express what it means to have the kind of concern for persons which is characteristic of God—and this is precisely what Jesus was trying to get his disciples to see. Granted, the Hebrew people misunderstood this. They wanted to obey the laws as ends in themselves; this was far easier than living in constant concern for the welfare of their neighbors. But when they *did* understand, they looked *behind* the laws to the Person of God himself. Then they could see that the laws were to teach them how to treat their neighbors. This would be the pattern of their lives if they had really given themselves in single-hearted loyalty to this God. The Decalogue is a "therefore" ethic: "I have brought you up out of Egypt; *therefore* you are to be my covenant people and to care about your neighbors as I care about them."[2]

This focus on persons is evident all the way through the Decalogue. An act is evil not as a matter of abstract thinking, but because of its destructive effect on human beings, whom God cares for. "Thou shalt not kill." The law points not at "killing" as an abstraction, but at the persons who suffer and die. "Thou shalt not commit adultery." This is not because there is something magical about marriage vows in the abstract, but because it is a person to whom a man is unfaithful when he breaks those vows. "Thou shalt not steal." It is not that property is sacred in itself, but that property represents the sweat and tears of other human beings. All these laws are simply a spelling out of what it means to affirm and to uphold the dignity of human life.

The ninth commandment makes it explicit. Not "Thou shalt not lie," calling for loyalty to abstract truth. Rather, "Thou shalt not bear false witness *against thy neighbor*." A lie is evil because the neighbor is hurt by it. Because this commandment is so clear about its relevance to persons, let us take it for our particular study. We will use it as an example illustrating how one may interpret many of the commandments. We will ask what it says to us about our response to a God who cares about persons.

A Look at the Ninth Commandment

Note, as we begin, the prevalence of false witness among us. Lies about people are the lies otherwise good folk are most tempted to tell. Highly respectable people who would never stoop to rob-

bery or adultery feel no qualms about the tale-bearing they do
every day. It is interesting that we expect rigorous honesty of the
scientist in his laboratory and would be appalled to hear that he
had reported falsely. But to speak falsehood about people? Nobody cares much about that. Let us then look closely at this ninth
commandment to see how it guides us in our human relations.

The ninth commandment was originally designed to support
the cause of justice in the courts. Justice would never be done, obviously, if witnesses in a trial did not speak the truth. But the spirit
of this commandment reaches much further, for we have broken it
when we say the things that harm other people. Elton Trueblood
has suggested that it ought to be rephrased in this way: *"Thou
shalt be meticulously honest in dealing with the reputations of
others."* He quotes an ancient Quaker question which all of us
ought to face: "Do you avoid tale bearing and detraction and are
you careful concerning the reputations of others?"[3]

In that light, consider the following questions:

1. *Our interest in each other*
   Think back over the conversations you have had today.
   a. What were the subjects you talked about?
   b. How many of the conversations had to do with people?
   c. What kinds of evaluations of other people's activities were
      made in these conversations—by you or by the people you
      were talking with?
      Examples—
      "He surely did a silly thing."
      "She did a good job on that paper."
      "He just oughtn't to have done that."
   d. Is there any reason to condemn ourselves for being interested
      in other people and what they do?

2. *Our concern for reputation*
   Most people want to be praised and cannot bear to be ridiculed.
   a. What evidence of this do you see in our society? What ways
      do we have of bestowing honors on people? Is any one of us
      really indifferent to being honored by others?
   b. What lies behind the Japanese custom of Hari-kari, where a

man commits suicide when he has "lost face"? Do we see this kind of impulse, though in less extreme form, in our own lives?

3. *Our responsibility for the reputations of others*
   a. What is the source of the blackmailer's power?
   b. In what ways do we threaten the reputations of our associates, short of thoroughgoing blackmail?
      For example are we involved in—
      Comments about business competitors?
      Professors discussing their colleagues?
      Mothers discussing other mother's children?
   c. In what way do we use "faint praise" of others to advance our own standing with our neighbors?
   d. How often do we spread slanders—or listen to them in silence raising no voice in protest?
      Examples—
      "The Jews are taking over the restaurant business."
      "That's what you can expect of Negroes."
      "That's Whitey for you."
      "He's a Communist, sure as you're born."
      "I don't really know how true it is, but I understand that she . . ."
   e. How does the ninth commandment speak to these actions of ours?

On the other hand, there may be some real problems involved in this concern for the neighbor's reputation. Consider these questions:

1. Does a concern for the neighbor's good name mean blinking at the reality of evil, like the monkey with his hands over his eyes? Note that the prophets harshly condemned the Israelites; Jesus scathingly indicted the Pharisees. The question: what was their motive in condemning?

2. Can truth-telling sometimes be harmful?
   How about the man who always tells the truth, whatever the

cost, however needlessly he may hurt people? What is his chief concern—the welfare of his neighbor or the purity of his own conscience? Are there times when concern for a person requires us to withhold the truth, or to tell a lie? Can you think of some situations of which this would be true?

Question for our consciences: Whose reputation are we usually trying to protect when we tell lies? That of others? Or our own?

Now, compare a New Testament passage which speaks to this same general concern: James 3:2–10.

1. What point is the writer making with his images of ships and forest fires? What sorts of fires is James referring to here?

2. No human being can tame the tongue, he says. Is it, then, completely uncontrollable? How would the tongue be affected if we really shared in God's concern for persons?

3. What is the contradiction in the "blessing and cursing" of verses 9–10?

By Way of Conclusion

Shakespeare's Iago said it well in *Othello* (Act III, scene iii, ll 154 ff.):

Good name in man and woman, dear my lord,
Is the immediate jewel of their souls.
Who steals my purse steals trash; 'tis something, nothing;
'Twas mine, 'tis his, and has been slave to thousands;
But he that filches from me my good name
Robs me of that which not enriches him,
And makes me poor indeed.

We know that "good name in man and woman" is tremendously important to us all. If, then, we really care about our neighbor, we will be meticulously careful about his good name. Responsible love for our brother will express itself in care for his reputation; it will, in fact, not abolish the ninth commandment, but fulfill it.

Is the ninth commandment obsolete? As absolute law, yes (that is, as law which we grit our teeth and obey, and let the chips fall where they may), but as a pattern which our response to God will ordinarily follow, not at all. For to say that we respond to God's action in what is happening around us—in the situation where we find ourselves—is not to say that we know nothing in advance about some general patterns that response will likely take.

We know what God cares about: *persons*. We know therefore what we must care about: *persons*. The Commandments point the way to caring.

THE SERMON FROM THE MOUNT

The Emphasis in Jesus' Teachings

"You have heard that it was said . . . but *I* say . . ." So Jesus prefaced his comments about the law in that group of teachings which Matthew has compiled for us in the Sermon on the Mount.

The Jewish people had settled for outward obedience to the Mosaic Law, oftentimes obeying the law but being very *un*-loving toward people. They had forgotten that the law was a means to an end, designed to show us how to act lovingly. They had made the law into an end in itself. This is the perennial danger of legalism— that we will bring our outward actions into conformity to law while leaving our inner attitudes completely untouched.

This is why Jesus was so harsh with the Pharisees and scribes in their righteousness—"righteousness," that is, in terms of meticulous obedience to the law. "Hypocrites!" he called them in Matthew 23. "You cleanse the outside of the cup and of the plate, but inside they are full of extortion and rapacity." "Whitewashed tombs!" he called them. "So you also outwardly appear righteous to men, but within you are full of hypocrisy and iniquity." "You tithe mint and dill and cummin, and have neglected the weightier matters of the law, justice and mercy and faith; these you ought to have done, without neglecting the others." It is not that they should

ignore the law ("without neglecting the others"); the problem is
that they have stopped with external obedience to it and have not
caught sight of the life of love toward which the law points.

So Jesus is seeking to fulfill the law, to point people to that
responsible love for others which the law was designed to guide.
"Not to abolish . . . but to fulfill," he says of his task, in Matthew
5:17. And in verses 21–48 of that chapter he goes on to describe
responsible love, which includes but goes far beyond outward obedience to the laws.

A slightly uncomfortable question bothers us here, however. It
is easy to see how Jesus was reinterpreting the law for his day, but
does he really give much guidance for us as we seek to respond to
God here and now? Our real problem is that what Jesus says is so
perfectionistic that it seems to speak very little to the realities of
our own situation. Sometimes we feel like the character in one of
Rose Macauley's novels who observed:

> 'All this Sermon on the Mount business . . . is most saddening.
> Because it's about impossibilities. You can receive a sacrament,
> and you can find salvation, but you cannot live the Sermon on
> the Mount.'[4]

"You, therefore, must be perfect," Jesus tells us, "as your heavenly Father is perfect." And that's what makes us wonder: who
among us arrives at *that?* The sermon is about impossibilities.

Just one comment about how we ought to look at the Sermon
on the Mount, and then we will consider two particular passages to
see what they say to us about our response to God.

How to Regard the Sermon

Jesus is pointing us to perfection, to a life lived in utterly self-
less love. What shall we make of that kind of demand laid upon
us? As with the Ten Commandments, there is no unanimity about
how the sermon is to be applied to our lives. Some call it a new
law, to be taken as a series of literal commandments; therefore we
ought to abolish our armies and refuse to take oaths and give to
every beggar on the street, regardless. Others say that the Sermon

on the Mount is not law for our lives but judgment upon our lives. Jesus' impossible injunctions are designed simply to make us recognize our sin and so throw ourselves upon God's mercy for salvation. Still others believe that the Sermon on the Mount has no relevance for us at all. Jesus intended it as an ethic only for the short interval before the end of the world—and since the world is still quite obviously with us, we are not bound by what Jesus says.

I believe that in the Sermon on the Mount we have definite guidance for the living of our lives, but that we must see Jesus' teaching here in the context of his larger teaching about the kingdom of God. He began his ministry in Galilee proclaiming, "The time is fulfilled, and the kingdom of God is at hand; repent, and believe in the gospel." (Mark 1:15) He was saying that the promised reign of God had already begun; the new age had dawned, when God would intervene in history to draw men to himself, enabling them to live the life of love he intended them to live. All this was a present reality, not just a future promise. Through Jesus Christ men could live in the kingdom *now*. The writer of the Hebrews was to say later that Christians are those who have already "tasted the goodness of the word of God and the powers of the age to come." (Heb. 6:5)

Jesus' message was that now men *can*—are able to—live lives that befit citizens of the kingdom of God, lives of openness to their neighbors and concern for their welfare. The Sermon on the Mount would be ridiculous if Jesus meant it only as a *demand;* the glory of it is that the sermon is more than a demand, it is an *offer*. Jesus is offering men citizenship in the kingdom.

This means that what Jesus is saying in the Sermon on the Mount might be called a "disciples' ethic." He is assuming that those who hear are already responding to God, already in the kingdom—that God is already enabling them to share in his love for people. This is ethical teaching for those who live in this world but have their true citizenship elsewhere.

If we are to interpret rightly what Jesus says in the Sermon on the Mount, then, we must see it in the perspective of the whole of his teaching. His ethical imperatives depend upon the glorious indicative, "The kingdom of heaven is at hand."

If we see it in this light, we can understand what Jesus is doing in the sermon. He is not so much legislating for us as describing for us life in the kingdom. He is giving us illustrations of what our lives would look like if we were really to respond to God and to be citizens of his kingdom. We would so participate in God's concerns that we would live in responsible love for the people around us.

To illustrate this approach to the whole sermon, let us now tackle two difficult portions of the Sermon on the Mount and see what we will make of them. What are these passages saying about God's concern for persons and the way in which citizens of his kingdom should share that concern?

A Study of Two Passages

Read Matt. 5:38–42—the question of "non-resistance."

1. A. D. Lindsay: ". . . the truest way to love your enemies or, for that matter, your friends may sometimes be to resist forcibly the evil they are trying to do. . . ."[5]

   Is this inconsistent with what Jesus is saying?

2. Would what Jesus says here really be good for society? Look for example at vs. 40. Does Jesus mean that we are not to stand up for legal rights? Isn't it to society's advantage that rules should be kept?

   Vs. 42. Is it good to encourage beggars who prey on people's sympathies? Should our giving not be intelligent and discriminating giving?

3. Is Jesus even concerned about the social consequences of what we do? If not, what *is* his concern?

   An interpretive note: Jesus is pointing out that his disciples are to be generous with all men, even those who do them evil. Go on to verses 43–48 and note what he says. The way to be children of our heavenly Father is to love others with the Father's generous love. He pours out rain and sunshine on all, whether they deserve it or not. In like manner we are to love generously and unstintingly, deserving and undeserving alike.

And God himself will enable us to love in this way—to act as his children should act.

Read Matt. 5:27–28, 31–32—the question of adultery
1. What is the connection between these two passages? Can you understand 31–32 apart from 27–28?

2. What was the comparative position of men and women in the society to which Jesus spoke?

3. Vss. 27–28. Is he saying that lustful desire is *as bad as* the actual act of adultery? (Compare vs. 22: Is anger as bad as murder?) What is Jesus' point? Is Jesus condemning all sexual desire? If not, what *is* he condemning?

   To what are advertisers appealing when they link their products with virile-looking men or sleekly dressed women? Is there any connection between this and the point Jesus is making here? What might this say about many movies, and much movie advertising? Note A. D. Lindsay's paraphrase: "Whosoever looks on a woman as just an object of desire or use is an adulterer." How does that sound to you? On that basis, can adultery take place *inside* as well as *outside* legal marriage?

4. Vss. 31–32. Does Jesus intend here to legislate for all Christians? (If so, he departs from his usual pattern of stressing inward attitudes more than outward behavior.) What is Jesus' concern here—the institution of marriage or the persons who are married?

   Jesus was denouncing here ". . . the fact of the man having this power over the woman and of men holding this view of women." (A. D. Lindsay) What power? What view? What was the divorce pattern under Mosaic Law? Who could get a divorce, who could not? On what grounds? What do Jesus' words have to say about treating people as persons?

   An interpretive note: Jesus is talking about the discipline of our impulses. Read verses 29–30. Obviously he does not intend to be taken *literally;* he is not asking us to inflict violence on our-

selves—cut off our hand, pluck out our eye. But he does intend
to be taken *seriously* about temptations that we cherish: we are
to cut them out of our lives in order that we may live abundantly. We are to discipline the impulses that give us fleeting
pleasure in order to know the lasting joy of fellowship with God.

To respond rightly to God is to have the same concern for persons that he does. But this is far beyond us and we recognize this
as we read the Sermon on the Mount. Shall we, then, say with the
Macauley character, "It's about impossibilities"? Well, recall that
in our discussion of the resurrection we talked about the new moral
power that is available to us. A. M. Hunter has said that "we are
not asked to scale the heights of the Sermon in our own unaided
strength: we are offered the continuing presence through the Spirit,
of him who promised, 'Lo, I am with you alway.' "[6]
That is the glorious paradox of the Christian life. God enables
us to do what he asks us to do. God himself provides the strength
for obeying his will. St. Augustine expressed this in his famous
prayer, "Give what Thou commandest; command what Thou
givest." We can be assured of the power of Christ through his
Spirit, and in that assurance the Sermon on the Mount becomes to
us not an oppressive burden but an exciting challenge.

GOD GUIDES, WE DECIDE

We have been saying that Jesus did not legislate; he never
prescribed some "action 103 B" to be fitted to "situation 103 B."
He was concerned not so much with outward actions as with the
inward springs of conduct—though, as Waldo Beach pointed out
clearly in *The Christian Life,* the two are not finally separable.
What Jesus did was to point new directions for our lives, to show us
that we need to move away from our preoccupation with ourselves
to a glad and free self-giving to others. He left it to us to work out
what that means in our everyday living. Christ does not do our
thinking for us. Rather, he leaves us free to perceive the issues and
to decide for ourselves.

Now, God provides guidance for us through the ethical teachings of the Bible. In the Ten Commandments and the Sermon on

the Mount, in Paul's letters, in the prophets—all the way through we find descriptions of how we will live with our neighbors if we share in God's concern for them. We will be forgiving to our brethren and generous with them. We will seek good even for our enemies. We will speak the truth in love and respect our neighbors' property. We will be faithful to those to whom we have committed ourselves—in marriage or parenthood or friendship. What the Bible has to say about ethics will never be obsolete insofar as it gives us a picture of love in action.

God gives guidance through the Bible, but he does not make our decisions for us. He wants us to be free, free to join him responsibly in the working out of his purposes. He wants us to be alert to the newness in the world. He wants us to be sensitive to the new things he is doing. "God speaks ever afresh to men," says Martin Dibelius, "by bringing them into new situations."[7] We cannot let ourselves be completely bound by the past if we want to hear the fresh things God is saying to us.

In response to God—but how do we determine the fitting response? Partly by discerning the patterns of love which come clear in the Bible. Our response is to a Person, and we know from the Bible that that Person is love. "Beloved, if God so loved us, we also ought to love one another."

CHAPTER 6

The Worship and Life of the Church

We have been studying how we can learn what God wants us to do. In the last chapters we have seen something of how the Bible helps guide us in our choices. Now we turn to the help we get from the church.

Through the Bible God draws us into fellowship with himself. Through the Bible God gives us light on the patterns our response will follow. It is God who does this; no human being can make the Bible speak to us. But at the same time no believer ever really reads the Bible by himself, for it is the church which gave him the Bible and it is within the fellowship of believers that he is most likely to read it with understanding.

In this chapter we will be discussing how our participation in that fellowship of believers helps us to know what God is doing and how we can appropriately respond to him. In the worship of the church, whether at 11 o'clock on Sunday, or in our homes, and in the whole life of the church—including discussion, study, and work together—we can help each other to see God more clearly and support each other as we seek to obey him.

OUR NEED FOR COMMUNITY

No man can know God in isolation from his brethren. From the very beginning the Christian faith has been a genuinely communal faith, not just the faith of a conglomeration of individuals. It is evident in the New Testament that for the early believers knowing Christ was inseparable from being in the Christian community. They had no knowledge of a merely "private relationship" to their Lord. So they described Christian existence as membership in a family, a household; as being part of a colony, a flock, a race; as membership in a body.

Reflected here is a basic truth about human beings: We are social creatures who come to full personhood only in communion with others. No one needs to rehearse what is common knowledge to all of us—the desperate fear of loneliness in our day, the yearning to *belong*. We see it reflected in the multifarious groups we have created—Rotary, Kiwanis, Lions, Knights of Columbus, Women's Clubs, DAR, UDC, college fraternities. We see it in our young people as they seek belongingness in sexual experimentation. We see it in the man who takes the transistor along so that he can hear a human voice while he waits on the corner for his wife.

Man's deepest need, however, is for fellowship with other men in the context of fellowship with God. T. S. Eliot has put it eloquently in "The Rock":

> What life have you if you have not life together?
> There is no life that is not in community
> And no community not lived in praise of God.[1]

The one full community is the church, where we share our lives with each other and with the one who has called us together.

When the Holy Spirit calls us to know Christ, then, he calls us at the same time to enter the church, and as we talk about the church in this chapter, we will be defining it in terms of the work of the Holy Spirit. Not that the Spirit works *only* in the church; far from it. He is at work in secular movements in our society; he is at work through individual lives which may not be identified with the institutional church at all (this we will be discussing in chapter 7). But the Spirit's work in the church is distinctive. There he is working through people who are *conscious* of their commitment to God, who have responsibly given themselves to his service through Jesus Christ, who is our Lord. And wherever Christians meet in fellowship, whether for worship or for discussion of their common task in loyalty to Christ, there is the church, the work of the Spirit of Christ himself.

We come into the church because we have been drawn by the Holy Spirit and know we belong there, not because we are seeking answers to our ethical questions; yet participation in the Body of Christ brings with it growing knowledge of the will of God and growing responsibility for obedience. The question we will be asking in this chapter is, How does our sharing in the fellowship of the church—its worship, its common life—sharpen our vision, enabling us to see more clearly God's work in our midst? How is it that being a member of Christ's Body helps to fit us for responding appropriately to what God is doing in our time. How does the church help us in making the ethical choices we all repeatedly face?

THE WORSHIP OF THE CHURCH

Look first at worship—worship, which reminds us whose we are and whom we serve. Before we ask about worship in our day, however, and how our lives can be refreshed and illuminated by it, let us take a brief excursion back to the time of Amos. Amos, like the other prophets, had some harsh things to say about the people's corporate worship. There were times, indeed, when he seemed to be pretty much "anti-church"—opposed to institutional religion as such, as though to suggest that the man who genuinely wants to serve God will have to do it outside the institutional patterns of religion. Let us ascertain what in fact Amos was saying.

Remember the situation as it was described in chapter 2 of this book. The wealthy of Israel were exploiting the poor and twisting the nation's laws to their own advantage, complacently assuming that God did not care (were they not giving him the worship he

Mr. Palmer

Mrs. Holliday
Eliz. Oliver
Ethel Baker
Nellie "
Ruth Lamb
Bertha Pope
Mrs. McBain)
Eliz. McClung
Mary Clark .

wanted?). The shrines were crowded—Bethel, Gilgal, and the others; how could God be angry with people who worshipped him faithfully? But Amos warned that God wanted something different from his people; unless they repented, their doom was sure.

A Study of Three Amos Passages

Amos 4:4–5.

> This is a bitterly ironical passage.
> What is the irony here?
> It sounds as though Amos is saying, "Go to the church and sin," as though he were completely repudiating the outward aspects of religion. Is he?

Amos 5:21–25.

> God through Amos is rejecting the people's offerings. Why?
> Had God himself not ordained the sacrificial pattern?
> Does Amos consider religious rituals wrong in themselves?
> Is he saying, "Go out and work for justice in society, and don't bother with worship?"

Amos 8:4–5.

> What is these Israelities' attitude toward religious observances like sabbaths and new moon feasts?
> What will God's response to those people be?

The Church Is Incarnate

As we think in this chapter about the worship of the church and ask how it helps us to know God's will and to obey, let us keep Amos' harsh judgment in mind. How different is *our* worship? Who of us enters the sanctuary on a Sunday morning really expecting anything to happen? Who of us is willing for God to shake us and change us in our worship, and send us out to live a different kind of life? Worship has become for us that part of the service we sit through as we wait for Dr. McTavish's sermon, and in the public reading of the Word we see our chance to reread the announcements in the bulletin—and we think that God is pleased by our mere presence in the pew!

Of course, the corporate worship of the church is not guaranteed to open our lives to the presence of God in his holiness. Langdon Gilkey tells of a conversation he had with a Quaker friend in New York. "I was raised a Quaker in a Quaker family, and grew up surrounded by a Quaker community—and the Inner Light spoke to all of us at the meetings we had together. But when we moved here to Poughkeepsie, and I began to sell stocks and bonds, all I could think of in that silence was the Dow-Jones stock averages. . . ."[2] We come into the sanctuary so immersed in the Dow-Jones averages, or the rising prices of food, or the frustrations of finding a house to live in, that these human preoccupations seem to completely shut out any vision of the holiness of God.

We need to be reminded once again that a God who incarnates himself in history does not draw us out of the realities of our situation to some radiant realm of pure spirituality; he meets us where we are. As the Bible is divine *and* human, not magically protected from the weaknesses of the human beings who wrote it, so with the church. God stoops to meet us in the church's worship, even worship offered by human beings who sometimes have the Dow-Jones averages on their minds!

We can expect that our worship will not be perfect and that there will be times when nothing happens. But God can speak to us even through the humanness of our worship. What we will be discussing in the following pages is what *can* happen in worship.

What Happens in Worship

Here is an example of how worship might bring guidance to one family.

The prelude was being played, a quiet piece. Jim and Sue were in the pew, with Susan; George had not yet come in from Sunday school. Let us in imagination enter the mother's mind.

Sue's thoughts wandered, as thoughts will. "Where's that George? Probably stopped to scuffle with those two Little League buddies in his class. 'Wolves' is really the right name for that team!! . . . If that boy comes bumbling in late again. . . . Hope Mr. Brooks' sermon won't be too long today. That marvelous roast in the oven—I couldn't bear for it to cook too long."

George came in breathless, just in time. The prelude ended, the worship service began.

The Call to Worship: "Make a joyful noise unto the LORD, all ye lands. Serve the LORD with gladness: come before his presence with singing. Know ye that the LORD he is God; it is he that hath made us, and not we ourselves; we are his people, and the sheep of his pasture." Then the Hymn of Adoration: "I Sing the Mighty Power of God," with Sue carrying the melody, and Jim singing a nice tenor. "There's not a plant or flower below, But makes thy glories known; And clouds arise, and tempests blow, By order from Thy throne." "Makes you feel sort of good," thought Sue; "reminds you that God is in control of things."

The Prayer of Confession: "Almighty and most merciful Father; We have erred and strayed from Thy ways like lost sheep. . . ." Sue frowned. "Why a prayer of confession?" she asked herself. "We're a pretty good family. We have our arguments, but really—we don't harm anybody. Reminds me of that terrible old hymn. How did it go? 'Alas, and did my Saviour bleed. . . .' Something about '. . . devote that sacred head for such a wretch as I!' I'm no wretch, and neither is Jim."

The Assurance of Pardon: "May Almighty God, who caused light to shine out of darkness, shine in your hearts, cleansing you from all your sins, and restoring you. . . ." Mr. Brooks' voice faded out; Sue was thinking about last week. Jim had called early one afternoon from downtown. Old Bill Sutton was in town— they'd been in college together. Could he bring Bill home for dinner and the evening? And that was the afternoon Sue's bridge club was meeting there, and she was stewing around getting ready. Of all times for Jim to call with *that* request. She blew her top. She called him inconsiderate. She told him he never cared about *her* affairs. Of course she relented and told him to bring Bill on—but it was still a sort of sore spot with her. And Jim? Jim hadn't been angry; just waited with his steady affection for the soreness to ease away. . . . That had been forgiveness. And—yes, she *had* sinned. She'd been thinking of herself, her affairs. Old Bill meant a lot to Jim. She could have been more gracious about the whole thing. "We have left undone those things which we ought to have done, and we have done those things which we ought not to have done . . ." If she needed forgiveness from Jim, how much more from God? And if Jim could forgive, how much more . . . ?

The Hymn of Thanksgiving: "Now Thank We All Our God."
". . . Hath blessed us on our way With countless gifts of love. . . ."
"He has," thought Sue; "oh, he *has!* Jim's steady love. The children. Our friends. That's the way we know God's love. And the
rain and the sun—in that first hymn. So much to thank him for.
And forgiveness." Sue missed some of the words while she was
singing. But she tuned in at the last: "The one eternal God, Whom
earth and heaven adore; For thus it was, is now, And shall be
evermore. Amen."

The Pastoral Prayer: petition and intercession. Mr. Brooks
prayed for our leaders in Washington, and for the leaders in Russia
and China. He prayed for the sick and the lonely. Sue was grateful for health and for people to love. "And I could be more aware
of people who don't have these. I've been meaning to go see old
Mrs. Jensen. Tomorrow morning; I'll do it."

The Reading of the Word: from Isaiah 40. "Have you not
known? Have you not heard? The LORD is the everlasting God, the
Creator of the ends of the earth." God is in control of history as
well as of nature. "That's what I was thinking a while ago," Sue
said to herself. "That first hymn. A sovereign God. The mighty
power of God. . . ."

The Sermon: God's sovereignty. God is sovereign over *all* men,
so there can be no outsiders to us. "But I told them we couldn't
take that foreign exchange student into our home this year. The
German boy. He's a foreigner—too hard to adjust to. An outsider?
Is he really an outsider?" God is sovereign over *all* of life, not just
the religious part. Real worship of the sovereign God ought to sen-
sitize us to God's claim on our trip to the ballot box, our attendance at PTA meetings, our spending at the shopping center. "Our
spending?" Sue asked herself. "What does God have to do with
that? Jim says I ought to watch our money more carefully; but
that's economics, not religion. What does Mr. Brooks mean?"

The Hymn of Dedication: "O Brother Man, Fold to Thy Heart
Thy Brother." "Gosh! We can't escape. Mr. Brooks keeps remind-
ing us that we have to care about other people. No outsiders.
Watch how I spend my money. Feed the widow and the fatherless.
Where pity dwells, the peace of God is there. . . . Mrs. Jensen.

Maybe we ought to think again about that German boy. . . ."

The Offering: "Why in the world did they change the order of service? Why does the offering come at the *end* now? Mr. Brooks did say something about dedication of ourselves. . . ."

The Doxology and Benediction: "Grant, O Lord, that what hath been said with our lips we may believe in our hearts, and what we believe in our hearts we may practice in our lives; through Jesus Christ our Lord. Amen."

* * *

Now they were in the car going home. Jim was driving more slowly than usual, for they were talking about the service.

George started it with his question. "Daddy, why have they moved the collection to the end? It used to be *before* the sermon?"

Sue added her bit. "I was wondering that same thing, George. I guess it has something to do with our dedicating ourselves. We give our money as just a token of something bigger. Right?"

Jim agreed. "And coming right after 'O Brother Man,' we could hardly miss what it meant. That's what dedication is: we serve God by serving other people. So we give our money to the church and that's a symbol that we're giving ourselves."

"Makes sense," George commented. "I guess the whole service is supposed to get us steamed up to dedication. And it's good for the collection to come last—sort of tops off the whole business."

Sue's thoughts had gone on ahead. "Mr. Brooks' sermon— ooh! Before I went to church I might have asked, Who *is* my brother? Now I have to ask, Who is *not* my brother? And the answer is, Nobody."

Jim was hesitant. "Honey, do you think we could reconsider having that German boy next year?"

"It hit you that way, too? I had that same thought. That thing in Isaiah about the Creator of the ends of the earth, God being in charge of it *all*—all men, Germans as well as us. And then, Mr. Brooks—pointing out what God's sovereignty means: we have to care about *all* men, nobody's really an outsider. Gosh! . . . But one thing I didn't get. He said that God's sovereignty has something to do with the way we spend money at the shopping center. I don't see . . .

Jim had evidently been thinking about it, too. "Well, maybe we've been assuming that one-tenth goes to God. I think Mr. Brooks was saying that God cares about all of it, not just a tenth. If he's sovereign over all of live . . . Well, here's Jake's place. I'll pull in, and George, will you run in and get the paper?"

Susan chimed in. "Can I go in, too?"

While the children were gone, Sue said it. "Jim, I realized something this morning. Confession, and forgiveness. Jim, you forgave me last week, when I blew my top over the phone. Maybe I'd thought of sin as big things—robbing banks, or something. I realized this morning it can be little things. I was worried about my own affairs—the refreshments for the bridge club. I forgot that you're important, too. And Old Bill is important to you. Thanks. . . ."

Jim reached over and squeezed her hand. The children came galloping back with the newspaper. Jim grinned at them. "Everybody ready to go home now?"

*   *   *

Worship can confront us with a sovereign God who claims the whole of our lives as our response to him. And worship can make us aware of our rebellion against God's rule—our sin. There is judgment in worship, if it is real worship.

But there will be plenty of times when nothing happens at all. God is in our worship, but we human beings are, too, and we are free. We always have to reckon with the incarnate nature of the church and with the human freedom God chooses to give us. So it is always possible that we will shut God out, will so twist our worship that, far from calling us out of narrow self-concern—as happened to Sue—it will only reinforce the selfish loyalties we already have. We may not want our comfort to be disturbed and will therefore say, as the people said to Isaiah (30:10–11):

> "Prophesy not to us what is right;
> speak to us smooth things,
> prophesy illusions, . . .
> let us hear no more of the Holy One of Israel."

This is the joy of our worship, however. God comes to us and wants to give himself to us, but he does not force himself on us. We have to open ourselves freely to this sensitizing encounter with our God. And when we do, the sovereign God can lift our sights and make us bigger people, fit servants of the God who cares for all.

THE SHARED LIFE OF THE CHURCH

In worship God calls us to direct encounter with himself. He is a Person who is present when we come to him in praise and confession, in repentance and self-dedication. In worship we are drawn into fellowship with him, so that our motives are cleansed and purified and we are sent out into the world to serve our "brotherman"—not just the nice people who like us, but whatever people God chooses to give us. The life of the church is broader than just worship, however, and in the church's study and teaching, its preaching, its fellowship of mutual support—in all of this common life—we cannot only help each other to interpret what God's service requires but also support each other in obedience.

Now, it is not the task of the church or of its leadership to set up ethical absolutes for its people. The church is not God's lawgiver, and we are all aware of the dismal things that can happen when it assumes this prerogative. When churchmen try to establish fixed laws, the tendency is to stress what is *not* to be done rather than what *is* to be done, and church history is full of the straining out of gnats and the swallowing of camels. Too often have churchmen harshly condemned the outward sins which can be easily seen, and smiled complacently at the inward pride which thanks God it is not like other men and so looks down on them. But this does not mean that we in the church cannot help each other in our own ethical thinking; within the fellowship of the church all of us can grow together in our understanding of what God is doing among us and how we Christians ought to be responding to him.

To take the context of the Christian message and relate it to the lives we live every day is not a job any one of us can do alone. We have said that no believer reads the Bible by himself; he reads it in the context of the life and teaching of the church. Likewise, no

believer makes ethical decisions all by himself; the thinking and attitudes of many other churchmen enter into his as he decides and
acts. The professional theologians, who spend all their time studying the ways of God with man, are there with him. The pastors
and teachers, who lead others in the study of the Biblical faith and
its relation to the facts of our lives, are there with him. And all of
his fellow-churchmen can be there, thinking with him, as together
they seek to understand what God requires of us in our day. None
of these is infallible, none speaks with absolute authority; but if the
church is the community of the Holy Spirit, then we can be assured
that God through his Spirit is working among us all and that he is
with us in our efforts to obey.

Follow Jim and Sue to their Young Adult Fellowship the next
Sunday and see what happens.

Honest Discussion in Groups

"I think you're just defining stewardship too broadly." Tom
Bridgeman was not the most vocal member of the Fellowship, but
this time he had gotten riled up.

"Seems to me it's inevitable, if you believe what Mr. Brooks
said last Sunday about the sovereignty of God." Bob Findlay was
the group's discussion leader, a good one and a thoughtful one. "If
God is sovereign over all life, then I'm responsible to him for how
I use my money in *every* realm—not just for the part I give to the
church. All week, as I've been working on this discussion of stewardship, Mr. Brooks' words have been nagging at me."

This was Sue's chance. "This has worried me too, Bob. I—I
think I agree with you, about God's caring, and all. And maybe we
are God's stewards—of 100 percent of our money and not just 10
percent. But, well, I just have a hard time drawing the connection.
Mr. Brooks talked about our spending at the shopping center. But
the things I spend money for—groceries and clothes and things:
the family *needs* them. God certainly doesn't begrudge that, does
he?"

"OK," said Bob. "Let's take a concrete case. Mary and I are
trying to decide whether to buy a color TV or not. Our black-and-
white is fine—but the kids are in high school now, and some of
their friends have color ones, and our kids are beginning to feel

—well, sort of left out. What should we do? We don't really *need* it, when you get right down to it."

Tom Bridgeman exploded. "I think you've hit my problem. I just don't see that it's God's business or anybody else's whether or not you buy a new TV. If you can afford it and you're not hurting anybody, then what's the problem? It's *your* budget; it's not a religious thing at all. What business is it of ours in a church group like this?"

Sue's thinking was beginning to crystallize. "When you put it that way, Tom, I just have to react. Anything we do is God's business, and that has to include how we spend our money. Maybe— *especially* how we spend our money, for look at how powerful money is."

"Well, that may be. But even so, it's still a private matter between a man and God. I don't think it's appropriate for us to talk about it in a group like this."

"But, Tom, we talk about other 'private' matters," said Jim, getting into the conversation. "We've studied our prayer life together, and we had a series on helping our children understand sex. Why should our pocketbooks be any more private than *that?*"

"I think part of our problem," said Bob Findlay, "is that we've all grown up in an era of economic individualism. We figure that how we earn our money and how we spend it are pretty much our business—within broad limits, of course. Remember three years ago, when our church school classes were studying *The Christian Life?* Beach had a chapter on Christian patterns of consumption, and we in my class were pretty well embarrassed by the whole thing. We sort of skimmed over it lightly—afraid to get into that subject too deeply. Isn't that part of it? We're just not used to letting anybody else in on our pocketbook decisions."

"But that's just where a lot of us need help, I think," commented Sue. "And why shouldn't we help each other, Bob? That color TV business: Jim and I'll be facing it pretty soon. George will be a teen-ager before long, and we're already feeling some of the kind of pressure you and Mary are under. There are lots of other things we could spend the money for; *our* black-and-white is perfectly OK, too. We don't really need a color set. So *we* need help on this, too."

A new voice was heard. "I vote with you, Sue." This was Mabel Rankin—mother of four, including two high schoolers. "Where *can* you discuss things that bother you if not in the church? If we're Christians, we ought to be able to share our problems with each other, and we ought to help each other with them. And that's the good thing about this group: I think we know each other well enough to do that. Will and I said after those discussions last year on sex that we've needed a group like this for years; those studies helped us tremendously."

"Mabel's right," said her husband. "That's part of what the church ought to be, isn't it—a community where we can help each other understand how to respond to God. We surely can't do it all by ourselves."

"And even if we don't all agree," said Sue, "surely we can trust each other enough to disagree—and even that can help all of us to think more clearly."

"All right. What about this color TV?" asked Bob. "The biggest problem, really, is the kids. Suppose Mary and I decide it's best to use that money another way—maybe to buy a refrigerator for a poor family we're sort of responsible for. Could we do that to our children? Suppose we end up being the only family with just a black-and-white. Is that fair?"

"Maybe that's another responsibility of this Fellowship," replied Jim. "Maybe it would help if several of us agreed on the same course of action; then we could sort of stick by each other. None of us would be the *only* ones not getting the color set or whatever."

"That's what meant so much to us after the sex discussions," added Will Rankin. "We knew that other kids besides ours were getting some of the same kinds of understandings we were giving ours. Sort of gave us a good feeling."

"OK," said Bob Findlay. "Now about that TV. . . ."

The Communion of Saints

What the members of that Young Adult Fellowship were talking about, really, was the communion of saints—believers giving themselves to each other in a genuine sharing of lives. In particular they were discussing how the saints can help each other to discern God's will and to respond to it in obedience.

This communion of saints is far bigger, however, than just one discussion group or one congregation. It reaches far beyond any of our denominations to embrace the whole body of God's people, wherever they are. So when we talk about the "shared life of the church" and how we learn there to respond fitly to God, we're talking about the *whole* church, the church universal.

But how do we expose ourselves to those other Christians— the ones outside the Reformed tradition? By reading, for one thing. *The Presbyterian Survey, The Church Herald* or *The Wachovia Moravian*—fine; but we need to have our horizons broadened. *Christianity and Crisis* or *Christian Century* or *Christianity Today; Religion in Life* or *Theology Today*—all of these are publications which face seriously the ethical problems of our time; all of them help us to bring our theology to bear on the decisions we make. How many have these magazines in their homes? Few, obviously; but how about the church library? These magazines can expose all of us to thinking which we ought to be open to—thinking that spans the breadth of the communion of saints today.

How about meeting with other Christians at the grass roots? Does all our discussing have to be with Presbyterians or our Reformed friends? Do our Methodist friends have nothing to say to us? Or the Catholics? One of the great new developments in today's church is the way many Catholics are opening up to their Protestant brethren. Often they are positively eager for discussion and sharing. We can join with them and be drawn out of the churchly provincialism that is so dangerous to us all.

This is the ecumenical movement we're discussing here. It is not just big conferences in Germany or Switzerland, producing all manner of mimeographed documents; it is also Christians at home, listening to each other and learning from each other. We have much to learn about God's work in our day; we ought to be free to learn from many different Christians.

It ought to be observed, though, that we are not *really* being ecumenical until we are willing to learn from the church of the past as well as from other churches in the present. The communion of saints spans all the ages of the church as well as the diverse traditions of the church today. As Leonard Griffith describes it, "On Sunday morning when we enter the sanctuary of God, we touch hands not only with the men and women whom we can see about us, but with a larger company than eye can see or mind imagine."[3]

We can learn from *all* the ages of the church, not just from our own immediate spiritual ancestors. Part of the parochialism to which we Protestants are prone is the tendency to assume that fruitful Christian thinking went into eclipse after the first century and did not emerge again till the Reformation. So we can rejoice in our opportunities to study the history of the church, as we did in 1965–66 and will be doing again and again. We can be reminded that something good *could* come out of the Dark Ages, assured that God has not left himself without witness in any era. We can have the joy of knowing Augustine's thinking in his *City of God,* or Thomas Aquinas' ideas on natural law, or Calvin's ideas about the church and civil government (which might give pause to Presbyterians who say the church has no social responsibility; Calvin's thinking is worth a study!).

The Bible is always the focus of our study, but there is collective wisdom in the life of the church which can enrich our interpretation of what the Bible has to say. Many in the Presbyterian and Reformed family have denied that we need to look to the tradition of the church at all; the Bible, they say, is all we need. The plain fact is, however, that we simply cannot disregard the accumulated experience of many generations of believers. We have seen that there are ambiguities in the Scriptures, and it would be folly simply to ignore what past generations of believers have found as they have devoutly wrestled with the Biblical texts. We can learn from Augustine and Calvin the pervasive reality of sin—a fact which must always figure in responsible ethical decisions. We can learn from Richard Hooker, the sixteenth-century Anglican, the dangers of extremism and the value of reason and judicious balance in our thinking. We can learn from Søren Kierkegaard the necessity for personal decision, whereby we become responsible selves.

Granted, the church and its thinkers, in whatever age, can be mistaken in judgment and even corrupted, and our looking to the past needs to be intelligent and discriminating. We can expect, however, that the God who is not too fastidious to meet us within the human limitations of history can speak to us through the tradition of the past as well as through the deliberations of Christians in our own day.

"We are really speaking nonsense when we try to restrict the revelation of God to our age. This is as great a distortion and a lie as to say that God's only revelation ocurred in some distant past."[4] Only dangerous pride and smugness could make us believe that none of our problems has ever been faced before or could make us forget that profound understandings of God came to men and women long ere our generation appeared on the scene. The church has been the community of the Holy Spirit from the very beginning, and the Spirit continues to speak in that community to-day.

*   *   *

People who live in periods of great change rarely discern with absolute clarity what is going on. Those who lived through the fall of Rome, or the revolutionary years of the Reformation knew that things were not what they used to be, and they wondered if they would ever return to normal. But how many of them had a clear vision of what God was doing, with no doubt of what they should do in response? So it is with us: ours is a time of revolution, leaving us often in confusion and uncertainty.

Part of our uncertainty is an inevitable result of our creaturely limitations, but perhaps the largest part is the result of sin. We persist in viewing all of life from our narrow little perspective with ourselves as center, and this distorts our vision of God's world. We in the Calvinist tradition know that we will never get completely away from this distortion, but we also know that being part of God's people helps to correct it. Worship smites our self-centeredness and gives us a broader concern than our own welfare; the fellowship of the church draws us out of our own lives and into participation in the broader life of the whole church.

The church is incarnate, yes; in this place of interaction between God and man, man is indubitably there! But awareness of man's limitation and sin ought not to obscure the fact that God is there, too, and is at work through the Holy Spirit, enabling us to see him at work, that we may fittingly respond.

Questions for Thought and Discussion

1. "Worship is a response to the presence of God, our reaction to the appearance of the holy."[5] But few people in our congregations have much awareness in worship of the holiness of God. Is there anything we could do about it?
   Example—
   a. ask the worship and work committee to plan a series of studies on the meaning of worship
   b. organize groups in the congregation to undertake community action projects
   c. encourage experimentation with the order of worship for Sunday morning services, e.g., ask college or high school groups to plan the worship: folk mass? dialogue sermon?
   d. other possibilities

2. How does the fact that some people get no message and most people get different messages from the same worship service tie in with the worshipers?
   a. individual differences
   b. individual problems
   c. individual prejudices
   d. individual sins

3. Sue at first assumed that because she did not rob banks, she was really not a sinner who needed forgiveness. Do we sometimes make that same assumption? Name some of the daily shortcomings and sins of which we decent people are often guilty.
   Example—
   a. we react in anger when colleague or friend points out an error we made
   b. we casually pack a towel with our things when we leave the motel
   c. we use the company car for a family outing

4. What are the factors that help to distort our vision of God's work?

5. Name some specific ways in which sharing in the fellowship of the church can help to "un-distort" our vision of what God is doing, through:
   a. worship
   b. fellowship and study
   c. the teaching ministry of the church

6. "For men who have themselves been re-created by the love of God, now become to some extent the incarnation of love. Having received love through another, they can now pass love on to the brother for whom they are responsible."[6]

   But how does this loving responsibility really get expressed? If we were to try to help each other with ethical decisions, wouldn't our discussions very soon become busybody meddling rather than sharing of lives? Think back to Jim and Sue's Young Adult group. Can you think of a course that discussion might take which would be "meddling" rather than "sharing"? How can your class better help each other in practical decisions?

CHAPTER 7

God in the World Around Us

God is at work in the world. This we were saying in chapter 3: the God who incarnates himself works not only in the sanctuary but also in the world, in the "secular"—in political campaigns and court decisions, in struggles against inflation and wars on poverty. "God so loved the *world*," says John—not just the church—"that he gave his only begotten son." Christ is the Lord of the world as well as of the church.

Now, in chapter 6 we were talking about our participation in the life of the church—its worship, its fellowship—seeing how this helps us to discern God's presence among us, and to make the right choices in response to him. This is indispensable; we saints need each other as we seek to respond to what God is doing. But we're always in danger of focusing all our attention on this gathering of the saints, assuming that it is here we meet God and nowhere else. If we keep our eyes turned inward on the gathered

Christian community, however, it is possible that, though we might see God's work in individual Christian lives, we will miss the grandeur of his presence in the people and events of the world around us.

This chapter aims at sharpening our eyesight so that we might see more clearly God at work in our world. To see God at work, we need to look at the history of our time and the great public events of our day, and we need to look at what is happening in the sphere of relationships among persons—the healing and restoration and creation of new life that is going on in lives all around us. If we would respond fittingly to what God is doing, we must be able to discern his presence. God is there, for the person who has eyes to see. Seeing him at work in the world helps us to know what in the world we ought to do.

THE TASK OF RECOGNIZING GOD'S ACTIVITY

The Task Must Be Done

The Hebrew prophets would never let us withdraw into our own private world and seek God's presence only there. Amos called the Israelites to see God's hand in the threat of national disaster, and to respond to that threat as response to God. Jeremiah urged the people of Judah to surrender to the Babylonians, for he believed they were the instrument of God's judgment; this would be the fitting response to the action of God.

The second half of Isaiah speaks perhaps more clearly than any other part of the Bible about the task of interpreting the times. Hark back to your study of *From Bondage to Freedom,* the section on Isaiah. Recall what was said there about Cyrus, and the Babylonians, and what God was about to do in the life of Israel. In that light, go back and read Isaiah 40 and 41, where the prophet is affirming his faith in the God who controls history and has chosen a special people to alert all the world to his presence. What is he saying about the job of interpretation? Consider the following questions:

1. *God is Creator of all and Lord of history: 40:12–16, 22–24; 41:2–4.*

a. What is God's relation to nature? To the events of human history—such as the rise and fall of rulers?
b. Who is it (41:2) who gets "stirred up . . . from the east" and "tramples kings under foot"? (Consult a commentary if you need historical background here.)

2. *God has chosen a people: 41:8–9, 20.*
   a. How is the world to know "that the hand of the LORD has done this"?
   b. What is the nature of the service to which the people of Israel are called?

The prophet is talking about the God who is active Lord of history and is saying that historical events, properly interpreted, reveal God's work and purpose in them. But they have to be interpreted, so God has called a nation of people to be his servants, to look with eyes of faith at history, and to see God's presence there. They are the ones who will interpret; they are called to enable *all* men to see and understand as they themselves see and understand.

The task has not changed. We in the church hear God saying, as did the exiles there in Babylon, "You are my servant, I have chosen you," and we know that a portion of our task is still the service of interpretation—helping people to know "that the hand of the LORD has done this." The church, as Harvey Cox puts it, "is that part of the world which is privileged to recognize and to celebrate what God is doing in and for the *whole* world."[1]

God is there, at work in the world around us. We need to see, and to help others to see.

The Difficulty of the Task

We are not Amos or Jeremiah or Deutero-Isaiah, and few among us would claim to discern God's work so clearly as to say without hesitation, "Thus saith the Lord." The evidence is ambiguous, and we know it, whether we look to international affairs and our nation's efforts (wise or unwise) to maintain freedom around the world, or look to domestic affairs and our government's efforts (wise or unwise) to stabilize the economy. What *God* is doing in all this is not always clear-cut, and we need not expect Christians to be unanimous in their judgments.

There are some special difficulties that beset us as we seek to interpret the signs of God's presence in the world around us. For one thing, God is not given to advertising himself. We never hear him shouting about his achievements; he does not attach banners to what he is doing so that we will be sure to give him credit. Rather, he goes quietly about his work, unconcerned for proper publicity. You recall that Jesus rejected the temptation to do his work in a spectacular way so that people would be compelled by amazement to believe (Luke 4:9–12). So with God: we cannot expect a great sign in the sky which will clear away all confusion and point clearly to the work of God in our midst.

A second difficulty is that God is not the only one at work around us; man is there, too, and what he does is all mixed up with what God does. In what way can we see God clearly at work as a doctor faces a dope addict? God is there in judgment and mercy, but human selfishness and ignorance are there, too. Someone introduced the addict to the drugs in the first place, and many people produced the insecurities that made addiction probable. God makes us free, and we act *against* God's purposes as often as we join ourselves with him. It is not easy to see clearly what God is doing, for we are surrounded by the confusing evidence of the work of man.

Perhaps the greatest hindrance of all to our seeing is our own self-interest; we comfortably assume that whatever suits our interests is certainly in line with God's will! It is hard to see God at work through people who disturb our comfort or threaten our profits, who hold us back as we seek to gain a greater share in this life's goods. The Negro rioting for better job opportunities hates the mayor concerned with law and order. The white segregationist battling against school integration hates the Supreme Court which made that integration inevitable. Each is likely to be blind to the hand of God in the forces arrayed against him.

In chapter 6 we talked about the power of worship to lift us out of preoccupation with our own welfare, and we will return to this subject in chapter 8 on prayer. But we ought not to minimize the fact that we tend to center our world in ourselves and our own interests, and it is terribly hard for us to look at those things that hurt us and say, "the hand of the Lord has done this."

All this should say to us that we will never be able to *prove,* scientifically and logically, God's presence in this event or that. No one ever has. The Hebrews never tried to *prove* that Yahweh was there in the exodus from Egypt, delivering his people from slavery and guiding them to the promised land. They simply confessed that God had enabled them to see, and invited others to join them in their faith. God had given them eyes of faith, through which they could see God's work in events where outsiders could see nothing divine at all, only the clash of human wills. "That 'lion's roar,' " as Paul Minear puts it, "which is most convincing to the prophet is least convincing to the nonbeliever."[2]

As with the Hebrews, so with us. The events that are taking place around us can be looked at from a merely human point of view. We can never prove to the agnostic that God is there. Moreover, even where people do share with us the faith that God *does* work in events, we may be far from agreement on the actual content of what he is doing in *this* event. As we have already seen, we dare not assert dogmatically that we are accurately reading the signs of the times.

We have to make our judgments of the evidence, then, in humility, recognize that other Christians may differ from us in their interpretation of what is happening. Some readers will not agree with this writer; there will rarely be unanimity within any group discussing this chapter.

The task of interpretation is ours, however, and though the evidence is ambiguous, we *do* have evidence to go on, for God has revealed to us something of the patterns in which he acts. Let us look at these patterns, for they help us to recognize what he is doing in our midst.

THE PATTERNS OF GOD'S ACTIVITY

How can we tell that a member of our family has been in the room? Well, there are pipe ashes in the ashtray. Or the newspaper is on the coffee table, left open to the "foods" section. Or a tennis racket is propped against the wall by the front door. These bits of evidence point us to the people we know and love, because they are reflections of their patterns of acting. The husband wants to finish off the day with a pipe and a book. The wife searches the Thursday paper for bargains at the supermarket. The young son spends his summer mornings at the tennis courts down at the park. We have lived with these people and are familiar with their patterns. We know how to read the evidence of their presence.

In like manner, we know something of what to expect of God, because he has made himself known to us through Jesus Christ. In Christ we know God's concern for wholeness in human life—fullness not only in man's relation to God but also in man's relations to his neighbors and in his own physical well-being. Moreover, in Christ we know how God works toward that wholeness; know that he works with us in the threefold pattern we discussed in chapter 3—the pattern of incarnation, crucifixion, and resurrection.

Because the God we serve is the God and Father of our Lord Jesus Christ, we can expect to see him working through people and within the mundane realities of sinful human life. He will not work toward achieving his ends through magic. Instead, he uses such instruments as the TV to alert people to their neighbor's needs, and federal taxation to enable us to share with the hungry in India. And his work will not be confined within stained-glass walls, nor to the saving and spiritualizing of individual souls. He will be at work also in the nearest slum and in city hall. He works through the material and the mundane to achieve his purposes.

Further, we know through the cross that our God is one who shares with us in the judgment for our sins. God is there in every situation where we men spit on each other (literally and figuratively) and refuse to trust each other as persons; he is there bringing upon us the judgment of suffering for what we have done, but he is also there to bear that suffering with us.

Lastly, we know because of the resurrection that God is at work in every event in restoration, in the bringing of new life. He is the God of the new creation, constantly working to restore to wholeness both individual lives and the patterns of our living together. As Waldo Beach has put it,

For the final faith of the Christian is that God judges in order to heal, that he casts down in order to renew, that within history he is constantly restoring life out of death and community out of disorder and warfare.[3]

This we know because the God whom we seek to serve is the God who raised Jesus Christ from the dead.

Here, then, is the general pattern of God's working, as he has made it known to us in Jesus Christ. Because we know this much about him, we can have an idea of what to look for in the world around us, and what kinds of things we can expect him to be doing. To see how knowledge of this pattern might help us to recognize God in action, let us look closely at two relatively contemporary events, asking, "What has God's hand wrought here?" And remember, this writer can only express what seems to her to be true; you must make your own analysis of God's role in these events.

TWO CASE STUDIES

God at Work in Watts—1965

Our nation has in recent years experienced tragic summers of widespread civil disorder. In 1965 it was Harlem and the disaster of Watts. In 1966 it was Cleveland, Omaha, Atlanta, Dayton, San Francisco, and twenty-four other cities. In 1967 Newark and Detroit were only the most tragic of the explosions of violence in the streets. In 1968 there was the murder in Memphis and its aftermath in a hundred cities. By the time you read this book, outbursts of violence will probably have occurred in other cities. How are we to understand these riots? What is God doing in them? Let's look at the Watts' riots in 1965 as a case study.

The facts were these: six days of rioting, 34 killed, 1,032 wounded, property damage amounting to upwards of fifty million dollars. What caused it? Official reports pointed to the usual problems of the ghetto—insufficient jobs, insufficient schooling, resentment of police. But behind these? A former Watts resident suggests that since the police are agents of the law, they reflect the "dominant American mode of life," a mode of life from which many Negroes are shut out. The law represents white values and white dominance.[4] It is the symbol of what the Los Angeles police chief said when peace was restored, "We're on top and they are on the bottom."[5] The cry "police brutality" is only the one-sixth of the iceberg which appears above water.

Pushing bitterness into violence was the increasing knowledge of the material abundance from which the people in Watts were shut out: a crystallizing factor was, as one writer put it, "the immediate proximity of the affluent society."[6] In the pioneer days of our national life, or even in the depression of the 1930's, poverty was made bearable by its being widely shared. But in an age of affluence, poverty takes on a different color, and for many Negroes,

> White existence, only steps away, glitters with conspicuous consumption. Even television becomes incendiary when it beams pictures of affluent homes and multitudinous consumer products to an aching poor, living in wretched hovels.[7]

Add to this vivid awareness of contrast the indifference and ignorance of many white Californians who didn't care to know about conditions in Watts. The commander of a National Guard unit sent into Watts estimated that three-fourths of his men had never seen or heard of this part of Los Angeles. "One of my fellows asked me: 'Do they sell this stuff?' He meant the rotten foodstuffs. Some of my men asked me: 'Do people live in these houses?' "[8]

> For most residents, Los Angeles is a comfortable city, psychologically as well as physically, because the unpleasant can be kept in its place—at a safe distance from most of the people.[9]

Encouraged, as some have suggested, by defiance of law in other parts of the country, the bitterness of Watts broke out into open violence, and "Get Whitey" was the battlecry of the day. As one Watts resident commented afterwards, "Man's got his foot on your neck, sooner or later you going to stop *asking* him to take it off."[10]

The story of Watts looks like simply the letting-loose of the worst of human evil and destructiveness. Yet Biblical faith claims that God is active in every event. How can we identify God's activity in this riot? Let us try to interpret this tragic riot through the threefold pattern we have found in God's activity revealed in Christ. That pattern is one of *incarnation, crucifixion,* and *resurrection.*

We have said that our incarnate God cares about the whole of human life including physical life in Watts. He is concerned with bodies, not just souls, and this means that we would expect him to be on the side of better living conditions for the people of the ghetto. Note that when God freed the Israelites from bondage in Egypt, it was not some sort of "spiritual" freedom he gave them, a spiritual ability to live happily within the conditions of outward slavery. God's deliverance, rather, included political deliverance; he freed the people in the most practical and earthly sense. In like manner we could expect him to be at work not just enabling the people of Watts to live triumphantly amid the harsh realities of their ghetto existence, but enabling them to have the kind of material surroundings which do not wither and stunt the human spirit. And if the whites, who are generally more affluent and could have helped in the situation, chose to ignore Watts because it was unpleasant, perhaps God chose this painful way of riots to breach their indifference.

Moreover, an incarnate God is not limited to working through the church; he can work through all sorts of influences we call "secular." Look back at the Hebrew prophets—Amos, Deutero-Isaiah, and the others. They testified that God used political and military events for getting things done in history. He used Assyrians, Babylonians, Persians—people who had never heard of him, even people who had heard and defied him—for doing his work in history. God can work through any people and any means he chooses.

It is interesting to note how many analyses of the Watts riots list television as a contributing factor—television which brings into the grubbiest slum a picture of gracious living. It is often said that there is no revolution where there is no hope. People do not rise up in revolt when they have no idea that life could be better; but as they begin to see other possibilities, frustration builds into bitterness and bitterness can break out into violence. Who can say that God has not been working through mundane, worldly influences—the TV, the vision of loaded supermarket shelves, the ads in magazines and newspapers—to move these people away from the wretched life in which many of them have been forced to live?

We have said, secondly, that the God of the cross is the God of judgment who exposes our sin and issues his divine No against it. In this riot God exposes to those with eyes of faith the sin of racism, discrimination, exploitation, and indifference. A teen-age girl in Watts shrieked at a white fireman who was battling the blazes, "White man, you started all this the day you brought the first slave to this country." And another screamed, "You created this monster and it's gonna consume you!"[11]

Judgment was there—judgment in the fear of white Angelenos who rushed out to buy guns for protecting themselves; judgment in death and destruction; judgment in the spread of riots and confusion to other cities in other parts of the nations. All of us, Negroes and whites, have participated in sowing the wind; all of us will continue to share in reaping the whirlwind.

But we Christians know also that the God of the cross shares with us in bearing the judgment upon our sin, that he is Love which identifies to the utmost with the beloved. We can see that suffering love manifested in those who identified themselves with Watts, who ministered to the people there despite bitterness and hostility and suffering. That love showed itself in a minister like Morris Samuel, who was one of the few whites who could walk safely in the streets during the riots. Father Samuel believed that the church had failed in its responsibility to these Negroes. "Christ was a revolutionary," he said, "but the Negro was never told that."[12] Father Samuel could have lived a comfortable life, but he chose to share the lot of a people in deep trouble.

God's love manifested itself in an outsider like Budd Schulberg, the writer. Shocked by overwhelming evidence of neglect in Watts, Schulberg offered to conduct a workshop, meeting weekly, to help people learn to write. Only two appeared for the first session, and for weeks Schulberg encountered fear, distrust, suspicion. What was this white guy after? Patiently he waited and worked, and finally he had a group of eighteen, from boys in their teens to unemployed middle-aged men. They would write poetry, read it to each other, criticize, try to help.[13] Here was Schulberg, who had many other uses for his Friday afternoons, sharing himself and his ability with men who needed his help.

Through all of this, we can see even in Watts the third dimension of God's work: the renewing, re-creating God at work in restoration and healing. Not only did good poetry come out of Budd Schulberg's group, but perhaps more important, a group spirit and willingness to help each other. People were being healed in that group, were coming to feel that they were human beings with something to offer. Small scale? Yes. But not everything that God does is spectacular.

Perhaps "the most effective agency now operating in Watts."[14] is the Westminister Neighborhood Association, begun by the Presbyterian Church well before the 1965 riots, now—at this writing— operating with the aid of Federal funds. With varied courses of study —arithmetic, reading, Negro history, and the like—the Association seeks to help unemployables fit themselves for jobs. This is renewal and restoration of human lives. Surely God is there, at work.

He is also at work in restoring, however, through other than church agencies. Los Angeles and indeed the whole nation were roused to concern by what had happened in Watts, and endless programs were organized in the hope of providing help—some of them realistic and effective, others hopelessly naïve. Programs like "Operation Bootstrap" and "Operation Head Start" for the young; training programs and employment assistance for unemployed adults; self-help programs like the Opportunities Industrialization Center; public funds for housing renewal. Money and concern poured into Watts in an attempt to close the great gaps left by previous neglect and indifference.[15]

"We're on top and they are on the bottom," said Chief Parker when the 1965 riots finally subsided. But problems remain, and it is this writer's conviction that God will continue to work against any situation where one group is on top, the other on the bottom. And wherever we see painful things happening which bring person-to-person dimensions to human relations instead of a "top" to "bottom" dimension, there we can say, "The hand of the Lord has done this."

All of which says to us, in the words of Harvey Cox, that "if we want to speak with God, then we had better find out something about the world because that is the only subject in which God is interested."[16] As many have pointed out, God is perhaps far less interested in "religion" than he is in "the world." This is not to say that we do not need the church—chapter 6 should have made that clear! It is to say, rather, that we will never have a clear view of what God is doing if we look for him only on Sundays.

If we are to respond fittingly to what God is doing, then, we need to have a thorough understanding of what is happening in the world. Watching TV? But it cannot be just entertainment. If we care about serving God, we need to be open to the serious analyses of the news which TV can bring to us—news in depth, documentaries—and we need to *demand* this from networks and producers. Reading? But it cannot be just the headlines in the daily papers. If we care about serving God, we need to carefully read the news, and thoughtful editorial comment. We need also to read magazines which often probe issues in depth—the *Saturday Evening Post, Look, Harper's* or *Atlantic*.

We in the church are that part of the world which God uses to interpret his actions to the rest of the world. But we will never be able to discern his work if we look for him only in Bible and church. Rather, they both should point us to the world, where he is at work and is calling us to join him.

God at Work Through a Loving Teacher

We might get to thinking that God's hand can be seen only in great national events. After all, Amos was addressing the whole nation: "Look! God is sending the Assyrians!" Deutero-Isaiah was addressing the whole group of the exiles: "Look! God is ordaining Cyrus to set you free!" We in our own analysis have looked to a race riot to ask what God is doing.

If we have eyes of faith, however, we will be able to discern

the presence of God in the lives of people right around us. Harvey
Cox has put it nicely: "We all stand in daily need of the God who
is as near to us as the nearest thou, because it is through the nearest thou that God bestows life on us daily."[17] And again, we can
recognize him in individual lives because we know in Christ the
general pattern of God's working. Let us look at the life of one of
the most distinguished women of our day, Helen Keller, and ask
how the God we know in Christ reached into her life through
Annie Sullivan Macy.

The story is familiar to all of us. Annie Sullivan, herself half-
blind, fresh out of a school for the blind in Boston, traveled to
Alabama to try to teach young Helen Keller—blind, deaf, and
therefore dumb. Annie Sullivan, orphan child of Irish immigrants,
took on at 20 a task so complicated that most veteran teachers
would have abandoned it in defeat. But through lifelong self-giving,
she enabled one like a little animal to become a full, rich human
being, known all over the world. Eyes of faith enable us to look at
these two lives being interwoven and to say, "The hand of the
Lord has done this."

Again let us look at this story in the Biblical categories of incarnation, crucifixion, ressurection. *First, we know that he is the
incarnate God, who works not quickly and spectacularly through
magic, but slowly and quietly through people. He worked through
people to touch the life of Annie Sullivan herself.* A desolate,
lonely little girl in an almshouse in Massachusetts, with a painful
affliction of the eyes, she was finally enabled to go to the Perkins'
Institute for the Blind to be educated. But she rebelled against
conformity to school patterns and the faculty despaired of being
able to teach her, until one English teacher volunteered to tame
her. Miss Annie Moore was wise and patient, and she taught young
Annie to read and write, but more than that, she taught her to be a
person—a person with a disciplined mind. And there were others,
persons who touched Annie Sullivan: Mrs. Sophia Hopkins, for example, who taught Annie how to dress properly. Through people,
God reached into the life of Annie Sullivan.[18]

It was through Annie Sullivan that God reached into Helen
Keller's pathetic existence and turned it into a life. *Secondly, it*

was the God of a cross who sent Annie Sullivan to Alabama; for Annie was to take on a life-long identification in love with this young child, an identification which would bring much suffering with it. Miss Keller herself said long afterward, "A sorrier situation never confronted a young woman on fire with a noble purpose."[19]

At their first meeting, seven-year-old Helen snarled like a wild animal, and Annie soon learned that not gentleness and affection would tame this little beast, but discipline. Many a struggle ensued, even exhausting physical battles in which Helen would howl with fury. Many a night Annie would cry herself to sleep in sheer frustration and exhaustion. "I think," said Helen later, "that at that time Teacher felt like the roots toiling in the dark and cold to build up the tissues of flowers."[20]

Annie absorbed endless hostility and violent opposition, taking all this upon herself in order to enable Helen to communicate. For she knew well that this was the way to lead the child from animal existence to humanity. Helen herself recognized this later. "Without a language of some sort one is not a human being; without speech one is not a complete human being."[21]

Third, through all this suffering love, a re-creating God was at work, restoring Helen Keller to the wholeness of personhood. There was the restoration of companionship through the power of communication, as Helen learned names—names for mother and father, little sister, and above all, Teacher. There was the ability to laugh and play, "a faculty-shaping element without which either study or skillful work is hardly possible."[22] There were endless channels for the expression of Helen's creativity—thought and love and speech and encouragement. Teacher's lifework, said Helen, was "my development as a human being."[23]

Anyone who reads of Helen Keller in later life—lecturer, world traveler, tireless laborer on behalf of the handicapped—might wonder how this could be; he who knows God in Christ will say, "The hand of the Lord has done this." And Helen Keller would agree. "She was lent to me from the Lord so that I might develop my own personality through darkness and silence. . . ."[24]

Granted, not everyone around us is a Helen Keller or an Annie Sullivan, but the God who through Annie Moore touched

Annie Sullivan, who in turn made a human being out of Helen Keller—that God is at work in plain people all around us. He does not wait until we are in social crisis to make himself known; "it is through the nearest thou that God bestows life on us daily." And because we know God through Jesus Christ, because we know something of the patterns of his working, we can recognize him as he does his loving work in our midst.

To Recognize His Work

God is at work in every event, working for human wholeness, for fullness of humanity. Oftentimes it is through the tragedy of judgment that he works, but always it is with the purpose of bringing new life. So we need to have eyes of faith, that we might see him in the things that happen in our world; and when we do . . .

When the sick are being healed, and broken creation is being repaired, restored, there we know God is at work. Where the hungry are being fed and the abandoned given shelter and warmth; where relationships among people are being strengthened, mended, there God is at work.

Where nations are learning to understand each other, and ideas are being shared and exchanged, there we see God at work. Where industry, seeing its responsibility to society, sacrifices profits to combat polluted water and befouled air; where a society works to help its aged, sick, retarded, poor—and maintains their "personhood" as it helps—there we see God at work.

Where a couple, troubled by marriage difficulties, listen again to the words of the wedding ceremony, and each learns again to put the other first: in plenty and in want, in sickness and in health; where a white man suddenly comes to understand, with the bottom of his heart, that this Negro is a person, there we see God at work.

But there are always other forces at work: man's sin which corrupts and hinders the work of God; man's freedom to rebel against God's purpose of love and to seek only his own good, not his neighbor's. God limits himself by our freedom; he does not force us to love. His time is eternity while ours is measured in the pain and toil of hours and seconds, decades and years; and it is sometimes difficult to see his hand.

But his hand is there, for those who have eyes to see. "But you, Israel, my servant, Jacob, whom I have chosen . . . 'You are my servant; I have chosen you . . .' that men may see and know, may consider and understand together, that the hand of the LORD has done this, the Holy One of Israel has created it."

Questions for Thought and Discussion

1. "It is not easy to see clearly what God is doing, for we are surrounded by the confusing evidence of the work of man" (p. 107). Explain this. How can the work of man likewise reveal what God is doing?
   Example—
   new medical discoveries
   discovery of new ways to lift people out of poverty
   other examples

2. In what specific ways does knowing a person well help us to understand what he is doing and to predict what he will do? How is our understanding of God's work related to this?

3. "It is not our responsibility to take Jesus Christ to the world; he is already there. It *is* our business to meet him there, work with him, and help others to recognize him." Do you agree or disagree with this quotation? Why?

4. To what extent, if any, does there have to be an element of "the crucifixion" in a situation in order for "resurrection" to take place? Explain your answer.

5. It has been suggested that we can find out about God's activities in the world today partly through our reading and the watching of television. How can we do this responsibly? When does our

reading become escapism or lusting after the flesh? When does our TV-watching become sloth, detachment?

How can we help ourselves and our children to be selective in their choices of books, magazines, TV programs? Why is this so important?

"We become what we read." Explain. Will Christian responsibility therefore cause us to read some new magazines, or some books we would rather avoid? Is there crucifixion here? Why are these uncomfortable to us?

CHAPTER 8

Prayer and the Service of God

We Christians have not been handed some precise calendar of events telling us what God will (for example) do on November 30, 1969 or March 5, 1970. Nor have we been given a precise rule book telling us what *we* must do on November 30 or March 5. But God has given us some clues and pointers to his activity in our midst. Now, how shall we put all these together into a coherent whole, so that we can discern what God is doing and respond fittingly to his acts?

The pointers are clear. God has revealed himself in Christ, and we can expect him to be an incarnate God, working through people and the mundane realities around us; a crucified God, judging our sin but suffering the consequences of it with us; a re-creating God, bringing healing and restoration to human life. God has given us the Bible, and we can expect him through this book to call us to response. God has given us the church, through whose worship and life we can expect God to lift us out of ourselves and into concern for his whole family. He has given us eyes to see him in the world around us, and minds to understand what we see.

It is in the life of prayer that all of these clues can be fitted together and crystallized into understanding. Prayer is that communion with God in which the revelation in Christ can become real to us. It is that communion in which our lives are opened to him so that he can speak to us through Bible and church. In the openness of that communion he is able to give us his perspective on the things that are happening, so that we can look at the events around us and recognize God's hand in them, saying, indeed, "the hand of the Lord has done this." Prayer can help to open our eyes so that we can read correctly the signs of the times.

But, practically speaking, in what way does prayer figure in the making of our decisions? In chapter 1 we described Jane and Ed Johnson as they faced a difficult dilemma involving their son and a neighbor's daughter. What would we mean if we advised them to seek God's guidance in prayer?

THE FACT AND NATURE OF GUIDANCE

Christians have always testified to the *fact* of the guidance of the Spirit. Jesus promised this as he talked to his most intimate disciples on that last night with them in the Upper Room. "I will not leave you desolate," he said to them; "I will come to you." "When the Spirit of truth comes, he will guide you into all the truth." And Christians know that Christ has kept his promise, that believers down through the ages have known the reality of the Spirit's guidance.

But in what form could the Johnsons look for this guidance to come? A direct message from heaven, giving them specific instructions as to what they should do? Some Christians would describe it in this way: God guides through concrete, personal address, through specific orders given to *this* Christian, *today*. Recall the Oxford Group Movement, a group of Christians who, as Daniel Jenkins describes it, "wait upon God at the beginning of the day with pencil in hand to note down any orders which may come for the day's work."[1]

Or is God's guidance something less direct, a sort of glorified common sense? The Christian simply studies the facts of the situation, holds them up to the ethical precepts taught by Jesus, and then proceeds to make his decision. If God speaks, it is through a man's reason and conscience, instructed both by the example of Jesus and by the best wisdom of the ages.

Many Christians would describe the guidance of God in less mechanical terms than the Oxford Group but in more intimate terms than just conscience and common sense. God's guidance comes to the believer neither as magical directive nor as mere human wisdom, but as the sharing of purposes within personal fellowship—a relationship between responsible persons. God does not suspend our responsibility by telling us precisely what to do; that would make us into mere instruments, computers programmed to reel off the proper thoughts and actions. He would not expect Ed Johnson to shift his mind into neutral, reduce his self-consciousness to passivity, and wait for God's direction to come. God expects a parent, rather, to make the fullest use of all his resources—mind, heart, and will—as he shares responsibly in God's work of healing and reconciliation. God calls us to be not passive instruments but responsible agents.

This is the work of prayer, then: not to elicit God's instructions by some process of magic, but to enable the Christian to "take every thought captive to obey Christ"—to share in the concerns of God. Prayer opens the believer's life to the transforming presence of the Spirit, so that he is able to move from a preoccupation with his own needs to a concern for his neighbor's needs; this is the loving concern he shares with God.

It is the difference between inventor with robot and father with child. The inventor builds his robot to respond exactly to every impulse that comes from the control board; what the robot does is simply reaction to electrical impulse. The father, on the other hand, builds *himself* into his child through continued personal communion: as the child grows up, he participates increasingly in the things his father cares about and is working for. The guidance the father gives to his child—and God gives to us—is the guidance of person to increasingly responsible person.

Something else ought to be said, too, about the way in which the Spirit guides: It is a continuous process, not just an answer to the on-the-spot appeal. God does not wait for the Johnsons to cry out to him in the crisis of decision. He has been involved all along as Jane and Ed have built their trusting relationship with their son. The Spirit has been with them as they have studied the New Testament understanding of responsible love; he has been with them as they have read about and discussed illegitimate births and forced marriages in our society; he has been with them as they have counseled with friends who have faced this situation in their own children's lives.

This is always true of the Spirit's work in our lives. As we accumulate over a period of time the understandings which will condition our thinking and action, the Spirit of truth is at work, helping us to keep from warping the evidence to fit our own predilections and prejudices. Facts do not determine our decisions, but no intelligent decision can be made without an understanding of the situation. The Spirit illumines our thinking as we study the facts, and enables us to see with a clarity which is not our own.

Quite obviously, the condition for receiving this kind of guidance is continuous openness to God in prayer. If God guided in a mechanical way, it would be sufficient to send up a prayer when the crisis of decision arose. But if God guides through transforming our concerns, then we need to live with God in constant communion. This is what Paul meant when he said in 1 Thessalonians 5:17, "Pray constantly," and in Ephesians 6:18, "Pray at all times in the Spirit." He was urging these people to make prayer such a habit of their minds that it would go on, as a sort of basic disposition toward God, even when it was not conscious prayer. Guy Bowden speaks of the father who is not always consciously thinking about his son, for many other things occupy his conscious attention during the day. But those things do not prevent his having continuing fatherly affection for the boy. Whenever the child *does* come into his consciousness, then his love for and relationship with the boy come into consciousness, and, says Bowden, "he knows that he has never ceased to love that child for a moment, though he has ceased to think of him."[2] Our love for God should be like that—a basic disposition of the heart which is there all the time, even when we are not *consciously* aware of his presence.

"Habitual guidance comes to habitual seeking . . . ," says George Stewart.[3] Sensitivity to God's presence among us and to the direction of his will is developed through continued humble seeking. "Ask, seek, knock," said Jesus, for God is more eager to give his Spirit than we are to ask.

THE CLEARING OF VISION IN PRAYER

It is not easy to see God at work, for our vision is blurred; we focus so intently on the things that affect us and our own people that what God cares about fades off into hazy distance. Ibsen accurately portrays us human beings in one scene in *Peer Gynt*. The hero has assumed that the people in the lunatic asylum are "outside themselves." Not at all, replies the director of the asylum.

> Outside themselves? Oh no, you're wrong.
> It's here that men are most themselves—
> Themselves and nothing but themselves—
> Sailing with outspread sails of self.
> Each shuts himself in a cask of self,
> The cask stopped with a bung of self
> And seasoned in a well of self.
> None has a tear for others' woes
> Or cares what any other thinks.
> We are ourselves in thought and voice—
> Ourselves up to the very limit. . . .[4]

We saw in chapter 6 that preoccupation with our own immediate interests blinds us to the sovereign God's concern for all men—Indonesian and Brazilian as well as American. We saw in chapter 7 that self-interest makes us identify God's work with the welfare of our own group, so that we have a hard time recognizing him when he works for the welfare of other groups at the expense of our comfort and our profit. Waldo Beach described our self-centered blindness in *The Christian Life,* saying that we worship false gods which reflect our own love of self. Money, security, status, comfort, Americanity—these are the deities before which we really bow, he said; and because we do, we simply cannot see the true God as he works among us. For he comes as one crucified, and he calls us to be willing to suffer with him, to be willing to give up comfort and status and security if the need of our neighbors, God's children, requires it. This is not the God we expect him to be, however, and want him to be, and we simply cannot perceive his work in our midst.

Genuine prayer helps to sharpen the dim vision caused by preoccupation with our own concerns. We have said that it opens us to the transforming and renewing power of the Holy Spirit. Paul has described for us what happens in Romans 6:3–11 and 8:9–17. The old self—"shut up in a cask of self"—is crucified with Christ. The person who really joins himself to the Christ of the cross has made a decisive break with the old gods—comfort and status and security and the power money can bring; these no longer dominate his life. Jane and Ed, whatever their final decision may be, are deeply concerned about the welfare of Louise and her parents, because protection of their own family's standing is not the final consideration with them. Moreover, the believer joined to Christ is raised up again, as Christ was raised, to newness of life—life in the Spirit. The Spirit enables him to be no longer a rebellious—and fearful—outsider, anxiously defending his own ego, but a child of God, secure in the Father's household, increasingly free to share the Father's sacrificial love for the rest of the family. The Johnsons do not have to be burdened by anxieties about their own position. They can be free to seek the welfare of these others to whom they are responsible.

Prayer opens us up to this kind of transformation by enabling us to be open to the presence of God's Spirit. The consequences are inevitable: as we children of the household share more and more in the Father's love and purpose, less and less are we concerned with the protection of our own ego. Less and less are we defensive about our own welfare, or that of our family, our class, our race. Increasingly we see things from God's perspective, see that his family includes more than just our own kind. And so our blurred vision begins to come clear in prayer. God, through his Spirit, helps to furl our "outspread sails of self" by drawing us into the utter security of his family where we can care for our brother's welfare as for our own.

With opened eyes, then, we can see God at work and discern what he would have us do. Now when he calls us to sacrifice for Indonesian or Brazilian, for employer or employee, for husband or wife, we more readily recognize him and see more clearly what he is doing, for we share increasingly in his sacrificial love for these others.

THE CONTEXT OF GUIDANCE

The Spirit *does* illuminate our thinking and our acting; this has been the testimony of countless Christians for twenty centuries. He lessens the blinding power of our self-centeredness and opens our eyes to recognize God at work, so that we who share his concerns may join him in his work. He is with us as we study the situation, enabling us to look honestly at the facts so that our work with God can be intelligent and effective.

The guidance of the Spirit, however, is not often given to me as an individual in isolation, off in a corner by myself. The illumination of *my* mind for the decisions *I* must make fits in with the whole context of God's self-revelation to men. So the church has always insisted that guidance comes most clearly to the people who are steeped in the thinking of the Bible, and to those who share with their Christian brothers in the community life of the church. Our prayer needs to be set in the context of our grappling with God's Word in the Scriptures and of our earnest listening to the testimony of God's people.

Prayer without the Bible can be meaningless. "The Bible is passport, guide and interpreter in the world of prayer," says Daniel Jenkins, "and if we neglect or ignore it can we wonder that we should feel lost and foreign in that world?"[5] It is not that prayer must grow out of *this particular* Bible reading, but that it grows out of a mind and heart so steeped in the Scriptures that it always uses the Bible as a point of reference. Our prayer is always in danger of falling into subjectivism; we are likely to come to prayer with head buzzing with our own problems—tensions with spouse or children perhaps, or with business partner or boss—so that we limit our prayer to this and nothing else. Prayer with Bible in hand, however, helps to focus our concern on God's kingdom, God's purposes. It lifts our eyes to see God's concern for the whole world, for that is what the Bible is all about.

The reverse is also true, however: The Bible needs to be read in the context of prayer; this we were saying back in chapter 4. The Bible is, after all, a book of history. It belongs to the past and would be to us simply a collection of curious facts if it were not somehow made contemporary for us. This is the work of the Holy Spirit through the believer's prayer. Without prayer, the Bible can be simply a dead record which has no relation to our life today.

The Spirit's guidance through prayer comes most clearly to people who are steeped in the thinking of the Bible, but his presence is also closely related to their sharing in the fellowship of the body of Christ. The person who depends on his own interpretation of God's action, while he is isolated from the church, is in danger of going off on all manner of false tangents.

"The breaking of bread and the prayers" was a characteristic activity of the early church. For the early Christians, the very idea of prayer meant prayer in and with the body of Christ. A New Testament Christian would likely have been baffled by the idea that prayer is an affair solely between the individual and God, going on independently of the community of believers. In the early church the fundamental form of prayer was common prayer; private prayer was just one aspect of the corporate praying of Christ's body.

Our prayer life today is poverty-stricken, partly because we have so little life together in the Christian community. We find a common life in the Scouts or the bowling club or the State Education Association. Here we often know genuine sharing and deep involvement in each other's lives. But rarely do we find the depth and richness of the common life of intercession, the common life which is our birthright as Christians and churchmen.

This does not mean, of course, that we can leave out the individual dimension of prayer. Each man must himself stand before God; no other can pray in his stead or make his decisions for him. Each Christian must put together for himself in prayer the evidence which he believes points toward the fitting response to what God has done. But the individual finds the setting for his own devotional life in the corporate life of the church. As he participates in the common prayers of the church family, saying "We" instead of "I" and focusing his attention on common concerns rather than his own individual cares and decisions, he can be delivered from his own subjectivity—his moods, his irritations, his personal successes and failures.

The individual Christian who seeks God's guidance all by himself is in danger of seeking it selfishly and therefore of not receiving it. Our prayer needs to be related to the life of the church and to the understandings of the Scriptures. When this happens, prayer can become a more effective instrument for opening our lives to the transforming power of the Holy Spirit. That Spirit lifts us out of our petty little self-concern and enables us not only to see the sovereign God at work, but also to join him in doing it.

THE CONDITION OF RECEIVING GUIDANCE

Archbishop Sodorblom of the Lutheran Church in Sweden once called his people to the privilege of serving and seeing the will of God for our day. He explained that his choice of the order of the words was a deliberate one: "serve and see." "For in the Kingdom of God no one can see so long as he remains merely a spectator. Those only who serve the will of God sacrificially can see the will of God."[6]

The condition for discerning what God is doing in our day is the willingness to respond in obedience. If "any man's will is to do his will," says Jesus, "he shall know whether the teaching is from God." (John 7:17) The one who would know God's mind must be willing to do God's will. The man who is willing to commit himself, to obey what he knows, is the man who will be moving constantly into deeper understandings of the purpose of God.

The prayer of this committed man becomes, then, the request to share in the work of the kingdom. It is an expression of willingness to share the concerns of God—the incarnate, crucified, recreating God—and to join him in his work for restoration and renewal in human life. So, real prayer is designed to help me find *my* place in God's work of re-creation, working toward wholeness in human life. But this is not abstract and general; it becomes quite specific and concrete. It becomes the prayer that the Spirit will guide me to do those things in *my* city which will make a Watts riot unnecessary. It becomes the prayer that the Spirit will alert me to the Annie Sullivan in *my* group who needs to be loved.

The Christian who would discern God's will must ask, seek, knock; undoubtedly. But further than that, he must be ready to obey what it is given to him to know. He who would see must serve.

FAITH, NOT SIGHT

Jane and Ed Johnson faced a complex and difficult decision; who would casually tell them what to do? But neither the Johnsons nor any of us is ever alone in the making of a decision. Jesus promised his disciples he would send them the Spirit, and he has kept his promise.

We walk by faith, however, and not by sight. Guidance is there for us, but it is never automatic and infallible, at least in our reception of it. The believer is not protected from making mistakes. We receive no immediate word from heaven assuring us that we have found the one course of action which is consonant with God's will. We simply go ahead and act, doing what we best understand to be the fitting response to God's actions, trusting in the love and wisdom and forgiveness of God. "The manifold wisdom of God is fully able to let those who are being saved be not yet fully wise, and to guide them even through their unwisdom at one and the same time into finer character and more fruitful service to His kingdom."[7]

That is the joy of it: God is willing to let us be "not yet fully wise," to allow us in our freedom to make mistakes. It is because he wants us to be not robots, but children of God, that he is willing to work patiently and graciously with us. He entrusts to us the responsibility of genuine decision, but all the while he is building himself and his love and concern into our lives as we open ourselves to his presence.

We have not been given a precise calendar of God's acts nor a precise rule book to direct our action in response. But God gives himself to us: he is with us throughout the whole process of decision-making. And because he is both sovereign and merciful, he can take even our mistakes and weave them into the pattern of his great ongoing purpose of reconciliation and redemption. What greater privilege than to serve a God like that?

Questions for Thought and Discussion

1. What is the difference between a passive instrument and a responsible agent? How does this difference encourage us to pray in order to find guidance?

2. Does corporate prayer—prayer with others in the church— mean anything to you? Why? What could or should it mean? What specific steps could your class take to revitalize the life of prayer?

3. Is "each kindly deed a prayer"? Why? Why not?

4. What is the relation between serving God and knowing God's will?

SECTION II

THE SOCIAL CONTEXT OF DECISION

Ethics is personal. Whatever may be the content of our response to God, no one of us can escape being personally responsible to God.

We do our best to escape, of course. Sometimes we are like children at a party, playing "Hot Potato." They pass the object rapidly—ever more rapidly as tension mounts!—from hand to hand; then, when the music stops, the one caught holding the object is out of the game. Great is the scrambling when that music stops; each wants to pass on the Hot Potato to somebody else.

We human beings have always been buck-passers. Look at the Garden of Eden. "The woman gave me the fruit," said Adam. "The serpent led me into it," said Eve. Who wants to take responsibility for a wrong decision? Look at us today. A mistake is made in the office, an order gets fouled up, the firm loses a good customer. Who is responsible? "Not I," says the shipping clerk; "the secretary misunderstood the order." "Not I," says the secretary; "the boss gave me a memo." "Not I," says the executive; "we just followed company policy." Who wants to take the responsibility for a wrong decision (and a miffed customer)?

Like children playing Hot Potato, we want to lose ourselves in the crowd; if *we* don't make the decisions, nobody can blame *us* for what happens. But there is no losing ourselves in the crowd when God is around. The old spiritual puts it bluntly:

> There's no hidin' place down here, hallelujah!
> There's no hidin' place down here.
> I went to the rock to hide my face,
> The rock cried out, 'NO HIDIN' PLACE!'
> There's no hidin' place down here.

The buck-passing stops here—with you and me. God is at work, and he calls *each of us* to respond fittingly. Ethics is personal.

To say that ethics is *personal,* however, is not to say that it is *individualistic,* as though we make our decisions uninfluenced by the people around us and without any consequence for the groups of which we are a part. The fact is that we make our decisions in a social context. What we decide to do is partially shaped by our community or communities—family, church, economic class, nation. And what we do affects all sorts of other people—not only the people around us, but also people whom we've never heard of and will never see.

How do we decide what we should do? We have been saying from the beginning of our study that our actions are answering actions; we make our decisions in response to what is happening. In Section I we were concerned with our *interpretation* of what is going on—how we discern the *meaning* of events. The lion roars, says Amos; the shepherd understands that the flock is in danger and acts to defend them. The trumpet blows; the people understand that the city is being attacked, and they spring to their posts. So with us: We need to understand what God has done and is doing, if we would respond fittingly to his presence in our midst. So we have been discussing how we can discern what God is up to, what clues he has given to help us recognize that "the hand of the Lord has done this."

In this section we will now move on to a consideration of the second aspect of our answering action: the fact that it takes place *within a social context.* Amos reminds us that God spoke *to Israel* —"the whole family which I brought up out of Egypt." For the fact is that the way we interpret the things that happen is strongly influenced by the communities of which we are a part.

We will be spending the next few weeks, then, talking about these groups which condition our thinking and which in turn are affected by what we do and say. In chapter 9 we will be asking, How wide is the community which shapes us? Do we listen to many different kinds of people or only to those who already think and react as we do? In chapters 10 and 11 we will be talking about the give-and-take decisions we make at home, and the way these affect both parents and children. Chapter 12 will focus our attention on the church and on the way in which we handle controversy in the life of congregation or denomination. In chapters 13 and 14 we will be talking about the decisions that are made in the business world—the world of work. We will seek to understand not only the ways in which we are both influencing and influenced by the people we encounter in office or shop or classroom or supermarket, but also the way in which the church can equip us for these encounters. In the last three chapters of this section—15, 16, and 17—we will discuss what is perhaps the greatest problem now confronting our society and our world: the population explosion. What does it portend for us, for our ability to live truly *human* lives? And what is our responsibility in the face of this increasing overcrowding of our planet? All the problems we are to discuss are presented here simply as samples. We will not have time or space to consider all the social problems of our time. But these will illustrate how our individual decisions are related to other people. And they will show how we may use what we have learned about ethics as response to God as we consider the complex areas of community life.

These are only *some* of the communities we are part of, and we have time to deal only with *some* of the areas of decision which confront us. Questions of war and peace, of race, of urban violence —matters like these will be touched on only obliquely. You will find no chapters devoted to those issues as such. Look back to Waldo Beach's *The Christian Life* for discussion of these things, and remember that the CLC study to be published three years from now will have a social focus. There is only so much space in one book and so much time for studying it, and a writer simply has to select.

We do need to look at the social context of our decisions, however, for though we are individuals, we are never *merely* individuals. We need to recognize both the joy and the responsibility of answering to God in the midst of the groups in which we are privileged to live. This will be our concern in Section II.

CHAPTER 9

How Broad Is Your Community?

THE OTHER PEOPLE WHO INFLUENCE US

The Fact of Social Conditioning

We give answer to God within a social context. God spoke *to Israel*—to "the whole family which I brought up out of Egypt." The way we interpret the things that happen is strongly influenced by the communities of which we are a part.

The fact is that our community helps to mold our consciences. As we look to see what God is doing in the world around us, we look from a certain viewpoint, conditioned by groups of which we have been a part, both past and present. What we see is colored by assumptions and by prejudices. We take things for granted because the people around us have always taken them for granted.

We can look back to our growing-up days and consider those groups to which we were intimately and directly related as we moved from childhood, to adolescence, to adulthood. The first group was our family, fundamental in importance. Here we picked up our attitudes toward people and the world, and our sense of values— convictions of what is important and what is not, what is worth pursuing in life and what is not. From our parents we learned how to react to income taxes and speeding motorists, to TV programs and books and magazines, to people of another color or another class, to food and trees and arguments and thunderstorms and dogs —and to God.

Moreover, because of the families we were born into, we find ourselves in certain economic and cultural brackets, and this has tremendous influence on our attitudes. We grow up accustomed to comfort (and assuming that everybody else enjoys it, too!), or accustomed to deprivation. We are thrown with certain groups as we grow up: some children in suburban schools, other children in schools in the inner city; teachers and administrators. All of these people help to build in us our prejudices and assumptions, our ambitions for ourselves, our expectations of life.

It is likely, too, that because of our family we happen to be in the church we are in. That church is another community that helps to shape our consciences—a community that may even assume a dominant role when our parents do not carry out their responsibility. If we grow up in congregations predominantly managerial and professional, we are likely to take a dim view of labor union activities. If we grow up in congregations predominantly of workers, we are likely to be suspicious of the motives of stockholders and boards of directors. If most members of our congregation are business people, we may suspect those eggheads of the university; if university people, we may scorn those money-grubbers in business. We absorb attitudes from each other in the community of the church and most often have no notion we are doing so, for we assume that *all* Christians naturally think as *our* group of Christians thinks.

These groups, to which we were directly related as we grew up, have all helped to shape our judgments of God's work and

"We always start with the little things that have been happening around our neighborhood."

Peg O'Connell in *Our Parish*. John Knox Press.

God's will. The larger groups in which we now participate as adults continue this molding process, unknown to ourselves. We are influenced by the people we work with: other mothers we meet regularly in the supermarket or over coffee; fellow-teachers at school; the fellows in the office. We get together at coffee break or at the water cooler and complain about those bureaucrats in

Washington, or those Jews down the street, or those narrow-minded people on the school board; and as we talk, attitudes are formed, suspicions comfirmed, prejudices strengthened. Our attitudes about right and wrong are molded in part by the organizations we meet with: Kiwanis or Elks, woman's club or labor union, PTA or bowling club. We listen to speakers and we talk to fellow-members, and if we hear the same philosophy week after week, we are not likely to question it.

We make our assumptions and are not often aware that we are making them, for our friends and colleagues rarely question our thought processes. Perhaps we are even less aware of the assumptions we pick up from the larger society of which we are a part. These are attitudes we have because we are Americans, or Southerners, or Midwesterners. We see the "American way" as the right way. The good life is, as Will Herberg has described it, "sanitary plumbing and freedom of opportunity, Coca-Cola and an intense faith in education,"[1] and we are a bit suspicious of "outsiders" who value other things more highly than these. We see the rural way as the right way, and we distrust those unstable folks in the city; or we see the urban way as the right way, and we have little use for those stubborn red-necks in the country. We are not aware that these are prejudices, because the people around us all share them. We Southerners cherish our history and reject the Yankee who interprets the Civil War differently. We Midwesterners cherish our individualism and reject those East-erners who talk about helping the masses. Seldom are we aware that we have taken on the coloration of our nation and region, and that others' viewpoints are both possible and valid.

The fact is inescapable: we are social selves. What we are and the way we think is to a great extent molded by the communities of which we are a part. This was certainly understood by the Biblical writers, who would have agreed with the German proverb, *"Ein Mensch ist kein Mensch"*—one man by himself is not a man at all. Without denying the responsibility of each individual (the Ten Commandments read *"Thou* shalt not"), they clearly asserted the corporate nature of human life. Achan sinned (Joshua 7) and his whole family shared in his punishment; David sinned (2 Sam.

24) and the whole nation suffered a plague. We are all one body, said Paul (1 Cor. 12), dependent upon each other as the head depends upon the feet, eye upon hand. The Biblical writers understood that our lives are bound together into one corporate whole.

Our experience validates the fact: we are social selves, each a part of the whole, each influencing and being influenced. But what shall we make of that fact?

How Shall We React to the Fact?

To know that we are influenced need not depress us; it can be reason for rejoicing. For it means that we human beings are so built that we can help each other, can share in each other's lives; and this is joy. It is the joy of families, where parents are helping children to grow up. It is the joy of friendship, where comrades share jokes and disappointments and exciting ideas. It is the joy of work, work together with others, where we can put our heads and hands together and be more productive than any could ever be by himself. If you have been in a Covenant Life Curriculum group where there has been real joint study, then look back over your own thinking and ask if there has been change; if there is evidence that as your group has struggled with new ideas, you have been molding each other's consciences. If so, then you know this joy, the joy of shared thought and decision.

There is danger here, however, for these molding influences can imprison us, can take away our freedom to think honestly and to respond with openness to God's work. The groups of which we are a part can narrow our potential for sympathy, making us incapable of ever imagining the feelings of the "outsider." We can find ourselves locked up in the prison cell of the thinking and imagination of our own kind of people.

Consider the discussion that took place one Sunday morning in a church school class in an upper-middle-class church in a Southern city. The discussion was of automation and layoffs and of what happens to the coal miner who no longer can find work in the mines. "Let the coal miner find work in industry," said many in the class. "But jobs are hard to find," pointed out one member. "And besides, the miner knows no other life than mining coal; how can he adjust?" "No problem there," said others. "A person can find joy in any work he does, just so he does it to the glory of God. Whether it is teaching or working in a factory or collecting garbage, no matter: there can be joy there for the man who has a vision of God's purpose." Thus spoke a group of teachers, and lawyers, and affluent business people who had never talked to a coal miner out of work, who had never themselves had to face the prospect of finding work they did not like and for which they were not trained. How could they really understand the coal miner's tragedy if they had known only teachers and lawyers and affluent business people? We talked earlier about blindness to what God is doing; here is deafness to what other groups might be saying.

In this situation we are not really free to think independently, for it is terribly difficult to transcend the prejudices of our group. How shall the member of that church school class recognize the limitations of the thinking that's going on? He has never heard those assumptions challenged, has never talked to the garbage man or the factory worker to ask him how he feels about his work. Had the coal miner been there that day, the class discussion might have taken a different turn!

The fundamental question each of us has to ask himself, then, is, *How broad is my community?* How many and how different are the groups which influence me, and of which am I aware as I make decisions? To what extent am I willing to expose myself to people not "my own kind," so as to be freed from the imprisonment of attitudes and ideas my group has always taken for granted?

It is this concern which is reflected in the American vision of the public school. Here was the place where children of all classes were to mingle together, where they could learn from each other and broaden each other's horizons, where each could grow in warmth of compassion and vividness of sympathy for others whose lives were different from his. Consider that dream. Could there be situations where it might be bad for parents to take their children out of a public school and send them to a private school? What would be the advantages and disadvantages of each kind of schooling? What factors should enter into making such a decision?

Perhaps that same concern was reflected in the vision of the early church. Rich and poor, masters and slaves, artisans, laborers, and merchants were all together in one body. This was the pattern of the Corinthian congregation and the Roman, the Philippian, the Berean, and the Ephesian. Consider that vision. Have we lost anything by developing homogeneous congregations of like-minded people? Have we gained anything? Would there be any advantages in having people of different economic levels gathered into one congregation? What would be the problems involved?

What would happen if a coal miner were a regular member of that church school class? It might mean that fewer things would be taken for granted! Consider the possibility that release and freedom can come when we have our assumptions challenged by people who are different. Are we really free to transcend the limitations of our group if we are not aware of other possibilities? Once the coal miner, or the sharecropper, or the millionaire, perhaps, poses an alternative, we can begin to think for ourselves. Freedom comes when we can take a stand *against* our group, if need be, in the interest of right and justice. Again, a Covenant Life Curriculum study group illustrates the point. If you have experienced greater breadth in your thinking by being exposed to different viewpoints, even within that relatively homogeneous group in your congregation, consider what an even broader span of persons might do to your thinking!

We will be molded by our community; this is a fact of life. The question is, how broad shall that community be? Shall it be so narrow that we remain prisoners of the ideas we have always taken for granted? Or shall it be broad enough to enlarge our sympathies, deepen our compassion, and enable us to participate imaginatively in the lives of the wide variety of people whom God loves and on whose behalf he is at work?

OUR RESPONSIBILITY TO OTHER PEOPLE

Who Is My Neighbor?

There is another side to the question. We have asked, How broad is the community which is to influence our thinking? Now we have to ask, How broad is the community for which we feel responsibility? Who is my neighbor?

Is my neighbor only the one who lives in proximity to me, who lives as I do, dresses as I do, works at the same kind of job and worships in the same kind of church? Does this mean that there can be "outsiders" for me, people for whom I need feel no responsibility? Need I share in the problems of just the family next door, the men and women at the office, my comrades on the golf

"WE'RE to blame for the riots?!...Why, I've never been in a ghetto in my life!"

Paul Conrad. Reprinted from the Los Angeles Times by permission of the Register and Tribune Syndicate

course? Or is there a sense in which I need to transcend my group, my kind of people, and care for my neighbor who may live in a slum in the heart of the city?

We hear it all the time, this drawing of the lines of neighborhood close about ourselves. I moved out to Garden Hills expressly to get away from the city; why should I sweat over the overcrowded downtown? I live in the city; why should I get worked up over the problems of the farmers (if they can't be efficient, let them move into the city and get a job)?

Many writers have noted that the people of Watts bitterly resented the indifference of most of the rest of Los Angeles. From the top of the Harbor Freeway one can see clearly the panorama of the impoverished area, and many commuting whites pass there twice a day. Most of them choose not to look, however, for it is not a pleasant experience. Los Angeles is a sprawling city, and as one writer noted, "To sprawl is to relax and feel comfortable. For most residents, Los Angeles is a comfortable city, psychologically as well as physically, because the unpleasant can be kept in its place—at a safe distance from most of the people."[2]

"That's *their* problem; we've got enough of our own." Is there any among us who has never said that? "Why should my tax money be spent on housing for the slums? Those people won't keep a place nice, anyway." "Why should they spend *my* money to clean up the Hudson River? The New Yorkers polluted it; let them un-pollute it." "Why should we worry about feeding the people of India? We have people right here at home who could use our help."

Who is my neighbor? Can there be a person so far away that his problems are no concern of mine? Well, I know what God's concern is: he cares for the whole, for *all* human beings. He does not value some groups more than others; he secks to reconcile *all* men to himself and to each other. And to the extent that I limit my responsibility to *a part* of humanity—to some groups and not to others, treating some as outsiders (whom I need not worry about)—to that extent I fall short of God's intention for my life.

Toward Broader Community

When a labor union leader urges his fellows to ease up on

wage pressure so as to fight inflation, when a corporation chairman appeals to the directors to share profits with the workers—these are steps toward God's broader community.

When white parents pass up the private school and send their child to public school to enlarge his sympathies; when a realtor decides in obedience to God to work for *all* people to have nice homes—these are steps toward God's broader community.

When a suburbanite campaigns for the bond issue to finance better schools in the slums, and the apartment-dweller downtown works for a rapid transit system for commuters—these are steps toward the neighborliness that knows no outsiders.

*   *   *

Ethics is personal, but it is not individualistic. We make responsible personal decisions, but we make them amidst the influences of the diverse groups we are part of, and what we do or refuse to do affects all sorts of other people, many of whom we will never see. The God who is at work among us cares for all men, on both sides of the tracks. So he calls us to broaden our horizons, to let ourselves be delivered from imprisonment within the narrow concerns of just one group so that we can share compassionately in God's work among a diversity of people.

In the chapters that follow we will be talking about the groups which influence us and which we in turn influence. God is at work in these communities of ours; how should we respond?

CHAPTER 10

Communicating Ethical
Values to Children

Here are three brief stories about the teaching that goes on in homes. Listen to them—one happy story, two unhappy.

Jane Johnson's mother was visiting them at Christmas time and, enthusiastic soul that she was, enjoying the Johnson family customs: the reading of the story from Luke 2 on Christmas Eve; the singing of a hymn before breakfast on Christmas morning; opening the packages one by one, so that each member of the family could share in the excitement of the others.

Christmas night, drifting off to sleep, Mrs. Sibley thought happily to herself: "I've enjoyed this. Boy, I'm lucky! Jane's family likes to do things the way we used to do them at home—when Jane and Freddy were children. Lucky. Makes it nice." Then she laughed herself awake. "Idiot!" she said out loud. "Where did

Jane get her ideas about Christmas?" Chuckling to herself, she gradually went off to sleep.

*   *   *

Leslie B., 17 years old, being interviewed by a writer for the *Saturday Evening Post,* explained why he drank. "After polishing off twelve cans of beer, I feel happy. I feel like a man instead of a kid. Nothing bothers me, and everything is funny. You know, it builds up your courage and your ego."

The interviewer asked him what his parents thought about all this. "My parents? All my life they tell me 'no' about drinking, and then I come home and see them . . . loaded!"[1]

*   *   *

Sara G., a young physical education instructor, came to the chairman of her department for counsel. "I had a letter today from one of the youngsters in the church where I worked last summer. Julie is 14, and she's pregnant, and she wants to know what to do."

"What about her family?" inquired Dr. B.

"Her father is away in the Army; she has no rapport with her mother. She turned to me because there just isn't anybody else."

"Well, haven't her parents taught her about sex?"

"The facts, yes. What to do, what not to do. But as I see it, they've never provided a relationship in which Julie felt important —felt that she was really a *person*."

"So she desperately sought in the sex relation the full attention of another person—something she'd never had at home. Right?"

"That's about the size of it."

TWO CONCLUSIONS AND A FACT

Three stories—one happy, two unhappy. What conclusions shall be drawn from them?

First, we adults communicate ethical values to young people by what we do and the attitudes we express. Words and teachings are secondary; they can only reinforce and interpret what children see and hear. They can have little impact if they contradict our deeds and attitudes.

Who should be surprised to see Jane and her family celebrating Christmas in that way? Her parents never had to say, "Go to now; let us enjoy Christmas as a family time; let us share together in the message of Christmas and in the giving of Christmas." They never had to *say* these things. They simply *did* them—and Jane and Freddy absorbed ideas from what went on in their home.

Who should be surprised to see Leslie B. guzzling beer? His parents can say "No" all they please, but it is not their *words* that Leslie has been hearing. What those parents have been teaching in words has not jibed with the way they live—and there is little question about which is the more powerful.

Second, ethical behavior is conceived in and produced by personal relationships. If the relationship between adults and children is a defective one, tense or indifferent, it is likely to produce behavior which may break adult hearts.

Consider Julie. She had no real security at home, so she sought it urgently in sex. Here was the only way she knew to find the assurance that somebody deeply cared about her as a person, that for *somebody* she was unique and irreplaceable. It is ironic that she should seek security and the assurance that someone cared in sexual expression, when it is possible that the boy cared not at all for her personally, but considered her simply an object for the gratification of his pleasure.

Consider Leslie. "It builds up your courage and your ego," he said to the interviewer. Why does he need to have his courage built up by beer? Surely it is at home and in the community of the church that a boy's security should be firmly established. It is here that he ought to find a sense of worth, an assurance that his life means something. It would seem that something is wrong, badly wrong, when a 17-year-old seeks courage in six-packs of beer.

The reality of it seems inescapable: the behavior of children is often determined by their relationships with the adults in their lives. If those relationships are sound and healthy, there is a good chance that the youngsters will be wholesome in their conduct. If the relationships are tense and anxious, if a youngster feels that he is constantly on trial, then there is grave danger that he may do wild things in order to prove to himself that he is a person.

Charles Schulz. © 1959 United Feature Syndicate.

These stories point us to a plain fact of life: all of us are involved in this business of communicating ethical values to children. It is parents, of course, who exert the primary influence; day in, day out, year after year, they are with their children— children who are watching and listening. Attitudes are expressed in facial expression and tone of voice; values and commitments come clear in what parents do and say. Parents are teaching whether they use words or not, for children see and hear—and follow.

Others besides parents, though, are communicating. Teachers see the young people every day in school and share with them ideas and excitements—as well as prejudices and resentments. Teachers in the church school have their effect, as do scout leaders and little league coaches. From all these adults young people are absorbing viewpoints and assumptions, ways of looking at life.

These are the "molding influences" we talked about in chapter 9; these adults help to color the thinking and shape the conduct of the young people as they grow up. By what we do and by the quality of our relations with these children, we participate in the making of persons.

TWO IMPERATIVES

The fact is inescapable: there are few adults who do not have some connection with young people, however indirect it might be. All of us are engaged in the enterprise of teaching ethics to young people. Two urgent imperatives are thereby laid upon us as Christians.

First, we need to get together on our stories. We need to see to it that what church school teachers and youth leaders try to tell these young people, and what parents *say* to their children, all fit in with what those young people *see* and hear in the adult lives around them.

Henry Resnik has told about some of his experiences as a high school teacher. He had tried to help his students in English class to see that turning in work they had not done was cheating, and immoral. Then one day the mother of one of his students came to him in great indignation; David had received only a "C" on a paper, which was an insult to his [David's] parents—who had helped him write it! As she put it, "Certainly if his parents write his papers with him he deserves to do better than a C—I mean, he's having expert help."[2]

The same mother went on, according to Resnik, to say that she and her cousin—"who taught history in high school, mind you"—had spent a whole evening working on a map for her daughter's history class; they had done a beautiful job, but the stupid history teacher had given the girl only 72 on the map.[3]

What teacher can convince his students that they should honestly do their own work when parents act otherwise? "It is quite clear," comments a newspaper editor

> . . . that one of the keys to anything remotely approaching a solution of this matter of wholesale cheating is the attitude of parents. If they put their children's grades above everything else, including their children's character, and even help the

children to cheat, the outlook would seem to be almost hope-less.[4]

What can the teacher accomplish if he teaches one thing in words and the parents teach another in actions? Consider the teacher of a senior high class in a church school, who is trying to help his young people catch a vision of service to God and to God's people. He challenges them to service in the community now. He challenges them to look toward sacrificial work for God in the future—the world mission of the church, the Peace Corps, teaching in a slum school. This is certainly a fine ideal, but what effect can this teaching have if there are boys in the class like Charlie B.?

My father has his own problems, and I don't expect him to devote all his spare time to me or to understand all of what I want to do. But I ought to get a few credits from him. I volunteered last summer to tutor some poor kids in reading in a town near here. My father laughed when I told him, and said if I were smart, I'd earn some money. We don't need the money, and he didn't want any of what I would have earned. But I wasn't getting paid for tutoring, so it was no good.[5]

The words spoken in church school will have very little mean-ing for these youngsters if they hear contradictory attitudes ex-pressed at home. The imperative is laid upon us: let's get together on the *content* of what all of us are teaching—verbally and non-verbally—to these young people who have been given to us as our responsibility. *There is a second imperative, too: we need to get together on the relationships within which these children are developing their ethical patterns.*

The Sea Scout leader is guiding his group in a study of family life and family responsibilities. They talk about ways in which family solidarity might be cemented, and one boy suggests that young people should be willing to talk things over with their parents. Parents need to know about and to share in the problems of their children. Fine; many parents would be pleased. But what does a discussion like this mean to Warren C.?

I haven't talked seriously with anyone around here in ten years. My father is not the type who sits and listens. He sits and tells you, when he bothers. I sit down to talk to my father and he falls asleep. If I take a problem to him, he immediately jumps into a stand and tells me what to do. That does me no good. I'm old enough for a discussion, not an ultimatum. One day I came home to tell my folks I had just gotten an "A" in Advanced Placement physics. My father and I got involved in something the minute I walked in the door, and it ended with him telling me I'm not old enough to have a serious opinion about anything. I walked out of the house. I never did tell him about the "A." . . . With the Navy next year and then college, if I'm lucky, this will be my last year at home.[6]

Family solidarity? What youngster can be taught to care for *that* when he meets no response from his parents?

A fourth grade teacher at school is trying to build class relationships where each child is accepted in his uniqueness. Not an easy job, that—to lead children to a respect for what each has to give so that they do not reject those who are different. One is a pint-sized scholar, another is kingpin on the playground. Each should be allowed to give what he has to give.

A fine ideal, though difficult to communicate. But the teacher could be building this kind of spirit in the class—unless she had many like Elsie Y. In Elsie's home are jealous parents, vying for the affection of their children. Insecurity is the problem: the father is galled to see Elsie's 11-year-old brother growing closer to his mother than to himself; the mother resents Elsie's obvious admiration of her father—such admiration that the child reflects his qualities in her 8-year-old life.

What teacher can build a spirit of mutual acceptance in the class at school when the children go home from school to competition, back-biting, and resentment? The urgent imperative is laid upon us: we need to get together—teachers, parents, and scout leaders; whatever our position or responsibility—on the relationships in which, far more than we realize, we are communicating ethical values to the young people in our midst.

QUESTIONS AND ANSWERS FOR ADULTS

Think again of Leslie B., 17 years old, whose parents said one thing in words and exactly the opposite with their lives. Think again of Julie, driven into sexual tragedy because her parents had never made her feel that she really mattered to anybody. In the light of these stories, none among us can avoid asking himself two crucial questions: How can I so order my life that what I say and what I do form together one seamless robe of consistency? How can I so order my relationships with these young people—my children, my students, these little boys I coach—so that when they leave me they go out feeling that they are *persons,* that their lives count, that they are significant?

It is obvious that we do not do these things by the gritting of the teeth or the tightening of the belt; the answer to these questions is not the simple exertion of willpower. The answer comes as each of us looks to his own relationship with God, seeking to be open to his presence within our individual lives, living in openness to his presence. And these are not just pious words, a sweet ideal; we are talking about an actual fact of the Christian life. Look at the way it would work.

Take, for instance, the parents of David, as they helped him with his paper for English. What was their real concern? David? Hardly! Is was their own egos they were coddling; they were desperate for their children to be admitted to good colleges so that they could say casually to their friends, "I heard from David today; he's at Yale, you know." So they were willing to push him to make high grades, even at the cost of cheating. The English teacher commented, "The new rule that cancels all others: Whatever will get the student ('my boy that I sacrificed everything for') into college is right."[7]

Suppose, however, that God's transforming power is let loose in these parents' lives, that in God's grace they are being made new creatures. Now they begin to share in Christ's concerns, begin to see things in his perspective. They begin to see that many things are more important than David's making it to the fanciest college. Increasingly more important for them now is the kind of integrity which does not need to deceive; it is that which they now want for their son—the kind of life in which he seeks his goals not by underhanded methods, but by honest expenditure of effort. Christ can enable those parents to think less of the satisfaction of their own egos, and more of the genuine welfare of their son.

Look at the parents of Charlie B. Here is a father who cannot see the point of sacrificial service—why work if there is no money in it? Money is power; with it you can order people around, and none can say you nay; surely one of life's more gratifying experiences! But Christ can begin the process of changing a man's sense of values, can begin to help him see that persons are more important than money. Christ can help a man to realize that human life is made for service, that here is where the satisfaction is—a real satisfaction that money by itself will never be able to buy.

Look at the father of Warren C. Here is a parent who is not really interested in his son as a person. He is centered in his own interests, and the boy is out on the fringes of his concern. Listen to his son? Not at all; he goes to sleep. When he *does* talk to him it is *to* him, not *with* him; his aim is always to dominate. But let that father begin to find the real security of being in Christ, a security that frees him from having to be constantly defending his own ego. Then you will see that man's life transformed. Now he is not compelled to assert and protect his sensitive ego by dominating his son's life; he can allow the boy to be a person in his own right, with thoughts and judgments that are worth listening to. And he can listen in genuine interest (not just the appearance of interest), for he knows that the boy—like his father, like all of us—needs to know that people are hearing what he says, needs to have people look him in the eye and acknowledge that he is there and important.

The Sea Scouts can discuss family solidarity all they please, but Warren C. will learn very little about sharing in families unless there is sharing in *his* family and unless he can talk to his parents, confident that they will listen. The God we know in Christ can take parents and make them into people who care.

Lastly, look at the parents of Elsie Y., who are jealous of each other. Why? Because each wants to be the center of the universe, each wants to be kingpin in the children's lives. Each wants the children to depend completely on *him*, dance attendance on *him*. But let Christ be at work in renewal and re-creation and there will be some changes made. In Christ a parent can have the basic security which frees him from dependence on his children's responsiveness, so that he need not try to envelop a child with his own life. In Christ a person's sense of value and of significance need not depend on having the lives of his children revolve around *him;* it depends on his being himself a child of God. In Christ a person can love undemandingly, allowing for his child's free response to other people.

It is at home that a child needs to learn about acceptance of others, about working together without jealousy. The fourth grade teacher can only take Elsie Y. and her classmates as they are and build class relationships on the foundation of attitudes that were built at home.

"If any man is in Christ, he is a new creation." The God who raised Christ from the dead can raise us up from immersion in our own ego and enable us genuinely to love and care for the people around us. These are not empty phrases; God's transforming power is available—if we are willing to be transformed.

How can I live a life of consistency between the words I speak and the deeds I do? How can I live in warm and trusting relationships with these youngsters for whom I am responsible? The answer is: we cannot, by ourselves. But if we are willing to be open to the creative power of God, he can begin to lift us beyond ourselves and make us greater than we are. He has called us to love as Christ loved us, and in his mercy he enables us to begin to do it.

CHAPTER 11

Decision-Making in Family Relationships

"O.K., folks; family council tonight."

Dinner was over; Aunt Mildred had gone to her room to get dressed for circle meeting. Ed Johnson had noted the strained silence at the dinner table and felt that it required no unusual intelligence to decide that something had gone wrong—and that the "something" had to do with Aunt Mildred. The family needed to look at this together.

Seven-thirty came; Aunt Mildred's friend honked for her and they went off together. Then the Johnson family settled down in the kitchen to thrash it out.

"So, what caused the trouble?" inquired Ed, looking from one child to another. "There *was* trouble, that's easy to see."

Each waited for the others, until Ted, feeling his responsibility as the eldest, spoke up. "I guess I'm the one who did it, Dad. I got fed up; she turned that TV off just one time too many."

"Yeah," said Mike, "I've *had* it! We step out to the kitchen to get a coke, and when we get back to the living room, there's the tube, blank, and we have to get it all turned on again. She does it all the time."

"Surely *that* needn't kill you," commented Mrs. Johnson, "just turning on the little switch."

"No," replied Ted, "I guess it's just that she acts like she owns the place and it's *her* TV instead of ours. If she doesn't like the noise, why doesn't she stay in her room?"

"So Ted blew his top, and that was it," added Mike. "She went charging off to her room. Boy, she didn't like it *one bit!*"

"O.K., boys, let's look at this," said their father. "Remember the family council last year—when we all decided we ought to invite Aunt Mildred to live with us a couple of years? We didn't *have* to do it; that's why we had to make a decision."

"And make it together," observed his wife. "We knew we'd all be in on it. Mike had to move in with Ted. We'd all have to make adjustments. We knew that."

"Yeah," replied Mike, "we decided. Uncle Frank had died and we worried about her. And I think it was right to do what we did; but golly, Mother, does she have to *take over* the place?"

"Let's think about it," said Mrs. Johnson. "Remember, she's never had any children. She's used to deciding about the TV herself—just she and Uncle Frank were there to watch it."

"And she's probably not used to our kind of noise," Sally chimed in.

"Who *could* be?" muttered her mother.

"Well, sure, but that doesn't give her the right to tell *us* what to do," said Ted. "Mother, can't you talk to her?"

"Yes, I think I can. But meanwhile, how about our responsibility? You boys need to try to understand what makes her react like that; try to see things from her point of view."

"And remember, son," added the father, "what we all said when we decided to ask her to come: we said she would need love and acceptance; we'd be willing to accept the difference she made in our lives."

"You're right, Dad. But—well—Mother, please talk to her.

And Mike and I will try to remember, but—well, it won't be easy."

"Not for any of us, Ted. But don't forget, she's a person. If we make her feel like an intruder rather than a member of the household . . . It's the responsibility of all of us to let her know we want her."

"O.K., Dad. We'll try."

DECISIONS WITHIN RELATIONSHIPS

This had been a shared decision in the Johnson family. The whole household would be affected by Aunt Mildred's coming; the whole family shared in the decision to invite her.

In chapter 10 we were talking about the importance of relationships, the need for parents to *listen* to children and to respect them as persons. Julie's parents had never made her feel that she was a real person, who mattered. Leslie turned to beer to build up his sense of worth. Warren C.'s father never discussed things with him; he *always* treated him as a child who could never have a serious opinion about anything.

Note that in the Johnson family, the children know that they are persons. They are not just things, to be pushed around as though they had no mind or will of their own, but persons—responsible, decision-making persons who have their significant share in weaving the fabric which is family life.

The decisions made at home are endless and infinitely varied. Can she or can she not watch TV? What time does he have to be in from the date? Shall Mother work outside the home? Shall they buy the trombone for Junior (will he really practice? and *what* about the neighbors' nerves—not to mention the family's!)? Jane and Ed Johnson believe in parental authority (when they say "No," that's what they mean), but they also believe that insofar as possible people ought to have a share in decisions that affect them. Just Ed make the decisions, and tell Jane what to do? Far from it. Jane make up her mind, and finagle Ed into going along with her? Emphatically not. The parents deliver ultimatums to their children ("You do so because I say so.")? Not in the Johnson household. For each one in the family is a *person,* a whole person, and the others respect him as such.

Now, what does it mean to be a whole person? Well, at least two things: to be aware of your own individuality, your separateness from other people; and to be able to respond to other people, to take responsibility for their welfare.

Consider this matter of individuality. We all need to know that we are individuals with our own identity, an identity that is not completely submerged in the family. Each of us needs to know that he's a person with a mind and will of his own, able to make decisions or at least to participate in decisions that affect him. Note that Ed and Jane said to the boys, "We all decided to invite Aunt Mildred. . . . We knew we'd all be in on it." And they implied, "We all have to adjust together to the consequences of our decision." Each person in the family had the chance to enlist his own individual thinking and willing in this common family enterprise.

We all need to know that we are *ourselves,* not just an extension of someone else's personality. Paul Tournier, the great Swiss physician, illustrates this nicely when he comments on the importance to a child of having a secret. The child becomes aware of his own individuality when he knows something that his parents do not know. "To know something which others do not, is to become a person, distinct from other persons."[1] But a child likes to *tell* secrets, too, for this means that *he* has the right to decide—to decide what he will tell and what he will hide. This is his decision and his alone to make. He is a person, who can take responsibility for himself.

Reuel L. Howe, who knows more than most people about human relations, is in accord with this understanding. As a child grows up, says Howe, he needs the care and supervision of his parents, but he also needs to be able to assert himself and his will, to be a person separate from his parents. For growing up requires the facing and making of decisions; only in this way does a child grow toward responsible maturity.

The objective of love, therefore, is to provide a relationship of firmness and tolerance within which a child may become autonomous and acquire a sense of self-control, self-esteem, and relationship with others. . . . Our aim is to help the child become a responsible participant in the crucial issues of life, and to preserve his integrity as a deciding person.[2]

If we love, then, we have to leave the other person, child or adult, free to do things his own way, to an extent consistent with his maturity. He must be free to stumble and make mistakes, free to receive the consequences of his errors. Not that a child is capable of making decisions for himself all along the line; that is foolishness. But from the beginning he needs to know that he is respected as a person, who can participate, insofar as he is capable, in decisions that affect him.

All of us have the basic need to realize our individuality, then. We need to recognize and respect ourselves as individual, decision-making persons, not play toys in someone else's hand. This is part of what it means to be a whole person. But there is another dimension of wholeness: the ability to respond to other people, to

"I can't play now. The establishment says I have to do the dishes."

George Dole. Copyright 1968 Saturday Review, Inc.

participate imaginatively in their lives. Recall Jane Johnson's words to her boys: "You boys need to try to understand what makes her react like that; try to see things from her point of view."

Martin Buber, one of the great Jewish theologians of our day, put this truth in his famous words: "Through the *Thou* a man becomes *I*."[3] "I become through my relation to the Thou; as I become *I*, I say *Thou*. All real living is meeting."[4] We become whole persons as we are able to be responsible for others; not to be withdrawn into our own separateness and ego, but able to share in and to participate in the lives of others. It is in Buber's words, to be able to "experience . . . the other side," to "feel from 'over there.'"[5]

If Ted Johnson is responding just to his own personal irritation, he will blow his top and lash out at Aunt Mildred, making her feel that she is an intruder rather than a welcomed member of the household. If, on the other hand, he can be helped to put himself imaginatively in her place (difficult task for an obstreperous boy!)—to feel what is happening "from the other side"—the chances of his responding with a degree of gentleness and patience are considerably increased, and he and his parents are better able to work out a constructive way to handle the situation.

It is in family relationships that we learn (or do not learn!) how to include the other fellow's welfare in our own decision-making, how to accept the difference the other fellow makes in our lives. It is not surprising to see husbands and wives having difficulty being considerate of each other's wishes when neither of them grew up with this kind of consideration in their own homes.

The psalmist declares that we are "fearfully and wonderfully made." (139:14, KJV) The way in which a person becomes a person is a fearful and wonderful process; we ought to have reverence for it and a profound concern to understand it. Each one of us emerges as an individual, unique and separate from all others, yet he does this within his relationships to those others.

Our service of infant baptism symbolizes both these dimensions of personhood. The minister calls the child by name, "Mary, I baptize thee . . ." identifying this child as a unique particular child of God, distinguished from every other child of God. He is accepted as an individual in his own right. Then the minister declares that this baptized child is a member of the household of faith, recognizing that he becomes a person only in relationships, only as part of a community.

So it is in the family. Each is an individual, needing to take responsibility for himself. But each also is a member of the family, needing the opportunity to relate responsibly to the welfare of the others. What would some family decisions look like if the family made assumptions like this?

THREE FAMILY DECISIONS

Husbands and Wives

A wife is champing at the bit, not finding complete fulfillment as a person in her household routine. She raises the question one night after the children have been put to bed. "I think I'll get me a job," she says to her husband.

"A job, honey? What for? We don't need the money. We're managing better these days."

"It's not the money. It's me. I need it. I don't know why, but I need it."

A history major in college, she misses the excitement of the coffee-cup discussions of campus days—an excitement she cannot find in conversation with elementary school children or with a husband who is tired at night. Note some possible husbandly reactions:

1. "Absolutely not. You're my wife, I'm supporting you. You'll stay home and take care of the children."

2. "Do whatever you want to do, honey—just so you arrange to have lunch for the kids and dinner on the table for me when I get home from work."

3. "Maybe we'd better talk about it. What do you mean 'I need it'?"

4. Other possible reactions?

Note the implications of each reaction for their relationship:

1. The husband makes the decisions and that's that! The wife is not to be a decision-making person herself, even where her own life and welfare are involved. He refuses to recognize her individuality and separateness.

2. The husband expects her to take care of her own life, not fully recognizing his involvement in what she does, his responsibility for her individual welfare and happiness.

3. The husband recognizes that this is a problem that involves them both. He knows that he needs to try to see "from the other side," to be involved in what is happening as *she* sees it. So he will listen to her and join with her in thinking it through.

Suppose they take option 3, to think through the problem together. Here are some matters which might be included in their thinking:

The Need: Why Does She Feel Dissatisfied?

1. The need for separateness as well as for belongingness.

2. The need to be an individual, not immersed in husband and children to the extent that she loses her individuality altogether.

Betty Friedan has stated the problem this way (in her controversial *The Feminine Mystique*):

The problem lay buried, unspoken, for many years in the minds of American women. It was a strange stirring, a sense of dissatisfaction, a yearning that women suffered in the middle of the twentieth century in the United States. Each suburban wife struggled with it alone. As she made the beds, shopped for groceries, matched slipcover material, ate peanut butter sandwiches with her children, chauffeured Cub Scouts and Brownies, lay beside her husband at night—she was

afraid to ask even of herself the silent question: "Is this all?"
. . . We can no longer ignore that voice within women that
says: "I want something more than my husband and my
children and my home."[6]

The Possibilities

1. Find a new perspective on her responsibilities and opportunities
   in the home; discover that they demand all the intellect and
   education any woman can muster.

   As Phyllis McGinley has put it:
   We who belong to that profession [of housewives] hold the
   fate of the world in our hands. It is our influence which will
   determine the culture of coming generations. We are the
   people who chiefly listen to the music, buy the books, attend
   the theater, prowl the art galleries, converse with the children.
   Our minds need to be rich and flexible for those duties.[7]

2. Recognize that this is not enough and move toward outside-
   the-home fulfillment as a person.
   a. Work in a part-time job which will allow her to get home
      before the children do.
   b. Work in a full-time job, arranging for an adult to be on hand
      when the children come home from school.
   c. Do volunteer work in the community—tutoring culturally
      deprived children, working in the Junior League Bargain
      Box, volunteer work on the church staff.
   d. Other options?

The Problems

1. Just any work won't give her the intellectual excitement she
   knew back in her college days.

2. It's difficult for her to find a paying job that can be adjusted
   to her own and her family's schedule.

3. The family does not need the money but the children *do* need
   to have Mother there when they come home. Though note

that there are studies which indicate that this may not be true:
". . . there is no definitive evidence that children are less happy,
healthy, adjusted, *because* their mothers work."[8] Other studies
showed that children of working mothers were less likely to be
either extremely aggressive or extremely inhibited, less likely
to do poorly in school, or to "lack a sense of personal worth"
than children of housewives.[9]

4. If she *does* work outside the home, she may have guilt feelings
   resulting from a fear that she is neglecting her family; and if
   she does not, she may fear that she is evading her responsibilities as a citizen.

Where Do They Go from Here?

1. How do husband and wife make a decision together about this?
2. Suppose he is reluctant to see her work outside the home. Does
   she yield to his wish, because of love for him? Or does he
   recognize her problem and yield to *her* wish, because of love
   for her?
3. What is God doing here? How can this couple be aware of his
   actions and respond to him as they respond to each other?

Decisions for Children, Remembering Their Personhood

The 16-year-old son has faithfully worked on Saturdays and
afternoons at a supermarket and has saved his money carefully
for months. Now he announces, "I want to buy a Honda." He
wants to be free; to be able to go where he wants to go, when he
wants to.

The parents are somewhat taken aback; they are painfully
aware of accident statistics involving motorcycles and motorbikes.
How shall they respond to their son's request?

Note some possible parental responses:

1. "No. It's too dangerous. We'll take you where you want to go."
2. "It's your money. Do what you want to with it."
3. "Let's talk about it. Why do you want the Honda?"
4. Other possibilities?

Note (as in our previous analysis) the implications of each response for their relationship with their son:

1. The parents are denying the boy's personal need for independence—for at least a responsible share in making a decision that affects him.
2. The parents are denying any real involvement in Tim's life and concerns. They don't really care.
3. They regard Tim as a person, but one who needs mature guidance. They are willing to listen to him, to enlist his aid in thinking the matter through.

Suppose they take option 3, to think through the problem together. Here are some matters that might enter into their discussion:

Pro—in favor of agreeing to the boy's request:
1. He has earned his money; he should decide how to spend it.
2. If he is mature enough to drive a car, why should he not own a Honda?
3. There would be greater convenience for the whole family—for his getting to school, staying late for football practice, and the like. (Mother could probably have the car more often.)
4. The other boys in his gang have them; he dreads being considered a square.
5. Teen-agers need to be independent, to assert their individuality as separate from their parents.

Con—problems the parents foresee:
1. The danger, first and foremost: a boy is far less safe on a Honda than in a car.
2. The idea of a Honda gang roaring around the streets at night.
3. Fascinations of riding could absorb too much time from studies.

Some Important Considerations

1. Parents have to make the decision on a major matter like this; a 16-year-old is not capable of running his own life without guidance. Some parents are afraid to say "No" to their children for fear of losing their affection or of the children's not being the most popular in their gang. To say "Yes" out of that kind of fear is to damage a child in the long run. He needs to grow into freedom to make decisions about right and wrong, wisdom and foolishness; not in response to social pressures, but in honest consideration of the issues involved. And he is more likely to learn this if he sees it in his parents!

2. Whether they say "Yea" or "Nay," however, such a decision needs to be made in full awareness of the boy's personhood. The parents should seek to understand what the boy wants and needs. They should seek to "see from the other side." Moreover, they need to have the kind of respect for his thinking and desires (goals) that will lead them to communicate to him the reasons for their decision, helping him to understand that what they do is not for their own convenience but for his welfare.

Where Do They Go from Here?

1. How do parents make a decision so that the son knows he has participated in it?

2. How do they convince him that their "Yea" or "Nay" is a result of their love and care for him?

3. What is God doing here? How can these parents be aware of his action? How can they respond to God as they respond to their son?

Decisions by the Family

Saturday afternoon the man of the house had been talking to a stranger out in the yard. He came in and reported to his wife.

"I knew it was coming. That was a real estate man. Wants us to sell before it's too late."

"It's his kind that stir up trouble, Jim. That series in the newspaper, remember—about blockbusters? They make folks panic and then they get everybody's money."

"Honey, the FOR SALE signs up the street scared me, long before I saw this guy. Six blocks away now; they'll be crossing Barnard Avenue before long. The Negroes'll take over our neighborhood, that's all there is to it."

"Not if we refuse to sell, Jim. Couldn't we get everybody together—and agree on this thing? Agree to stand pat? Remember what happened to Aunt Sara and Uncle Bill's neighborhood. They all got together and formed a council or something, and promised each other they wouldn't sell out. And when a few Negroes moved in, they discovered nobody got leprosy or anything. . . . Might be nice neighbors—who knows?"

"Sounds good. Wish we could do that—get folks to stand pat. But they won't; you know that. And could we risk it? We just can't afford to lose money on the house. And the children . . . the schools . . ."

"But those folks *have* to have some place to live. And wouldn't the city be better off—be more peaceful—if we could all live side by side? I read in the *Daily News* about that suburb in Philadelphia, and that place in northern Virginia. They've done it there, and they haven't had many problems. Don't we have some kind of responsibility here, to more people than just us?"

"Yeah. I agree. But if it means sacrificing our security, no; that's our first responsibility—the children. We can't take a financial loss, Helen, when *they'd* be the ones to suffer in the future."

"Jim, the children ought to be in on this. They're old enough to know, and to help. They'd have to leave their friends if we moved. We're all in this together."

"Agreed. We'll talk about it at supper."

*   *   *

"I don't understand, Mama." This was 8-year-old Sara Jane talking. "Why don't people want these other folks to come to our neighborhood? What if we wanted to move to a new neighborhood and people said they didn't want us? How would we feel?"

(TO THE READER: Sara Jane is asking her parents to "experience from the other side." What should they say to her in reply?)

Said Tom: "Dad, Mr. Jarman says I'm in line to be editor of the Catawampus next year. Could we wait till year after next—so I can finish school before we move?"

Replied his father: "That may be too late, son. It's property values I'm worried about."

Sara Jane was puzzled. "What does that mean, Dad?"

"You wouldn't understand it all, honey. But when these people move into your community, then your house is not worth as much."

"*Why*, Dad?"

(TO THE READER: A child's question—asking her father to sort out myth from reality. How should the father answer the question?)

Sara Jane was worried. "I'd hate to leave my friends here."

"But they'll be moving, too, dear, most of them. Really, most everybody will."

"If *everybody* moves away, the Negro people will know we don't like them. But in Sunday school I learned that God loves everybody, and we should, too. How can we make the Negro people feel bad like that?"

(TO THE READER: What does the father say to *that* one?)

Other matters the family might think about:
1. The parents' concern that the children be properly prepared for college. Is there reality in the fear that the quality of the neighborhood schools might be lowered?
2. The parents' concern about the kind of companions their children would gang with. Likely comments from the children: Sara Jane: "There are Negro children in my class already. Some are my good friends."

Tom: "I bet some of them would be nicer to have around than that runny-nosed Bassett kid who plays with Sara Jane!"

3. The possibility of persuading some of their neighbors to stay, in the security of mutual support. But if that doesn't work, they might be left behind—too late to sell the house.

What should this family do? What is God doing here? How can this family be aware of his action? How can they respond to God as they act in this situation?

GOD AND MAN

We make our decisions in response to God, whatever those decisions may be. They may be large or small: can she watch TV? what time should he come home? shall Mother work? shall we buy that trombone? But they are not obscure and unimportant, for it is out of such material that character is woven, and the quality of the relationships within which these decisions are made is of crucial significance. We need to look, then, at God's relationships with us men; if in our decisions at home we want to be responsive to God, we need to ask how he deals with us, his children.

It ought to be said for one thing that God does not deny our freedom; rather, he works in and through and with it. God has the power to manipulate us in any way he chooses, but he does not choose to make puppets of us. He wants us to be persons— whole persons—and that means that we must be free. His dealings with us, then, are personal and not manipulative. In the last resort, we must respond to God from our own thinking and with the consent of our own will. Every one of us is always a "Thou" to God—a person with will and personality—and not an "It" to be shoved around at will.

Look at the way Jesus dealt with people. He always resisted the temptation to *compel* men's allegiance by a spectacular display of power, like flinging himself from the pinnacle of the temple and being miraculously saved from injury by God's angels. Read again the story of Jesus' temptation in Luke 4, and note how he steadfastly refused to take shortcuts to men's loyalty; he wanted them to respond to him freely, with the full consent of their wills.

Or recall that people were always asking him to provide signs and proofs of his power, signs from heaven (see Matt. 16:1–4), and he would say to them, "Think for yourself, read the signs of the times, judge the evidence in your own freedom. Don't ask me to *compel* your faith." Or recall the time when the disciples asked Jesus to call down fire from heaven on a Samaritan village that had not responded to their witnessing (Luke 9:51–56); Jesus rebuked them, saying, "You do not know what manner of spirit you are of—this is not God's way of doing things, but the way of impatient men."

God patiently respects our freedom, so he allows us to stumble and make mistakes. But it needs to be said, secondly, that *God sticks with us and shares our lot even when we do make those mistakes*. Nothing that we children of God might do can make God turn his back on us. Not that he condones the evil we do; the wrath of God is just as much a reality for the New Testament as for the Old. But God eagerly seeks us out, to draw us back to himself: the father goes rushing out to meet the returning prodigal; the shepherd leaves the flock to search for the lost one; the woman diligently sweeps the house to find the lost coin. God accepts us and forgives us and loves us in spite of all, and he stands beside us to share in our lot, whatever that may be.

As we respond to that kind of God, we can begin to develop that kind of relationship in our homes. We who know God's patient respect for our freedom can reflect the freedom of the others in our family. We can even learn that spouse and children are different from us and they may not always do things the way we would do them; in fact, they may *need* to do things differently, for the sake of their own integrity. Dissension and disagreement can be there among us, but it can be worked out as among responsible persons. The young girl can speak her own desires and judgments, not having to fear that she will be stomped on because she disagrees with her parent. The boy will know that he can freely discuss things with his father and not be subjected to a dogmatic harangue in the style of Warren C. God seeks our free response to himself; in like manner, we can respect the freedom and personhood of the members of our families.

Furthermore, we who know God's forgiveness and mercy for our own sins and short-comings can be forgiving and understanding of the hurtful things the people in our family do. Again it is not that evil is condoned; there has to be reprimand for bad things done. But there must also be willingness to accept and love and forgive in spite of all, and to share with each other even in the consequences of each other's mistakes.

"We love because he first loved us," says John in his First Letter (1 John 4:19). God the Father loves us, his children, and respects us always as persons. So we, as we respond to him, are enabled increasingly to have that kind of love in our homes. "Little children, let us not love in word or speech but in deed and in truth." (1 John 3:18)

CHAPTER 12

Controversy and Community in the Church

"Of such is the basic issue in religion today. Of such will come the split in the Church if it should ever be divided asunder."[1] Thus spoke not long ago one of the major periodicals in the Presbyterian Church, U.S. There are issues in the church, this magazine was saying, that have caused such grave controversy that they may finally split that denomination asunder.

It is a truism to say that Christians differ on issues. Controversy is there: in the congregation, in the denomination, even unto the edge of the abyss of schism, as our quotation above suggests. But all this is embarrassing to us who love the church, since it somehow contradicts our image of the church. "Behold how these Christians love one another"—*this* is the picture we want the world to have of us, not the picture of a scrapping, quarrelsome group who can never come to agreement on anything. We listen with sympathy to Paul's plea to the quarreling Christians in Corinth: "I appeal to you, brethren, by the name of our Lord Jesus Christ, that all of you agree that there be no dissensions among you, but that you be united in the same mind and the same judgment." (1 Cor. 1:10) This is what we feel the church should be like.

So what shall we do with controversy? Shall we sweep it under the rug, and speak in the church only of non-controversial matters? Shall we push on toward schism and organize ourselves into separate communities, each made up of like-minded folks who can be counted on always to agree? Shall we learn to live with controversy in the church?

How we personally decide about right and wrong, how we respond to God, is in part a matter of our relationship to other people. In the last two chapters we have discussed ethical decision in the context of the family. This chapter will describe something of what it means to respond to God in our church relationships.

CASE STUDY OF CONTROVERSY

To see an example of the problems Christians have in getting along with others in the church, let us take one illustration.

Let us look at the "basic issue" of which a Presbyterian publication could say, "of such will come the split." Let us face the question head on, asking ourselves what *we* think about it. As you discuss it in your class session, you may find that the differences of view found within Presbyterian and Reformed denominations are reflected right in your class. Thoroughly study this matter for yourself, and be prepared to discuss it when you join your group in the church. The discussion itself may demonstrate what it means to differ within the unity of the church, the body of Christ.

The basic issue referred to in the opening quotation has to do with the fundamental question, What is the mission of the church? Is it to be used by God in saving and nurturing individual persons, and only that? Or is the church to be used by God *also* for reconciliation in society?

Look at two characteristic statements of these two points of view. The Lay Committee of the National Council of Churches said in 1954:

Our committee believes that church organizations should devote
their time and energy to saving souls and making Christians out
of people; that once people have become Christians, they will
evolve a government which can be depended upon to administer
the affairs of state wisely and well.[2]

Dr. Harvey Cox, of Harvard Divinity School, said to a Baptist
student conference:

> It is the world, the political world and not the church, which
> is the arena of God's renewing and liberating activity. The
> church participates in this liberation only insofar as it partici-
> pates in the world. To turn our back on the world is to turn
> our back on the place where God is at work.[3]

If we look specifically at the Presbyterian Church, U.S., we
see the same dichotomy in thinking about the church's mission,
though the second position would not be stated so extremely as to
deny that God is at work in the church *as well as* in the world. Two
independent publications in this denomination, which take somewhat
different positions on many matters (is this bad?), differ considerably on the question at hand. Look at these two quotations from *The
Presbyterian Journal:*

> The Lord Jesus came to establish a spiritual kingdom. Jesus
> said to the man who asked Him to be arbiter in a dispute with
> his brother over their inheritance, "Man, who made Me a
> judge and a divider over you?" How wise is our Confession of
> Faith when it declares that the church is not to meddle with
> civil affairs.
>
> The New Testament program is to bring men into trans-
> forming relationship to Jesus Christ that they may go forth into
> their world to honor Him and obey Him. Why is this not widely
> understood? As Christian citizens they will play a mighty part
> in the lifting up of society. This was the program of Jesus. This
> was the program of the apostles. This ought still to be the pro-
> gram of the church. Our Lord's kingdom on earth is a spiritual
> kingdom.[4]

From an article by a writer in the *Dallas Morning News, The Journal* quotes with approval:

> Isn't this the message the church needs to grasp today? . . . "We are convinced," declares the group (the Presbyterian Lay Committee), "that the church has been diverted from her true mission, through public pronouncements and political activity in civil affairs. We believe that the one effective way to establish the kingdom of God is by the regeneration of individual men through the preaching of the Gospel of reconciliation.
>
> "There is a desperate need for the church to manifest her faith in God and thus develop further her spiritual power. The mission of the church is to call all men to redemption and only as she redeems individual people will society be effectively transformed."
>
> . . . Which is the better and more effective way—to have preachers in the picket lines or Christian laymen in the legislature?[5]

The *Presbyterian Outlook* would answer differently the question of the mission of the church. In one article the writer pointed out that

> . . . persons and social structures are so intermeshed that the church can work for nothing less than the conversion of each in relation to the other. Racial prejudice, for example, sends its roots deep into the proud egoism of the human heart. What but the gospel can truly strike home to that pride and replace it with repentance? But racial discrimination, in its institutional forms, feeds such pride day after day in our society. How can we preach repentance to this dimension of both self and society, if we fail to see both as subject to the judgment and forgiveness of God?[6]

In another *Outlook* article the writer analyzed the relevance of the Apostles' Creed for the mission of the church, and made this comment:

No province of individual or corporate existence and experience is ever apart from God's living, ultimate, intense, personal concern. Every breath you breathe, every face you
encounter, everything you touch, has the potential of a particular holiness because God is there!...If God's province is
where two or three people meet for any reason, then economics, civics, and politics should never be classified as "fundamentally secular concerns." In fact, the whole idea of "things
secular" is contrary to the biblical doctrine of God. . . . If,
therefore, no human institution escapes the purview of God,
so, also, should no human institution escape the vital concern
of the people of God.[7]

Think through these statements on this basic issue which
threatens to divide a denomination, and consider the following
questions:

1. *Where would you take your stand on this issue?*
   Which of the above statements do you agree with most?
   Which do you think is the sounder? Can you state reasons why?
   Which of these statements come closer, as you see it, to describing the Biblical idea of the task of God's people? Can you
   think of specific passages from the New Testament which support your viewpoint?

2. *Can you see any validity in the other point of view?*
   Can you state some reasons for espousing the other view?
   Can you think of Scripture passages which support this view-
   point?

3. Review in your own mind what we said in chapter 9 about how
   our views are molded by the groups of which we are a part.
   *Can you look back in your own life and identify influences
   which have helped you to your present attitude on the issue at
   hand?*

4. Study the following passages from the New Testament:
   a. Matt. 26:47–56.
      What is Jesus' reaction to the use of force—worldly power—
      in his defense?

What does he mean by, "But how then [i.e., if the disciples used force] shall scriptures be fulfilled, that it must be so?"
b. Luke 12:13–15.
Why does Jesus refuse to intervene in a quarrel over an inheritance?
What is the main point of this story, as expressed in vs. 15?
c. John 18:33–36.
What is the specific context of the oft-quoted statement in vs. 36?
Does Jesus intend to be making a general statement about his concern or lack of concern for this world?
d. Luke 4:14–30.
What is Jesus saying about his task? Does "to preach the gospel to the poor" (vs. 18) include concern for their *material* welfare?
When in vss. 25–27 he talks about Elijah's ministry to a Phoenician woman and Elisha's ministry to a Syrian leper, what sort of comment is he making about the "segregation" in Jew-Gentile relations?
Why were the synagogue folks so angry at what he said?
e. Matt. 25:31–46.
What is Jesus saying here about the Christian's responsibility for the material needs of men?
Does this necessarily suggest a concern for the *structures* of society? Does it help much to feed the hungry without addressing yourself to the causes of the hunger?

You will note as you study these five passages that the first three seem to lend a certain amount of support to the view that the church's mission is solely a spiritual one, concerned with individual salvation rather than with social change. The latter two point to the understanding of the church's task as including efforts to transform society. You might ponder the question, Can either position be finally proved from specific Biblical passages?

STUDY OF ONE SEEMINGLY AMBIGUOUS BIBLICAL PASSAGE

Church members often find it difficult to agree with each other on questions of doctrine or church policy, such as "What

is the mission of the church?" We often differ, too, on our interpretation of the Bible.

Look now at a passage which is familiar to all of us but for
parts of which there might be legitimately differing interpretations.
Turn to Jesus' "high priestly prayer" in John 17; read the whole
prayer, but in your study, focus particularly on verses 6–19. Note
that Jesus says that the disciples are to be *"In* the world" (vss. 11,
12, 15, 18), but not *"of* the world." (vss. 14, 16)

The word "world" as used in the New Testament does not
usually refer to the cosmos in the sense of the universe, or the
whole created order; it means, rather, the world as the arena of
human relations, especially human relations under "natural" conditions—the world of the "natural man." As William Barclay puts
it, "The world" is "human society organizing itself without God."[8]

Here are questions to be pondered:

1. *"I am not praying for the world."* (*vs. 9*)
   a. Is this to say that "the world," or human society, is beyond
      praying for?
      Compare vss. 20–21; also 3:16–17; 6:51.
   b. To get perspective: For whom is Jesus praying in 17:1–5?
      6–19? 20–26?

2. *"They are not of the world."* (*vss. 14, 16*)
   Literally, they are not *out of* the world—not derived from it,
   produced by it; their character and conduct is produced by God,
   not by the patterns of men.
   a. Does this mean the believer is detached from the world and
      therefore not concerned with conditions in the world?
   b. Does being pilgrims here—citizens of another world—
      mean that we have no further dependence upon and re-
      sponsibility for the affairs of human society?

3. *"I have sent them into the world."* (*vs. 18*)
   Christ did not serve God off in a cloister. He served in the
   midst of the turmoil of human life, and so must those who are his
   followers. It is *within the world* that the Christian life is to be
   lived.

    a. Does this necessarily mean that the church is to concern itself with social matters? Could this not refer to personal evangelism, seeking men out *where they are* in everyday life?

    b. Christians have their work cut out for them in the world where the people are; is John Wesley right, however, in saying, " 'You have nothing to do but to save souls' "?⁹

4. *"Sanctify them in the truth."* (*vs. 17*)

"To sanctify" is to set something apart from ordinary life for God's use (used of the temple and things in the temple).

    a. When Christ asks that his disciples be sanctified, is he suggesting that they be withdrawn from everyday life in the world?

    b. Or could it mean being set apart for a task, which is to go back into the world and be used in transforming the world?

WE CAN EXPECT TO DIFFER

Work through those questions on John 17, and be prepared to talk it all over in class. It is entirely possible that you will discover in your class discussions that equally honest and sincere Christians will differ in their interpretations of these words of Jesus. You may have found, too, that you have differed in your earlier discussions of the mission of the church. How shall we handle this fact of disagreement among Christian brothers?

One of our problems in responding to the reality of differences is that somehow this does not jibe with our idea of Christian community. We expect the church to be a place where there are no tensions at all, since, after all, these are Christian people with whom we are dealing. We interpret unity in the church to mean a condition in which there are no ruffled feathers of disagreement, where everyone is thinking alike. It becomes then something of a sacrilege to disagree with our fellow-churchmen, and we are acutely embarrassed when controversy does arise among us.

What many of us expect in the church is a special feeling of harmony—intellectual, spiritual, and social: this is what we mean by unity. We try, therefore, to surround ourselves with people who think as we do. Dr. Charles E. S. Kraemer commented to the Presbyterian, U.S. General Assembly in 1966, that our tendency is to "hunt around until we can find some group made up of people with whom we always agree, who will always tell us that we are right, who will never challenge us or disturb us . . ."[10]

The fact is, however, that uniformity has never been the prerequisite for unity—a fact for which we can be grateful since we'll never find a group where everybody is always in agreement! Moreover, it would not be good for us if we *could* find such a group. To quote Dr. Kraemer again:

> As long as we are sinners, and this means among other things that we lean strongly in our own favor, the kind of counsel we need is not always and only of people who will tell us invariably that we are right. . . . For the good of the church, for the good of our own immortal souls we need to be challenged, to be reminded, to be bestirred, to be disturbed.[11]

We will not be challenged and disturbed by the people who always agree with us. If we know that to be true, then we can understand why God intends for the church to be heterogeneous, as witness Paul's metaphor of the church as a body: many members, different from each other but drawn into wholeness by Christ the head. God uses our very differences from and with each other to challenge us all to deeper thinking.

What, then, is the true nature of Christian community? A Christian community is, first of all, made up of *people who know God and who know therefore their own finiteness and sin.* Having encountered God, we know that we are creatures and therefore finite; we cannot possibly grasp the whole truth, ever. We recognize our dependence upon others who may have grasped some different facets of the truth. We need them to supplement our own understandings of an issue. But more than that, having encountered God, we know that we are sinners, which means among other things that we lean strongly in our own favor. We have seen in previous chapters how the vision of each of us is narrowed by self-interest; those things seem true and right to us which are conducive to our own comfort and well-being, or to the well-being of those around us. But to be confronted by God is to become aware of this fact about ourselves and to be open to having our horizons broadened.

A Christian community, then, is a group of people who because of their relationship to God know their partiality and sin, and are willing to confess these things to each other and to the world. That kind of confession means that they are people who will speak in humility and be willing to listen to others who differ, and to learn from them.

A Christian community, secondly, is a group of *people who know God and rejoice in the security of being loved by him.* Secure in his love, we need not always be proving ourselves, proving the rightness of our own ideas. Moreover, we are secure enough to let our brothers be free to think differently, express things differently, and still love and trust them as brothers. "God does not will that I should fashion the other person according to the image that seems good to me," Dietrich Bonhoeffer observed, "that is, in my own image; rather, in his very freedom from me God made this person in His image."[12] It is the person who rests secure in God's love who is free enough to let his brother be free. A real Christian community is made up of such people as that.

Christian unity, then, is not something *we* achieve by ironing out all the human differences that exist among us; rather, it is something that is given to us by God *in the midst of our differences.* He gives it to us by drawing all of us into loyalty to himself, a loyalty in which we know the humility of the knowledge of our sin and experience the security of knowing God's grace. But this does not mean that we lose our individuality. Paul reminds us in Ephesians 2:15 that Christ brought Jew and Gentile into oneness —and could there ever be any two groups further apart than those two?—but there is no indication that they ceased to be Jews and Gentiles in the process. Differences remained; if you need evidence, read the story Luke tells of the first council of the church (Acts 15), where tensions between Jews and Gentiles came to a head and had somehow to be reconciled.

The fact is that unity in Christ is even more striking where

"Henry, don't be a troublemaker!"

Peg O'Connell in *Our Parish*. John Knox Press.

there is oneness in the midst of difference. Where there is opposition on the human level, even conflict of wills, there the unity that is in Christ shines out even more brightly. For where two Christians are in collision, a collision that cannot be resolved by human resources, their loyalty to Christ can point them beyond their differences to that One who is above them both, and in whom they are both one. Christian unity does not mean ignoring or suppressing differences; it means accepting each other and differing with each other within our common bond of loyalty to Christ. Says Bonhoeffer:

> The decisive passages in the New Testament do not say: one theology and one rite, one opinion upon all things both public and private, and one mode of conduct in life. But they say: one body and one Spirit, one Lord, one faith, one baptism, one God and Father of us all. . . .[13]

THE HOUSEHOLD OF FAITH

The New Testament writers knew what they were doing when they used images of *home* to describe the church. The church is the household of faith, they said; it is the family of God, the company of those who know God as Father. It is an appropriate image, for what we have been saying here about the quality of relationships in the church is exactly what we were saying in chapter 11 about the family. The family that is a congregation *ought* to have the kinds of relationships that our family life *ought* to have.

In the family there ought to be respect for the individuality and freedom of each. Each needs to be allowed to be different; there ought not to be the forcing of all into one mold, whether that is the pattern of Father's thinking, or Mother's, or whose ever. Further, there ought to be acceptance and understanding at home, a willingness to be so involved in each other's lives that each tries to "experience from the other side." This means real listening to each other, unlike some of the parents described in chapter 9, who either went to sleep when a teen-age son wanted to talk, or simply handed out ultimatums which brooked no discussion.

So it ought to be in the church: each of us granting to our brothers the freedom to think differently, each of us listening to the others in recognition that no one has the whole truth. Now, in some ways it is easier to do these things at home. I can put up with cantankerousness in my spouse and children, for they are mine; they belong to me, willy-nilly, and we all know that if things are rough today we will work them out tomorrow. But the people in my church are different: I have not committed myself to them

"Crazy!"　　　　　　　　　　　　　　　"Crazy!"

John Ruge. Copyright 1968 *Saturday Review*, Inc.

as I have to my family, and the compulsion to stick with these brethren when they are being ornery is not nearly so strong. I can get away from them—and that is precisely what I am tempted to do when disagreement begins to make me uncomfortable. I'm tempted to pull out, to go and find people who will not ruffle my feathers, who will preserve my serenity by agreeing with me.

We are called to respond to God, however, and God never tries to get away from us, no matter how stubborn and irritating we may be. And this, after all, is what it all boils down to: we are called to treat our brethren, at home or in the church, as God treats us—as *persons*. God wants us to know full personhood, and to that end he accords to us genuine freedom, even when it means he must suffer with us in our mistakes. And we must do likewise with those whom he has given us as neighbors. If we act in response to God, then our fundamental concern will be not always to prove that we are right and to argue everyone into agreement, but to see that these others become persons, whole persons, in the fullest, richest sense. "I am come that they may have life," said

Jesus, "and have it abundantly." This is God's primary concern; if we are to respond to him, it must likewise be ours.

The Issue
I almost understood today:
Almost knew the reasoning
Behind this thought
Which contradicts my own.

I almost listened
And caught sincerity in the words
I had hoped to label "sham"
Because they sounded new.

I almost saw it:
Almost looked from another side
And found all-new vistas
With horizons re-arranged.

Almost.

And, had I not retreated
To the ease of familiar patterns
Where thoughts repose and never venture,
I might have changed my mind.[14]

CHAPTER 13

Christian Decisions on the Job

A group of bankers met regularly for a year to talk about the ethical dimensions of their work. Late in the year's discussion one of the members of the group asked the question, "Well, could Jesus Christ have been a good banker?" An officer in one of the nation's largest banks replied, "Yes, I suppose so—in a small town."[1]

Implied in that officer's statement is his nagging conviction that bankers face all sorts of moral ambiguities in their work, that the banker has to do some things which he cannot quite square with his moral responsibility as a disciple of Jesus Christ. As a Christian person he can seek to follow Christ in his private life— his family relationships, his clubs, and such. But when he gets into his banking business—at least in a large bank—then he finds a different sort of situation.

The fact that these bankers were meeting together for discussion, however, indicates that there are many who do not accept the situation complacently, for their group was only one of many groups like it—people in varied occupations getting together to discuss the meaning of discipleship on the job. In recent years more and more people have wanted to meet with other Christians in their occupation, to explore with these colleagues how to relate *being a Christian* to *doing the job*.

In Section II of this book we have been talking about how all our discussions about right and wrong involve other people. Moving outward from ourselves, we are thinking of larger and larger contexts in which we must decide how to respond to God. Chapters 10 and 11 dealt with the circle of our family. Chapter 12 dealt with the larger circle, the church. This chapter moves out to consider a larger circle still. How do I respond to God among all the people in the world of my work?

SOME PROBLEMS IN RELATING CHRISTIANITY AND WORK

Now, one who wants to relate his faith to the doing of his job encounters many difficulties along the way. For one thing, so many of us have numbers of our decisions made for us by others; we are not really free to make on-the-job decisions in response to God, since so often we simply carry out policies set by others. In the great corporate structures where many of us work, we find ourselves on the lower rungs of the ladder. The company lays out the policy; we carry it out. We are told what to do and when to do it. Our problem as Christians in such cases is not so much how to make decisions, how to choose between alternative courses of action, but rather, what shall we do when the company sets policies that go against the grain of our consciences as Christians? We have to eat; our families have to eat. How can we set ourselves against the policies which are determined by those on whom our livelihood depends?

A second difficulty is that even in situations where we *can* make decisions, sometimes it is hard to have a genuinely Christian perspective on our work, to see how our job fits into God's overall purpose. We all know the old story of the three masons who were working on a cathedral. When someone asked them what they were doing, one answered, "I am laying these stones one on the other in order to build a wall." The second mason answered, "I am working so that I can buy the things my family needs—food and clothing and shelter." The third mason said, "I am building a house of God so that people may come and worship and be joyful."[2]

Fine, for the medieval man who could see that he was directly involved in the building of a church and know that most of his friends and neighbors would worship there. It was easy for him to see how his work was related to God. But even there we see that two out of the three saw no such relationship. For us it may be even more unlikely. We sell automobiles for a living, or pound typewriters, or draw designs for new products, and how all this fits into the work God is doing in the world is a bit beyond us. How, then, can we respond to God in doing these jobs? By what criteria can we make decisions when we are not building cathedrals but just earning a living?

There is a third difficulty for us if we want to relate our faith to doing the job, and that is the terrible complexity of so many of the decisions we face in our work. All the way through this study we have been talking about the complexity of ethical decisions, but nowhere is it more real than on the job. We have to do our work in a world of sinners, and there are all sorts of doubtful practices in almost *any* work. What do we do? Do we join in without asking any questions? Do we take a stand on principle at the risk of losing our jobs? Then where are we, and what have we gained?

Moreover, it is rare that we will really be faced with a clear-cut choice between good and evil; more often it will be a decision between alternatives, both of which are partly good and partly evil. Hans-Reudi Weber tells of a young pharmacist who had recently opened his own business and was working hard to make a go of it and to build a solid reputation in the neighborhood. He bought a large supply of a medicine highly regarded by the doctors he knew, but a few months later a superior product was put on the market. To meet popular demand he bought a large supply of this. Now, what was he to do with the stock that was outdated. It was good, but something better was available. To discard the original

"You bit me, I bit you back. Shall we consider the incident closed?"

Chon Day. © 1968, by *Harper's Magazine,* Inc.

supply, however, would involve a financial loss he simply could not afford.[3]

Now, this is no black-and-white decision between pure good and pure evil. To sell the older drug would not be to foist upon the public something that was dangerous; the drug had been perfectly satisfactory two months before. However, if he were to sell it now, he would not be providing the best possible product for his customers. On the other hand, if he were to scrap it all, he might take such a financial loss that his business would be endangered. He had a family to support, and he wanted to continue to serve the community as a druggist. So what was he to do? How do you think he should decide between the goods and evils in the options available to him?

All these difficulties tend to make Christians want to throw up their hands and say, "I'll go to church on Sunday and I'll try to be Christian with my family and friends, but I just won't worry about my faith when I go to work on Monday. I've got to make a living, and there's no use getting an ulcer over it." But the Christian who does this will still have to face those disturbing words of Paul to the Corinthians (1 Cor. 10:31), "Whatever you do, do all to the glory of God." It is difficult to leave your job out of that "whatever." What we need to do, then, is to develop what two British writers have called the "art of responsible compromise,"[4] the ability to work within the realities of the situation and find the relatively best option. There is danger here, of course; the danger of rationalizing or slipping into moral cynicism. But this need not be an irresponsible, cynical drifting with the tide; it can mean recognizing that all of us sin, that none will stay 100 percent pure and yet that all of us need to live with a continuing sense of the tension between what *is* and what *ought to be*.

Let us look now at four specific on-the-job decisions and ask in regard to each, What would responsible compromise involve?

FOUR CASE STUDIES

Low Man on the Totem Pole: Can He Protest?

Tompkins is *very* junior in his corporation, but he hopes to be rising gradually to the top. At the level where he now finds himself, he has to travel for the company during most of every week. Monday through Friday he is on the road, making contacts with customers and suppliers throughout his region. This is a good position; from here he can go right on up.

There are problems here for Tompkins, however, severe problems, for he realizes that in this kind of life he's not being a full person. He is a good company man, and he thoroughly enjoys his work, but what sort of husband and father can he be, or citizen in his community, or deacon in his church? He is at home on weekends, and he tries to crowd into those two days a whole personal life. He and his wife work hard at having a good time; but desperate fun is no fun at all. He tries to discipline the children, but he wants to play with them, too, and the children are thoroughly confused by Sunday night. He loves his church and would like to put time into it, but the Diaconate meets on Wednesday nights.

He has the same problem with the Community Fund drive and the Optimist circus and the School Board election campaign: the meetings are during the week and he is simply left out.

"This is no life," he says to Wilson, his best friend, one Saturday on the golf course. "Should I quit this rat race? But if I did—what then?"

Tompkins is only one man, and as a self he is unique, but his name is legion—the man who cannot set policies himself but must work within and live with policies that disturb his conscience. The young accountant in an accounting firm who finds himself helping clients cheat on their income tax: orders from above. The young secretary in the office, sending out letters she knows are dishonest: orders from the boss. There are many of us, folks who must decide what to do when company policy requires of us behavior which makes us uneasy.

So what does Wilson suggest that Tompkins do? Quit his job? Well and good for a single man, but Tompkins has a wife and three children, and the family man cannot casually toss over a job. The irony of it would be that if Tompkins took that course, he would be doing it out of love for his family, but his very act might plunge his family into financial insecurity. Would that be loving?

Moreover, if he gave up his job, he would be giving up the opportunity to rise to the top, to rise to a position where *he* would have influence on policy—and could perhaps change the pattern of putting one man regularly on the road. (Wilson being an honest man and a good friend might point out that Tompkins' motives are mixed here: rising to the top would give him a hand in policy, yes, but it would also give him a great deal more money and a considerable hunk of prestige. Tompkins' ego is not uninvolved as he thinks about *that* prospect!)

In the conversation, Wilson might raise two or three questions for Tompkins' thinking.

WILSON: Basically you have to ask (and you have to ask this any time the company treads on your conscience), Is this worth losing my job over? Is this of central importance, or is it only peripheral?

TOMPKINS: My family is right central!!

WILSON: Right. Maybe that's the nature of the decision you have
to make. Which is of first importance: a decent family life,
even on less income; greater financial security for all of you,
but ulcers and tensions for you; or emotional danger for those
children growing up?

TOMPKINS: That's rough. I want the kids to have the chance for
good schools and knowing nice people. I want Liz to have a
decent station wagon; I don't want the other wives looking
down on her. If I risked losing my job . . .

WILSON: One more question: Would Liz stand behind you if you
decided to protest this thing? Would she be willing to risk the
cut in income in order to get her husband back?

TOMPKINS: I could talk it over with her.

WILSON: You'd better. You're in this thing together. And if you
two agree on it, would it hurt to go to the V.P. and ask about
the possibilities of a change in the pattern? You're just assuming that if you made a protest, you'd be fired; you don't *know*
that. Maybe they'd be willing to scatter out the travel responsibilities; those guys at the top have just forgotten what it's
like to be young and to have a young family!

TOMPKINS: Suppose I go, and the V.P. says *no soap*.

WILSON: Well, then I guess you'd really have to face it. . . .

Questions for You to Think About

1. What are the different claims on Tompkins?
   responsibility to his company
   responsibility to provide financially for his family
   responsibility to give time to his family
   others

   How does a person balance out these claims when he can't meet
   them all?

2. How can Tompkins respond to God as he responds to the
people in this situation?

3. What do you think Tompkins should do?

Brass Knuckles on Monday

One member of that bankers' discussion group made an honest confession. "I love to go to church on Sunday and be inspired with the Christian message, but on Monday I have to put on the brass knuckles."[5] Even those people who are in a position to have a hand in policy-making—who work in a small firm, or who have arrived at the upper echelons of a big one—are still not *completely* free to do what is right as they conceive of the right in response to God's activity among us. Said another of the bankers, "Our ethics are set by the fact of competition."[6] It is well for a Christian to want to obey God, but he must also stay in business!

Jamison is salesman for a small food wholesaling firm—so small, indeed, that Jamison is *the* salesman! He works with congenial people in the firm, people who believe in integrity and honesty in dealing with their customers. Jamison calls on the buyer for a large restaurant chain. Here is a potential customer who would be a big one. There would be fat sales for the company if these folks would buy. The buyer is willing, provided Jamison is willing to give him personally a 5 percent kickback.

The salesman is in a bind. The company policy is straightforward: one price, for quality foods. No rebates. But sales to these restaurants would be worth all sorts of rebates. Does the company's policy make sense? He calls on another buyer. The conversation is not a long one; Jamison does not get the business. The buyer never *says* that it is because there's no rebate, but Jamison is sure this is the reason. Other companies do it; it's a usual pattern. Why should a restaurant buyer pass up the chance to feather his own nest a bit? Will Jamison's firm be able to stay in business if they do not yield a bit on this?

Jamison sits down in Bertram's office to talk it over. Bertram and his cousin have been running this business for a good while, and Jamison respects the integrity of both.

"Competition can surely draw blood, Bertram. We're losing business to those other guys. Can we afford to keep on doing this?"

"Do they all do it?"

"Looks to me like they do. I've lost three sales in the last two days. And you know our foods are the best—and they know it, too. How long can we keep on doing this?"

"We don't want to run a dishonest business."

"No, but are rebates all that wrong? Really, now: I give my customers gifts at Christmas. Is that wrong? And is that any different from a 5 percent kickback to Olson up there at the Candlelights office?"

"Why don't we get Martin and the others in and thrash it out?"

"I think we ought to. And even if they decide kickbacks are wrong, we've still got to ask what we're going to do. Our competitors give the rebates and they get the business. Do we have to do a little compromising to stay in business?"

"Go see if Martin's in his office. . . ."

Questions for You to Think About

1. What are the options open to these people?

2. *Is* there any difference between Christmas gifts and a 5 percent kickback? What difference?

3. Is this issue important enough for Christians to risk losing sales and profits? Bertram and Martin and Jamison all have families to support; can they afford to buck the pattern on this issue?

4. How can they respond to God as they respond to the people in this situation?

5. What should they do?

Two Problems for Professionals

The business world and the professional world are somewhat different. Most often the professional does not face the same dilemmas that the Tompkinses and the Jamisons of this world must live with and make some sense out of. The professional's decisions are no less agonizing, but often they are different.

Take competition, for an example. Now, of course, there *is* competition in the professional world, but usually the doctor does not have to scrounge for patients nor the teacher for pupils. Theirs is not often Jamison's dilemma of what to do to stay in business.

Orders from higher up is another example. Often the professional is on his own, and he makes his own decisions about when he will travel and how he shall use his time. He will not often find himself facing the kind of situation that Tompkins has to deal with.

Now, there are many ways in which the professional's freedom is limited. The Medical Society or the Bar Association imposes certain patterns upon him, and there may be some of those patterns which disturb his conscience. The teacher must answer to the chairman of the department, and sometimes the chairman's policies are not what the teacher would choose. There are limitations on the professional's freedom. Moreover, oftentimes a teacher has to operate in the midst of cut-throat politics on a university campus, where departments knife each other in the back and vie with each other for public attention.

The fact remains, however, that the ethical problems these people face are different from those of the businessman. Often it is not a matter of how to stick to principle and still meet the competition, but rather, how to handle conflicting responsibilities to *persons*. The doctor has a patient with a terminal illness; shall he tell him the truth? Shall he prolong the man's life artificially, at terrible financial and emotional cost to the family? These are not the decisions which confront the businessman, but they are no less disturbing than the dilemmas which Tompkins and Wilson and Jamison and Bertram must face. Look at these two hard ones:

A. The Investment of Time and Energy

Jean Frazier teaches political science in the local junior college. She spends fifteen hours a week in class, and nobody blows a whistle on the rest of her time. Sounds good. Hours and hours of leisure. Except for the constant study and preparation always hanging over her: reading a stream of books and articles; revising last year's class lectures; writing detailed comments on student papers (how else can she help them to think more clearly and critically about the political issues of the day?). Beyond all that, there are

the endless demands to speak in the community: the League of
Women Voters, the Rotary Club, church groups. Her problem is
that she has let these demands so stack up on her time that now
she has begun to sleep fitfully: waking up in the night, she worries
over getting it all done. Three extra speeches in the week to come
—speeches about issues in the upcoming election—and already
she has been skimping on class preparations.

Another request comes, and the crisis of decision is upon her.
This time it's the adult group in her own church. Will she take
over the teaching of their church school class after Christmas?
The studies have to do with social ethics and political problems,
so she ought to be able to do it with minimum preparation—she
has all that at her fingertips.

All that at her fingertips! Little do they realize, Jean thinks
to herself, the hours she has to study to do that sort of thing. So
—how does she decide what to do? Jean lies awake that night and
tries to decide about priorities in the use of her time.

1. What is her first responsibility?
   to the institution which actually pays her salary, having em-
        ployed her to meet classes? (Yes, but she is not missing
        any classes, even with all these outside activities.)
   to the citizens whose taxes support the college and who hon-
        estly want to be themselves more intelligent voters—and
        have a right to ask that the college help them to that end?
2. What responsibility does she have to her fellow-churchmen?
   Surely they have a special claim on her time?
3. How can she balance all these claims upon her time?
4. What is the proper stewardship of her considerable understanding of political and social issues?
5. How can she respond to God as she responds to this committee's request?

Jean goes to an older friend in the church for guidance. What
should that friend say?

B. The Development of Budding Young Professionals

Kendrick is a lawyer, a battle-scarred veteran of many cases.
A young law student is working with him this summer, a cousin of

the senior partner in the firm. After a couple of weeks, it becomes obvious to Kendrick that this young Segram just hasn't got what it takes. Of course, he is only 22, and allowance ought to be made for undeveloped potentialities. And he has a clear, sharp mind, with a quick grasp of legal intricacies. But the plain fact is that that high-pitched voice and the not-quite-pleasant personality would be fatal to the youngster; the boy just won't inspire confidence. The professors at the law school should have discouraged him; but then, he has the brains, and the highest average in the class; what would they tell him? Kendrick lies awake at night, turning it over and over in his mind. What should he do?

"It's really not my business. The boy's just here for the summer; why should I feel called upon to step in? And yet, if nobody stops him, the boy is heading for disillusionment and failure. If nobody else is willing to, shouldn't I?

"But how can I be sure the boy won't make it? Who am I to play God in somebody else's life?

"Well, after all, I've been in this game a while; I've learned to read the signs. God gave me brains and judgment, and he made me responsible for using them to help other people. Has God given me that boy for the summer, to help the kid face the truth about himself? Would I be failing God if I sidestepped this thing? After all, why did old Segram put him with me for this work? Millard could be teaching him as much as I am. Or Hall. Is God involved in this?

"Suppose I go to old Segram to talk to him about the boy, and he doesn't like it, and we end up with strained relations? Is it worth the risk? Why should I risk a good relationship in the firm for the sake of a youngster who has no real claim on me?"

Why, indeed? How should Kendrick work out this decision?

1. Does the boy have any real claim on Kendrick? What claims does old Segram have? How about Kendrick's responsibility to

himself? Are there other claims here—indirect ones? the Bar? the courts?

2. How can Kendrick discern the action of God in this situation? How can he respond to God as he responds to these people?

3. What should he do?

WHERE THE CHURCH MEETS THE WORLD

"The laity of the Church," says Hendrik Kraemer, are "dispersed in and through the world. . .[and] the real uninterrupted dialogue between Church and world happens through them. They form the daily repeated projection of the Church into the world. They embody the meeting of Church and World."[7] It is Christians at work, on the job, who speak (or do not speak) of God to the world, and they speak far more effectively than any clergyman can. For when a salesman talks to other salesmen about their responsibility to God in dealing with customers, they listen; he knows their problems from the inside. When they see him struggle through a decision and take the costly course because he believes it to be God's will, they may hear God calling them to go and do likewise.

This is partly what is meant by those who talk about the "ministry of the laity." They are not talking about piling up more and more ecclesiastical responsibilities on the laymen and laywomen so that they will take over in the church the work of the ordained clergyman or the professional staff; rather, they are talking about Christians who minister to people where they are, who act in response to God in the cafeteria of the big corporation, in the purchasing office of the restaurant chain, in the classroom of the community college, in the book-lined study of the lawyer.

Jesus said, "You are the salt of the earth"; you are to be scattered out in the world, to influence it, to lead it in obedience to God. What the world needs is "salty Christians,"[8] disciples of Christ who, as they make the difficult decisions on the job, will make those decisions in honest response to God, trusting that he is involved in the situation with them. For Christians like that will be speaking about God in the most effective language there is— the language of their lives.

CHAPTER 14

Equipping the Saints

What the world needs, says Hans-Reudi Weber, is "salty Christians."[1] Jesus said, "You are the salt of the earth," to be scattered out in the world, influencing people for God wherever you are. This is to say that the church is not meant to be a group of people all bunched together, taking care of their own needs in a self-centered way; rather, the church is to be scattered out as salt is sprinkled over food. As Christians face ethical dilemmas on their jobs, they are speaking for Christ—speaking with their lives. In the way they do their jobs and the way they treat other people, they are being ministers of Jesus Christ. When the salesman Jamison sits down with Bertram and Martin, and the lawyer Kendrick works with young Segram, these men *are* the church, scattered like salt.

But how can we be equipped for this kind of ministry? How

can we maintain our saltiness? At this point let us break into the
pattern we have been following—the pattern of exploring a few of
the many kinds of decisions we face in our group life—to discuss
in this chapter how we in the church can help each other to be
salty Christians in our daily work.

The fact of the matter is that though we must scatter out in
the world, we still need to gather together periodically as a church.
Weber illustrates this need as he tells of two Christian insurance
agents who protested the dishonesty at city hall and found that
this jeopardized their jobs. They then had to ask themselves about
their responsibilities to their families, their fellow citizens, and
their employer, as well as to God. For this reason, comments
Weber, "it is necessary for Christians in the world to be able to
'return to the fold,' to bring their lives to the altar for prayer and
offering, and to meet with their fellows for encouragement, counsel, and training."[2]

We need, then, to live in a rhythm of "withdrawal" and
"return," of "disengagement" from the world and then "engage-
ment" again. In the last chapter we looked at the kinds of choices
Christians face on the job. We battered Christians, facing difficult
and costly decisions in our work life, can turn with a deep sense
of need to the gathered life of the church. There we seek insight
and a sense of direction, and the courage to do what we believe to
be God's will.

How can the "gathered church" help us in the decision we
must make as separately we deal with others in the everyday
world of work?

"TO EQUIP THE SAINTS"

We who are the laity—the ordinary church members—are the
frontline troops of the church. Since time immemorial, Christians
have been called "soldiers of Christ"—no outworn metaphor,
since it is believers, and especially laymen, who fight Christ's
battles in the world. This means that the church in its gathered
life should serve as a boot camp or training camp for the troops,
to train them before they are sent up to the front lines. The place
of gathering of the saints ought to be the place where the Christian

pharmacist or salesman or teacher can think through his responsibility to God on the job.

Instead, we often get to thinking that the boot camp life is an end in itself.

It is as if army training for frontline service always took second place to preparation for formal parades and/or the unit concert—and a new wave of enthusiasm for a more efficient army simply meant *more and more time* spent on parades and concert rehearsals, so that recruits ended up by having even less time and opportunity for battle training.[3]

Now, we do talk about the "ministry of the laity," but so often what we mean by that is laymen working in the organized, institutional work of the church. They teach the classes and visit the sick, keep the books and organize the stewardship campaign. The ministry of many of our laity is turned inward on the life of the congregation, and men and women are challenged to give their energies solely to maintaining the ongoing life of the institution.

We need to conceive of the work of the gathered church, however, as Paul conceived of it. "And his gifts were that some should be apostles," said Paul to the Ephesians (4:11, 12), "some prophets, some evangelists, some pastors and teachers, for the equipment of the saints for the work of ministry." The church is given its leaders by God not to carry out the church's ministry themselves, but to prepare and equip the members for *their* ministry. Each member has his own task to perform, and the apostles and prophets and preachers and teachers are given to fit him for that particular task.

What we ought to be doing in the gathered church, then, is letting ourselves be fitted to do God's work in the world. And this means not just discussing but being called to real responsibility—to decision and action. We can discuss and discuss in the church, but too often we let it stop there.

Discussion can range from China to Peru and maintain the high-minded impartiality of the irresponsible. Responsibility involves the necessity of choosing one line of action, of committing oneself to it, of taking one's stand alongside other people. The life of the congregation does not train people to do this.[4]

But we *need* to be trained to do this. When we gather in the congregation, we need to be challenged both to decide and to act. Let us see what this would involve.

Guidance for Decision

Consider Jamison, the salesman. What kind of help does he need? For one thing, he needs guidance—help with thinking through the dilemmas he faces on the job. It is not that the gathered church ought to tell him what to do. Rather, he needs fellow-Christians who will listen to him, share with him, think through his problems with him.

One thing that would help Jamison would be consultation with other Christian salesmen, the opportunity to sit down with men who face the same dilemmas he does. This can be done at the level of the local congregation. In one congregation in Denver, doctors would get together regularly at an early morning hour to worship together and think through the ethical tensions they encountered as Christians in their professional life. A church in Washington held periodic weekend retreats for people in varied vocational fields; two full days would be devoted to enabling these people to face together the kinds of situations in their work in which they had to carry out their Christian ministry.[5]

Increasingly, this kind of thing is going on at the denominational level. Week-long conferences on theology and vocation are being held, and weekend retreats, in which medical people or teachers or secretaries or beauticians gather from all over the denomination to meet with theologians for no-holds-barred discussions on what obedience means on the job. These are times of corporate thinking, where nobody is there to tell the others what's what, but all are there to think honestly together about ways of responding to God.

At the ecumenical level, too, the saints are gathering more

and more often to share with each other some of the difficulties of
on-the-job decisions. "Lay centers" and "lay academies" developed in Europe, but it is a pattern which Americans are finding
useful. Many American Christians are finding the opportunity to
attend seminars at places like the Christian Faith and Life Community in Austin, Texas, or the Detroit Industrial Mission. These
are continuing institutes and not just occasional gatherings; their
whole reason for being is to enable Christians to take more seriously the meaning of discipleship in the world.

Chapter 13 began with mention of a group of bankers who met
in Chicago to face the ethical ambiguities of their work. This was
part of a project initiated and carried out by the Department of the
Church and Economic Life of the National Council of Churches.
In other cities building contractors met together over a period of
a year, deeply concerned about the question of bidding in the context of competition; public relations men met to consider the
problems of truth and personal integrity in advertising. In all of
these groups there was honest facing of dilemmas, and Christians
were met together to help each other find a way through them.

Jamison needs guidance as he undertakes to make decisions
in his work as salesman, and the gathered church can make it
possible for him to meet with other Christian salesmen for that
purpose. He also needs, though, the guidance of Christians who
are in other occupations. They can provide perspective sometimes
where his fellow-salesmen cannot. So he needs to sit down with
folks who share his faith and can be trusted to share his problems.

Now, there may be groups already at hand for such a need.
It may be that the group studying the Convenant Life Curriculum
together has developed the kind of rapport within which a person
would be willing to talk honestly about his problems. Circles of
the women of the church, young adult groups, or men's groups
have been known to develop a real sense of community. And yet,
if we are realistic, we have to admit that groups like that are
mighty hard to come by—groups where there is real openness
with each other and caring for one another.

Part of our problem is that traditionally we have assumed
that when around the church building, we Christians are not to

admit that we have problems and tensions. We are to leave our
family arguments and frustrations from the weekday world at
home, and arrive smiling and well-adjusted when it is time for
church school to begin. How, then, are we to break through this
pink-tinted frosting in our group discussions? How can we build
the kind of group relations in which people are willing to be honest
with each other, to open up and tell about their own dilemmas,
and to listen to others tell about theirs? This is a question for you
and your class. What would have to happen in the group with
which you are studying this book in order for real openness to
become a possibility?

Now, it ought to be pointed out that there is always a danger
which goes along with the building up of a real sense of community and sharing—the danger of ingrownness, of exclusiveness,
of cliquishness. The deeper is the shared life of a group, the more
difficult it is to give an outsider the sense of belonging. But somehow it seems worth the risk, if Jamison finds that he can talk and
listen and be helped by the group to discern more clearly what is
involved in responding to God. This is a matter worth the consideration of any group in the church.

Encouragement for Action

It is not enough, however, to have fellow-Christians helping
you decide *what* to do; you also need to have folks standing by
when you *do* it—standing by to give you the courage you need,
and to help you make the costly decision when necessary. If junior
executive Tompkins decides to risk his job by asking for a slow-
down in his traveling, he needs to know that there are those who
care, and who are willing to share with him in what is happening.

There are many ways in which the gathered congregation can
provide encouragement for its members—en-*courage*-ment in the
literal sense. For one thing, a church could act to help each person
know that he is a minister of Christ in his daily life and that the
congregation recognizes this and stands with him in it. Some congregations hold commissioning services for their members, to send
them out as ministers in their weekday tasks. One church calls it
a service of ordination. The terminology is not important, but the
content of understanding is tremendously significant.

The Church of the Saviour in Washington explains it this way. "Ordination means that the individual's sense of call is confirmed by his own Christian community."[6] In that service of ordination the minister says these significant words:

> Today, _____(name)_____ has come to acknowledge to God and to us that the work he does each day takes place on holy ground. He comes to ask God's blessing on his work and for guidance in making each act he performs pleasing in God's sight. He comes to give back to God the work which God has given him to do. In turn, we in the Christian community come to offer _____(name)_____ the strength and love and encouragement which our being together in Christ makes possible.

And after the participant takes his vows, the minister says further:

> Is is fitting that the dedication of your work to God be sealed

with the strengthening devotion of your Christian community.
___(Sponsor),___ by placing his hand on your shoulder, offers
ourselves to you as channels of the empowering grace of the
Body of Christ, pledging our love, interest, and encouragement
in the work you have dedicated to God's care and guidance.[7]

A person commissioned in that way to his work in the world
would be likely to take his responsibilities seriously, and would
know that the Christian community goes with him as he tackles
those responsibilities. The congregation could encourage its members, secondly, by helping them to realize that all of us live by grace
in an imperfect world. In its teaching and preaching the gathered
church needs to emphasize the reality of sin, not just in our individual lives but in the patterns of our society. We make decisions
among shades of gray—we have said this over and over—and this
is partly because we function within social patterns that were shot
through with selfishness and the hunger for power before we ever
arrived on the scene. The church needs to help us face the reality
of this, so that we will not demand of ourselves the impossibility
of an utterly pure conscience.

In this imperfect world, however, we can have the assurance
of God's forgiving love, and the church needs to remind us of this
again and again. George Webber has put it nicely: "Faith in God's
redeeming love can resolve the impossible tension between high
ethical idealism and the practical necessity of life in community."[8]
No Christian, then, need drive himself to be the embodiment of
moral perfection in situations where no perfect decisions are possible; he can know that if he seeks to be obedient according to his
best judgment, he can have the assurance of the forgiving love of
a justifying God.

Atkinson is a veteran accountant and a devoted churchman
who over the years has been in three different churches and has
been church treasurer in each. All his life Atkinson has driven
himself to earn the respect and approval of the people around him
—and has driven others in the same way. In a discussion of God's
forgiveness in his church school class, it suddenly came clear to
him, "This means ME!" That group had made him know that he
belonged with them, whether people liked him and agreed with him

or not; and through their discussion they had shown him that likewise he was a child of God, no matter what. Atkinson was a
different man on his job that week!

It is not only in the general preaching and teaching of the
gathered congregation, however, that encouragement of the saints
can take place. There can be definite structures set up to provide
the kind of support that salty Christians need. One Reformed
church has set up specific groups for sharing in the concerns of the
daily job. Groups of ten persons each meet weekly; each week one
person reports to the others something of what has happened in
his ministry in the past few weeks. He tells the group how he feels
he is succeeding or failing as a minister on his job. Then the group
talks over his problems with him, helping him to get perspective on
his work and assuring him the support of the Christian community
he represents.[9] A somewhat formal structure? Yes, but perhaps a
principle worth considering.

More likely, perhaps, would be the possibility of finding
"senior laity" to teach and to work with younger ones who are in
the same occupation. The Christian realtor who has been in business for a long time can help the discouraged youngster. The Christian teacher who has been at it for twenty years and is still a
Christian can help the novice who is feeling the pressures of the
work. "These senior, worldly, battered, often very tired laity may
surely claim to know something of the mind of Christ for their
particular calling and daily routine."[10] And they have what it takes
to sustain and support the junior laity who are just beginning to face
the problems of their jobs.

Commissioning services, the preaching of the grace of God,
small groups for mutual support all help to give courage to the
Jamisons and the Kendricks and the Tompkinses who take seriously their responsibilities as ministers of Christ amid the dilemmas
and frustrations of daily work. But suppose Tompkins is encouraged to risk his job and he loses it. What then? Shall the support
of his Christian brethren be expressed only in words? If there is
any reality to the mutual concern of the Christian community,
then surely it needs to be expressed tangibly when a Christian,
working in a sinful world, makes the kind of decision that costs
him his job.

This is not easy, and we know it. On a denominational-wide basis, one group of churchmen contributed $25.00 apiece for the relief of ministers who might lose their pulpits because of their stand on racial matters. Here was an expression of community concern and sharing, but it was a specialized concern of people who cared especially about the church's social witness. In some churches there is a discretionary fund set aside in the church budget to be administered by a deacons' committee or by the pastor or by some other small group. This would be used to tide a family over till a new job could be found, and to have a budgeted fund of this kind would seem to be a practical way of going at the problem. The point is that where a person acting in response to God suffers severe financial loss, the rest of us need to share in his plight not only with sympathy but with hard cash.

One more way in which the gathered community can share with the Tompkinses who lose their jobs: there can be a quiet canvass of those in the congregation who themselves are employers and have contact with other employers. If Tompkins were not competent to do a job, it would not be fair to ask other employers to take him on (or would it? What would be a Christian responsibility here?). But if he is fully competent and lost the job because of the stand he took, there need be no hesitation. Here a concerned group in a church school class might go quietly to work to canvass the possibilities. Or they might enlist the services of the pastor, or the teacher of the class, or others in the congregation whose counsel and help would be valuable.

The congregation of the Church of the Saviour pledge to each member "our love, interest, and encouragement in the work you have dedicated to God's care and guidance." A congregation of people who have that kind of concern for each other will find practical ways of making that concern real.

GARRISON FOR THE TROOPS

Douglas Blatherwick, a British writer, expresses his admiration for the Salvation Army, but he points out what to him seems an error in their way of doing things: they call their headquarters "The Citadel." This suggests to Blatherwick a sort of fortress mentality, an inclination to pull in the drawbridge and be safe against the outside world. A better word, he feels, would be "The Garrison," where men are trained for and sent out to the battle.

That is what we have been saying in this chapter about the church. It is a garrison, not a fortress; a place for training the troops. The saints gather not simply to insure the safety and continuity of the institution, but to be equipped for their work of ministry.

So it is that the Christian life is a rhythm of withdrawal and return: leaving the job in order to be nourished in the worship and life of the gathered church; returning to the job in sharpened awareness that this is a ministry carried out in response to God.

The participant in the ordination service of the Church of the Saviour says these words: "Enabled by Christ's love for me, I shall endeavor to make each day's work a sacrament."[11] That is the intent and the purpose of a salty Christian.

CHAPTER 15

Christian Responsibility on a Crowded Planet

According to United Nations estimates, world population is growing by 8,000 every hour or approximately 70,000,000 a year. A number equal to the population of France, Belgium, and Holland taken together is being added every year to the people living on this earth![1]

. . . if present fertility and mortality trends continue, a long-range projection by the National Academy of Sciences foresees that in about 650 years there will be one person per square foot throughout the United States, and in less than 1,500 years the weight of the United States' population will exceed the mass of the earth, that is, 6,588,000,000,000, 000,000,000 tons![2]

"God speaks ever afresh to men," says Martin Dibelius, "by

bringing them into new situations."[3] "New occasions teach new duties," says James Russell Lowell, and here is a "new occasion" to take the breath away. The population explosion is bringing change on a scale we have never known before, and it confronts us with all manner of decisions, for the sheer mass of the world's growing population threatens to outstrip our ability to produce and distribute food. Change always forces us to make choices, but this change makes the choices more awesome than ever before. How shall we respond to God in this new situation into which he has brought us?

Note that as we have discussed some examples of the many kinds of decisions we face in our day, our concern in this section of the book has been moving out in ever-widening circles. Talking about the social context of our ethical decisions—the groups in the midst of which we must respond to God—we talked first of the family, and the ways in which we make decisions there. Then we spoke of the congregation, and how we can handle controversy in our church life. We moved then to a consideration of the kinds of dilemmas we face in the public life of work, on the job. Now we come to a consideration of the largest community—the whole of American society, indeed, the whole world.

But why should our hair get gray in worrying about the world, we ask. "I'll worry about my family and the people I know; we have enough problems right here at home. Are there people hungry in India? Well, why don't they practice birth control? When they begin taking some responsibility for themselves, then they have a right to ask for help from me. Until then, I'll not worry about them."

Recall, however, the question we were raising in chapter 8: "How broad is your community?" Who are my neighbors? Just those who live up the street, or sit in the next pew, or work at the next desk? Can I limit my concern to those who are like me, who share my culture, who agree with my way of doing things? The answer is quite clearly "No." If God is really sovereign over all that is, if he created all men and loves all men, then my loyalty to people and my concern for them cannot stop with my own group. If I am to respond to a sovereign God, then I must recognize that my neighbor is not only the man next door but also the man in Wyoming, and the man in India—and the man in China!

THE PROBLEM OF POPULATION

The facts are familiar to us; we see them in newspapers and magazines, and we hear about them over radio and TV. We know that after long centuries of stability, suddenly the world's population has taken a sharp spurt upward. We see charts that make the change vivid for us—charts like this one:

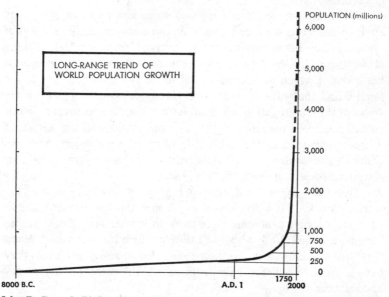

John D. Durand, "A Long-Range View of World Population Growth," (Adapted) The Annals of The American Academy of Political and Social Science, Vol. 369, Jan. 1967.

The possible consequences of this population explosion are familiar to us, too. We hear of the danger to the world's standards of living, even of the threat of starvation if the tide is not turned. We see cartoons like this grim one of Fischetti's on page 215.

The causes of all this are not very clear. The explosive increase in population dates from about 1930, according to most experts on the subject. It is not, however, that the actual number

AT THE END MAN CREATED...

John Fischetti. Courtesy *Richmond Times-Dispatch* and Publishers-Hall Syndicate.

of births has risen; rather, the death rates have dramatically fallen and the balance between the two has been radically upset. The past generation or two in our world's history have seen the development of disease control on an international level. Health campaigns carried out by groups like the World Health Organization have won spectacular victories in the battle with diseases that have been the scourge of mankind. Malaria, yaws, sleeping sickness are not the universal terror they were in the old days; new insecticides and antibiotics have enabled many nations to cut their death rates spectacularly.

In the old days a life expectancy of 35 years was pretty good for any society. Now, however, the average life span is more than 70 years in the developed countries of the world. Before the advent of modern health methods, it was expected that one out of every four or five babies born would not survive the first year; now in the developed countries the figure is closer to one out of fifty. With the old balance—however tragic it was—between birth rate and death rate now radically upset, the world's population has surged upward, and the experts predict that by 1985 we will have 5,000,-000,000 people on our planet, while by 2000 there will be about 7,000,000,000 jostling each other for space.

Back in 1964 the *New York Times* reported 63,000,000 births that year and commented editorially:

> This news is just as important as any this newspaper can print. . . . It means more in the long run than elections, economic trends, catastrophes and international crises. If the human race is to survive on anything higher than a slum basis, something will have to give—presumably the birth rate. Such is today's biggest news—and greatest problem.[4]

Pressure in Underdeveloped Lands

Back in the nineteenth century the British economist Thomas Malthus raised the question of whether our planet can provide enough food for increasing numbers of people. For some time few took him seriously; technology enabled us to stay well ahead of the population growth. But lately people have been raising again that question of Malthus': can we provide decent living standards for the great hordes now peopling the earth?

The effects of rising population pressures are being felt almost everywhere in the world, but the burden is greatest in those areas which are economically less well-developed. Whatever economic growth may be achieved in India or Malaysia or Chile is offset by the increase in the population. Food production may go up, but there are just more mouths to feed, and these nations must sprint desperately in order to simply stand still.

To complicate the problem, the masses of the people in many of these lands are already hungry. One scholar estimates that of the present population in the world, 10 to 15 percent are severely undernourished, while up to 50 percent suffer from some degree of hunger or malnutrition or both. Merely to maintain present levels of nutrition with the expected population increase would demand a doubling in our total food supplies; but to bring many of the world's peoples to adequate diets would require far more than that.[5] And even if the United States farm surplus were to be distributed among the world's hungry people, it would provide about a cup of rice a week—not much help for the undernourished!

The added frustration in these countries is the burden of

illiteracy and religious tradition. The desperate hunger in a land like India is increasing as the numbers of the people are burgeoning, but teaching birth control to illiterate people sometimes seems a hopeless task—especially when adults want to have many children to care for them in old age. Moreover, the Hindu belief that all animal life is sacred means that good steak or roast beef roams around the streets while nobody dares lay a hand on the animals. The cattle, utterly safe themselves, often damage the crops which are so desperately needed by the human beings around them.

> The world of the American citizen who sleeps between clean sheets and the world of the Calcutta citizen who sleeps in rags on the street are so far apart that they baffle the imagination of the American who has not seen this world of hunger and poverty.[6]

We must very soon find ways of slowing down the world's population growth if we would save people from the wretchedness of hunger.

Pressure in the United States

It can't happen here. For one thing, there has been some indication that our population growth has slowed. Moreover, we can produce enough food, whatever the increase; we even have enough space for uncounted millions, if you take into consideration all the vast reaches of land on this continent, especially the sparsely populated regions of the West. We Americans have been somewhat reluctant to see any real threat in our own population growth. We discuss with horror the population explosion in the rest of the world, but often we see no relation between the high birth rate in our land and what goes on elsewhere, for we can take care of ourselves.

It is likely that we *can* produce enough material goods for our foreseeable future population. The threat of the population increase here is not so much to the material side of life as to the *quality* of American life; an increase of 100 million people could erode some of our most cherished patterns of living. Consider some illustrations.

Suppose we have plenty of food and clothing, fine; but in what sort of atmosphere will we be living? As more and more people are concentrated in our cities, with more and more industries to provide for them and more and more automobiles to get them to work, what will happen to the air we breathe? Already our governments at all levels are undertaking costly programs for air purification. What will happen when we have half again as many people? And what will happen to our water supply? The increasingly severe droughts of recent years in the northeastern part of our country are omens of things to come. We have hardly even glimpsed the terrific demands we will be making on our sources of water as there are more and more people to use it. We have traditionally assumed that we would always have pure air to breathe and clean water to drink; these may be ours no longer.

Consider what is happening to the open spaces around us. Countryside that used to be open and green and soul-satisfying is being bulldozed under at 3,000 acres a day—1.1 million acres every year. And it's not just that the countryside is receding from the cities, so that we have to go farther and farther to get a walk in the country; rather, it is disappearing completely as cities and their subdivisions merge into each other. The Fort Worth-Dallas area; the Florida east coast; the Eastern seaboard from Norfolk to Boston—for people who live in these areas a picnic or walk in the open country is becoming well-nigh impossible.

All of which puts tremendous pressure on the parks and recreational facilities we do have. More and more people, with shorter hours and higher pay, want to use our park facilities. The forecast is for an increase in visits to our National Parks from 63 million in 1959, to 240 million in 1980, to over 400 million by 2000. This means that we *must* have more space to keep open for public use; but with land prices skyrocketing, which of us is willing to vote more taxes for himself in order to keep the outdoors available for all of us? (That's a question we Christians ought to ask ourselves!)

John Stuart Mill foresaw the problem back in the nineteenth century:

A population may be too crowded, though all be amply

supplied with food and raiment. It is not good for man to be kept perforce at all times in the presence of his species. A world from which solitude is extirpated is a very poor ideal. Solitude, in the sense of being often alone, is essential to any depth of meditation or of character; and solitude in the presence of natural beauty and grandeur is the cradle of thoughts and aspirations which are not only good for the individual, but which society could ill do without. Nor is there much satisfaction in contemplating the world with nothing left to the spontaneous activity of nature; with every rood of land brought into cultivation . . . and scarcely a place left where a wild shrub or flower could grow without being eradicated as a weed in the name of improved agriculture.[7]

Consider what is already happening to the quality of the education we can provide for our young people. By 1971—NEXT YEAR—high school students will number 15,000,000—a 50 percent increase since 1960. Will communities be willing to impose stiff new taxes upon themselves to provide for more teachers and more classroom space? The alternative is having their children studying in increasingly crowded classrooms. (Again we ought to ask, What is our responsibility as Christians here? What sort of decisions ought we to make as citizens?)

The number of community junior colleges among us is rapidly increasing, and taxpayers must support these. The four-year colleges and universities will have 12,000,000 students by 1980— *triple* the 1960 number. Building buildings, finding and training teachers: these are difficult. But even more important, Can we maintain the spirit of free inquiry when education is carried on in this mass way? These are decisions with which the population explosion confronts us—even us Americans.

Most crucial of all, however, is the important question of freedom; the more people there are crowded together, the greater is the need for regulation of our lives by all kinds of governments. When families lived ten miles apart they could be free; they could do what they wanted to do without bothering anybody else. But now that we are being jammed close together there simply have to be more rules to keep us from stepping on each other's toes. We may see, for instance, more and more limitations placed on our private use of our land. Some suggest that in the future, homeowners may not be allowed the luxury of growing flowers instead of vegetables in their backyards. Perhaps if space gets tight, we may not even be allowed a backyard! We may see intensive controls placed on our means of transportation. We individuals may prefer the privacy of our own cars for getting to work, but the time may come when that will be a luxury no longer permitted to commuters, especially when we realize that automobiles move people at a rate one-seventh that of buses, and only one-twentieth that of rail facilities. When there are so many of us, we may not be free to decide for ourselves.[8]

As population increases, of course, so will the economy and the gross national product. But J. Kenneth Galbraith has pointed out, tongue in cheek:

> It is hard to suppose that penultimate Western man, stalled in the ultimate traffic jam and slowly succumbing to carbon monoxide will be especially enchanted to hear from the last survivor that in the preceding year the Gross National Product went up by a record amount.[9]

It can happen here, and it is happening now. These things await us in our future unless we can somehow stabilize our population.

THE CHALLENGE TO DECISION

"God speaks ever afresh to men by bringing them into new situations."[10] What is God saying through the frightening new situations we have been describing here? What would it mean for us to hear and to respond in obedience?

To Share with Our Neighbors

Most of us have recognized our obligation to feed the hungry, to share what we have with those who are in need. We Americans have done a tremendous helping job: our churches through agencies like Church World Service, our government through programs like Food for Peace (Public Law 480), our individuals through

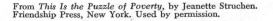

Oh, yes?

Love thy neighbor as thyself? Each year people in the U. S. spend $11.1 billion on alcohol, $8.1 billion on tobacco, and $6.5 billion on beauty and grooming. Yet the foreign aid bill passed by Congress in 1965 provided only slightly more than $3 billion to help other countries.

From *This Is the Puzzle of Poverty*, by Jeanette Struchen. Friendship Press, New York. Used by permission.

the multitudinous agencies like CARE and Christian Children's Fund. We send millions of dollars worth of goods abroad each year. No other people in history have taken upon themselves as we have done the responsibility of helping needy neighbors.

Yet it is often pointed out that with our potential, and the need of the world, what we do is just not enough. One writer has noted that the "direct economic grants" of our government to other nations "amount to about one-twelfth of what Americans spend on cigarettes each year."[11] Consider these three questions:

1. Can we support a national agricultural policy that restricts food production in order to improve domestic agricultural prices, while much of the rest of the world goes hungry? North America has 10 percent of the world's population and 31 percent of its food production, and this ratio is not likely to change much in the future. One writer has said, "Restricting food production in this kind of world is an immoral, politically dangerous, economically indefensible answer."[12]

What is your reaction to his statement? What are the possible alternatives if we want to protect our farmers from suffering from low prices? What about subsidies paid directly to the farmer to maintain his income but not to maintain artificially high prices to the consumer, while allowing the farmer to produce as much as he can?

2. What should we Americans do directly about the hunger of India and her neighbors? It has been suggested that we and the other Western nations ought to devote one percent of our national income to helping the less developed nations get on their feet. But there are thorny problems involved here. One, we see so much abuse of the financial aid we are already giving: local politicians get the money and use it to maintain their own power, and it never reaches the poor who need the help. We feel that we are just pouring our money down a rat hole (and this is true of our efforts to fight domestic poverty, too). Second, we see so little progress: why should we keep trying? The spectacular results from Marshall Plan aid in Europe made us know those efforts were worthy. But to try to aid India and Pakistan and Burundi when they have not even begun with an industrial revolution—what good does it all do?

3. Suppose we believe that as Christians we *are* obligated to try to feed the hungry people of the world. So what happens if in the future the people of Red China become desperate and her leaders ask us for help, for trade or direct aid, or both? China has undertaken a massive agricultural program, but the *Wall Street Journal* has said that their chances of becoming self-sufficient are slight.[13] So the possibility of a plea to us is not impossible. How would we meet it? Paul said to the Romans (12:20), "If your enemy is hungry, feed him." How do we take this? Literally? Disregard it? Paul Simon raises this question and comments on it: "But no enemy is ever popular, and the passage is obviously directed to help those with whom you literally violently disagree."[14] But if we were to help them, would this not make China stronger to oppress other nations?

Discipline Begins at Home

It can't happen here. We have no problem. Whatever trouble the world is having with population, it's those other countries who are causing it. Whatever trouble we might possibly have in our country, it's the poor who are causing it, the poor who multiply like rabbits.

But it can happen here. Our *rate of population increase* may have slowed recently, but the actual population is still going up and up. And it's not only the poor who are causing the problem. The middle and upper income groups are accounting for more than three-fourths of American births; they and their children will produce most of the extra 100,000,000 Americans who will likely join us by the year 2000. The population pressure among us poses some questions which we as Christians have to face.

1. Should we as a nation go all-out to provide birth control help to the poor? There is still a good deal of political harassment of those public officials who try to give this help to women on relief. In many communities hospitals and clinics are simply not free to prescribe contraceptives and to assist couples who want to use them. Do we Christians have a responsibility here in the creation of a climate of public opinion?

2. Some nations, like Japan, have effectively cut their birth rate by making abortions available virtually upon request. In the United States there are about .2 abortions for every 100 births, whereas Japan has more abortions than births—about 140 to 100. There is considerable pressure in the United States for liberalization of our fairly rigid state laws, most of which allow abortion only to save the mother's life. Should Christians support this move to make abortions more readily available—for instance, in cases of rape or incest, or if there is a substanial risk that the baby would be deformed? Should we go even further and allow abortion to prevent the birth of an "unwanted child"—the pregnancy of the unmarried girl or the wife with too many children?

Consider these two statements. Which makes more sense to you? Why?

Those who condemn any liberalization of existing laws insist that from the moment of conception a new human life exists. Thus . . . to terminate that life virtually amounts to murder.

". . . The unborn child is from the very first a child. It is still developing and has no independent life. But it is a man and not a thing, not a mere part of the mother's body. . . . He who destroys germinating life kills a man and thus ventures the monstrous thing of decreeing concerning the life and death of a fellow man whose life is given by God and, therefore, like his own, belongs to Him."

". . . At no time and under no circumstances has Anglo-Saxon law ever sanctioned the destruction of one human being —however useless and unwanted such a person may be—for the purpose of securing or increasing the health or happiness of other individuals."

That is a point worth pondering. Once society, even for the most high-minded reasons, begins to decree which life shall continue and which shall end, the most serious questions arise about where such policies might eventually lead.[15]

*   *   *

It is obviously better . . . to eliminate a mass of growing tissue within the womb than to require a mother to deliver a child who is defective, or the product of rape, or likely to damage the mother's health—mental or physical.

. . . Suppose a child is unwanted. Suppose the prospective mother is unmarried and unable to give the child a warm, loving home. Or suppose the parents have too many children already, and addition of another would aggravate a bad situation. Isn't abortion preferable to permitting the child's birth under such tragic circumstances?

". . . Is it better to produce a child at all costs, however conceived, however damaged, whatever the threat it poses to the mother's well-being and that of other members of the family, whether it elicits suicide, or psychosis, or is fore-ordained to live in a series of foster homes—anything, rather than remove some cells which have not yet become a sentient human being?"[16]

3. What about our personal decisions about family size? We used to think it was a religious and patriotic duty to rear large

families. Now, even though we rarely think of it as duty, we still consider it a right that each couple has. "The number of children we have is nobody's business but ours as parents. We like children; we have the right to have as many as we can support."

But consider these three statements. How do you react to them?

We can no longer say that families should have as many children as they wish. We cannot now, as a people, continue to extol a way of life which—however much we enjoy it in the present—will ultimately turn the earth from a habitable place into a grim, overcrowded prison, where individuals will survive only by stepping over the bodies of those struck down by hunger and despair.[17]

. . . the bearing of a large family can no longer be construed as a social contribution. In fact, if our rate of increase continues high, it will become necessary to be even blunter: by pointing out that those who elect to have more than two—or at the very most, three—children necessary for replacement, are indulging themselves at the expense of the rest of society.[18]

Many responsible, well-educated people who are vaguely aware of the population explosion apparently are unable to connect it with their own lives. How else to account for the college graduates who cheerfully—and with no sense of sin— produce four, five, and six children? What they do not grasp, evidently, is that the question is a moral one. To put it baldly, anyone who increases the total number of people in an overcrowded world adds to the likelihood of war.

Once this simple mathematical truth is widely understood, it may lead to the acceptance of a new commandment ordained by natural law: Thou Shalt Not Produce More Than Two Children.[19]

(Obviously no one can endorse all the quotations in this chapter. Which seem the most Christian to you?)

The Challenge to Decision

"God speaks ever afresh to men by bringing them into new situations." An overcrowded planet: this is a situation we human beings have never faced before. The chart on p. 214 shows that for millennia we of the human species bumped along with only the barest increase in population; our numbers were stable because of the balance between birth rate and death rate. But in our generation we are facing a new and frightening situation. The consequences will be overwhelming if we do not find a way to de-fuse the population bomb that is ticking away.

Through this new situation God is speaking to us; our task is to be alert to what he has to say. There are thorny questions here, but there is no dodging them. A sovereign God cares about what is happening, not only in our own group but in the whole nation and the world. With what decisions shall we respond to him?

CHAPTER 16

Population and Personhood

The ideal set up by the Party was something huge, terrible, and glittering—a world of steel and concrete, of monstrous machines and terrifying weapons—a nation of warriors and fanatics, marching forward in perfect unity, all thinking the same thoughts and shouting the same slogans, perpetually working, fighting, triumphing, persecuting—three hundred million people all with the same face.[1]

This is George Orwell's nightmare, in *Nineteen Eighty-Four:* the nightmare of three hundred million people who have lost their personhood. No thoughts of their own, no private loyalties; millions of people all with the same face—this is the grim picture Orwell paints for us in his frightening fantasy.

In chapter 15 we were saying that we Americans are in no

immediate danger of starvation, whatever our population increase might be. The threat to us from the population explosion is not a threat to our material abundance but to the *quality* of life we live as persons: the kind of air we breathe, the kind of education our children will get, and above all, the kind of freedom we will have to be real persons. The more people, the more crowded we will be; and all crowded in together, we might find ourselves moving toward the deadly uniformity which Orwell visualizes.

In Orwell's "Oceania" the greatest crime is to have your own thoughts, your own private affections. And Orwell's "hero," Winston Smith, is sensitive enough to know what has happened. "We are the dead," says Smith, again and again. We are "unpersons." In losing their individual uniqueness and their ability to love other people, their very personhood has been destroyed.

Nineteen Eighty-Four is only a construct of the author's imagination, and for that we are grateful; there has never been an Oceania or a Big Brother, never a society which has been that regimented. And yet, in the crowded life we Americans are increasingly facing, there are all manner of threats to *our* personhood. Now, this does not mean that some power-hungry government, in Washington or elsewhere, is trying to play Big Brother and make faceless millions out of us. The fact is that in a populous, complex society, we *have* to have a strong central government, for the problems of our society—poverty and racial tension, urban sprawl, mass education, air pollution—are beyond the capacity of individuals or local communities to solve. Effective government can actually *free* us by tackling the overwhelming social problems that threaten to strangle our common life. No, it is society itself—an overcrowded society—which is making it more difficult for us to be the full, whole persons God intends for us to be.

Recall what we were saying in chapter 11 about personhood, about what it means to be a whole person. It means recognition of one's own uniqueness and individuality; one needs to recognize and respect himself as an individual, decision-making person, separate from other people, with a responsibility all his own. But this does not mean withdrawal into one's own separateness and ego, for along with individuality must go the ability to respond to other people, to be responsible for them, to participate imaginatively in their lives.

Personhood, then, involves both individuality and community. We need to inquire now how the population explosion poses threats to both of these, and to ask with what sorts of decisions we are thereby confronted.

THE THREAT TO PRIVACY

Nosy Americans

A foreign visitor described modern Americans as people who are as "friendly as puppies—and just as nosy."[2] Because we tend to be nosy, and because there are more and more of us to *be* nosy, we are finding less and less privacy for the living of our own individual lives.

It has not always been thus among Americans. Back in frontier days families lived far apart and took care of themselves. Parents made the decisions in their own families. They read what few books they could get their hands on. They thought whatever thoughts they pleased, orthodox or unorthodox. Privacy was well-nigh complete in the early days of our nation. Even in the largest city of the time—Philadelphia, with 30,000 people—one would be let alone if he wished.

Today things are different. Consider the denizens of large apartment houses who cannot help hearing each other's most intimate conversations and who, aware that they themselves will be heard, become careful about what they say. Even in the suburbs where neighbors cannot hear every word of a conversation, it is still difficult to live your own life without interference. Recall Jimmy Breslin's comments in "Let's Quit the Suburbs" (Appendix, chapter 9). He complained that neighbors pressured him to build a basket-weave fence—so that his home would be exactly like everybody else's!

Neighbors are nosy, and so are employers. The majority of people today work for large organizations of one kind or another, a far cry from the individual self-sufficiency of the frontier. The bigger the organization, the tighter must be the rein in the hands of the managers. And if they cannot know the employees personally, thus building bonds of trust, then often they must resort to compiling information about them—information that will point to trustworthiness or untrustworthiness, loyalty or disloyalty. Endless questionnaires, fat dossiers in files; lie detectors; bugging devices that pick up conversations in employees' washrooms—a person becomes a number, not really a person, and yet at the same time his innermost thoughts are to be laid bare to his employers.

Neighbors are nosy, employers are nosy, and in this electronic age nosiness can become automated. *Newsweek* pointed out several years ago that we are moving into an Orwellian world in which there are all sorts of possibilities of prying into our private lives. The estimate is that each day at least 10,000 electronic transmitters eavesdrop on the conversations of U.S. citizens, and these electronic bugging devices are becoming more insidious. They include FM radio transmitters the size of a lump of sugar; infra-red cameras that can photograph in pitch darkness; transmitters which can be sewed into clothes, even capped into teeth by a dentist.[3]

Moreover, there is the surveillance of our lives by computers. Each year, more and more information about individual lives is being stored away in the gigantic memories of these machines. This is good, for it enables the government to catch the tax dodgers and the criminals. But is there danger here, too? Organized knowledge can be potential power in the hands of the people who control it. And what happens when a man's whole past is held in the memory of a computer? Every false step he has made is there in that mechanical brain, to be held against him when he applies for a job or a credit account, or runs for public office. Is it possible that this kind of computerized memory could make us into machines, not persons? A machine moves along its predetermined course, with no possibility of change within itself; a person can grow out of his past; grow into a different future. We have always assumed that a person could start over again, afresh. Will this become impossible in this day of computers?

Increasingly our lives are being scrutinized, so much that one scholar calls this the "Goldfish Age."[4] The consequence is predictable: people will become watchful and suspicious, on their guard lest they say the wrong thing to the wrong person. "A hallmark of totalitarian societies," observed the American Civil Liberties Union, "is that the people are apprehensive of being overheard or spied upon."[5]

George Orwell has pictured vividly the threat to privacy in the future against which he warns. Two-way television sets enable officials in *Nineteen Eighty-Four* to spy constantly on everyone.

The telescreen received and transmitted simultaneously. Any sound that Winston made, above the level of a very low whisper, would be picked up by it; moreover, so long as he remained within the field of vision which the metal plaque commanded, he could be seen as well as heard. There was of course no way of knowing whether you were being watched at any given moment. How often, or on what system, the Thought Police plugged in on any individual wire was guesswork. It was even conceivable that they watched everybody all the time. But at any rate they could plug in your wire whenever they wanted to. You had to live—did live, from habit that became instinct—in the assumption that every sound you made was overheard, and, except in darkness, every moment scrutinized.[6]

To live in wariness from habit become instinct is a chilling prospect for any of us. Increasingly it is becoming a reality for many Americans.[7] The result is that we are being robbed of our privilege of being eccentric; when the public has access to all your inmost thoughts, you hesitate to think thoughts that are different and unpopular. Thoreau once observed, "If a man does not keep pace with his companions, perhaps it is because he hears a different drummer. Let him step to the music which he hears, however measured or far away."[8] But in the Goldfish Age, it becomes more and more difficult to step to a different drummer.

How in the midst of all these intrusions into our private lives shall we maintain our individuality? Consider some questions which you can think over for yourself and also which can be discussed when your CLC group meets together.

1. How can I protect *myself* from this sort of thing? Are there times when I need to say, "None of your business"? When would that be?

2. What can I do to protect the privacy and individuality of others?
   a. How can a child be trained to respect the privacy of others (and the property of others)? What does a child learn from the way his parents treat him?
   b. What are some of our attitudes toward others who think and say unorthodox things?
   c. Are there organizations dedicated to protecting individual rights—freedom of speech, freedom of worship? What sort of support could we give?
   d. How about our own neighborhood? What could we do there to protect the privacy of all of us from nosy neighbors?

   If the . . . depersonalizing forces continue undiminished, will the time come when a man can no longer enter a closet to pray in secret, enjoy solitude, keep a trust, hold an unconventional opinion, cover from public view some private part of his being? Is the world of *1984,* the world of Big Brotherism, a dreadful certainty rather than a titillating fantasy?[9]

Noise: Trespass upon Privacy

One urban planner, living amid the noise of a modern apartment building, called the noise there "a new form of trespass, a new invasion of privacy."[10]

Unseen, but all too perfectly heard, are domestic strife (and bliss), digestive strains, telephone bells ("Is it ours or theirs?") new hi-fis and old TV commercials. Pounding on the wall is no solution: it is all too likely to collapse.[11]

Noise is all around us: intruding noise, unignorable noise. You cannot lie on the beach enjoying your own private world, thinking your own private thoughts; the man lying a few feet away has his transistor going full blast, and it is beyond human capacity to shut it out of your attention. You cannot choose to spend a peaceful Sunday afternoon in the park with the children; the expressway runs nearby, and the roar of the trucks drowns out any attempt at conversation. With more and more people all around, our nation's noise level is rising, doing perhaps untold psychological and physiological damage to us. Vance Packard quotes a scientist on the subject. "Audiologist Joseph Krimsky has stated that the capacity of noise to annihilate privacy is not only aggravating life's stresses but can produce pathological changes in the auditory system and reduce sensitiveness to the nuances of sound and music."[12] And the frustration of it all is that we as individuals seem helpless; we cannot freely choose *not* to be victimized by noise, for it is all around us, trespassing upon the privacy of our thoughts. Over a half century ago the great German scientist Robert Koch predicted: "The day will come when man will have to fight noise as inexorably as cholera and plague."[13] That day may already have arrived.

What is the problem? Noise is usually defined as "unwanted sound." Measured in decibels—the smallest difference in loudness that the human ear can pick up—here is the way assorted noises stack up.

A noise of 100 decibels can cause physical discomfort, and the close-up roar of a jet engine can produce actual pain. Reactions to noise vary, of course, since, as *Newsweek* noted, "one

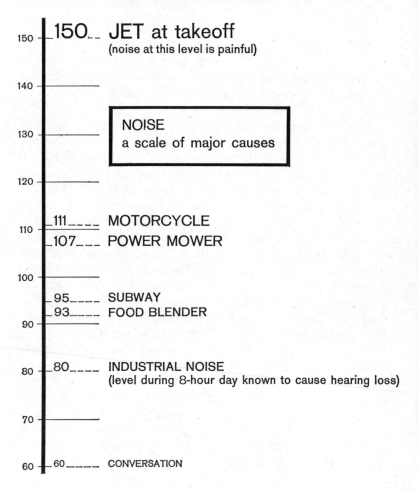

DECIBELS—standard units of measure for intensity of sound

150 — **150**   **JET at takeoff**
(noise at this level is painful)

140

NOISE
a scale of major causes

130

120

110 — 111   MOTORCYCLE
107   POWER MOWER

100

95   SUBWAY
93   FOOD BLENDER

90

80 — 80   INDUSTRIAL NOISE
(level during 8-hour day known to cause hearing loss)

70

60 — 60   CONVERSATION

man's sonata can be another man's stress."[14] There are clear in-
dications, however, of the kinds of things noise can do to us. It
can, of course, impair hearing and even cause complete deafness.
The hairs in the inner ear pick up vibrations to be transmitted to
the nerves leading to the brain, and these hairs simply wear out
when subjected to a continuous bombardment of loud noise. A
person exposed continuously to eighty decibels or more will gradually find himself less and less able to perceive distinct sounds like
spoken words. And though the average person is not exposed to
sustained sound of this intensity, the fact is that there are more
and more powered, mechanical noisemakers both in the home and
in the community, and many doctors suggest that community noise
levels are rapidly approaching the danger point.

Perhaps of more crucial significance would be the psychological effects of noise which medical men are beginning to discern.
The experts say that our ears go on listening while our brains sort
out the sounds by an effort of concentration; we get accustomed to
continuous clatter and are not aware of the toll in energy which
the noise is taking. For this reason physicians are suspecting that
noise contributes to irritability and fatigue and even to neurosis
and psychosis.

And there is no escape. In the old days we could get out in
the country and revel in the peace and quiet of it all. Now one is
hard put to it to be out of earshot of a super-highway, and of jets
streaking overhead. Automobiles are bad enough at 70 decibels,
but trucks roar along the highway at over 100 decibels. Tomorrow
will be worse. There will be more people, all of them wanting to be
on the move; so more traffic, more noise in the future. There is no
rest for weary ears.

All of which confronts us with decisions. Consider these questions for your own thinking and for discussion with your class.

1. How much are we ourselves contributing to the din?
   According to the *Dallas News,* "it [noise] will be suffered until
   we Americans grow up. Invention and precaution will help
   some. But self-restraint and consideration for others are nine-
   tenths of noise abatement."[15]

    a. What is my attitude toward my neighbor's personhood? Does his comfort matter to me?

    b. How is my attitude apparent as I—
       play my transistor radio on the beach? out in the woods? use my power mower?
       entertain my friends at an evening party?
       play my radio, TV, hi-fi?

    c. Have my neighbors had to complain to me about my noise or my family's noise?

2. What can be done through community structures?

    a. What are the possibilities of community regulation? Many communities now have ordinances regulating the sound-proofing of walls, the decibel level of appliances, and penalizing individuals who play radios, phonographs and such loudly between 11 P.M. and 7 A.M.

    b. What avenues are open for plain citizens like us to *demand* abatement of noise in our community?

    c. What can be done about the increase in traffic noises? Trucks can be adequately muffled; how can we effectively demand that this be done?

    d. Can traffic noise—autos, trucks, airplanes—be effectively controlled at the local level?

Norman Cousins has laid the challenge at our door:

> Whether or not they realize it, the American people are waging unremitting war against themselves. The weapons are tranquility-smashers and are fitted out with decibel warheads. They penetrate all known cranial barriers and invade the innermost core of an individual's privacy, impeding the processes of sequential thought, breaking down the sensibilities, and unhinging the capacity for serenity. The noise level is rising and the level of common sanity is falling. . . .
>
> We live at a time when thought alone represents the differences between safety and total madness. One of the prime requirements of such thought is privacy and a little silence, at least now and then. We will get it once we attach value to it.[16]

THE THREAT TO COMMUNITY

Personhood and Involvement

The other side of personhood is community. Individuality is essential to being a person, and we need the privilege of privacy if we are to become uniquely ourselves. But individuality needs to be balanced by caring for others, for real personhood does not allow for withdrawing into separateness for the protection of one's own ego. To be a whole person requires the ability to be involved in other's lives: to love them, to care for their welfare, even to be willing to suffer for and with them.

We have been talking about all the threats to our individuality —to privacy, to the right to be different—and it would be natural to assume that we are being *forced* into corporate living, willy-nilly. One would think we can't help having a sense of interdependence and community. But this is not necessarily so; the fact is that often-times these very invasions of our privacy stir up such reaction in us that we are likely to withdraw from involvement with others.

Consider how natural it is. A man sits a few feet away from us at the beach with his transistor blaring, forcing us to listen: it's likely that we'll lie there and seethe, becoming less and less interested in that guy's welfare as a person, more and more receptive to the idea of having something bad happen to him. The point comes when we'd be delighted to see scuffling children splatter him *and* his radio with sand and sea water. This man has destroyed any vague feelings of good will we might have had toward him; now we couldn't care less. The strands of community have been loosened because he has invaded our privacy.

Or consider the way we turn to air-conditioners; they are perhaps the best maintainers of privacy we have so far developed. Not only does the air-conditioner keep us cool, but it also shuts out the outside world—the noise of it, the smell of it, all the things that can irritate even in a small town these days. Insulated by air-conditioning, we can be spared the heart-catching sound of the siren on the ambulance, or the crump of car against car down at the corner (somebody ignored that stop sign again). The low hum of the air-conditioner can muffle all annoyances from the outside, and can even make us unaware of a cry for help in the street. We can be safely swathed in our privacy, and the strands of community are frayed thereby.

As the population increases, the struggle for privacy will grow more and more desperate, and people will be less and less eager to be involved with their neighbors. As people are crowded together in apartment houses, for instance, they are not at all sure they want to be intimate with the people next door; there are so *many* people next door! If you can ignore the folks who live nearby there'll be time for people elsewhere whom you yourself choose. Harvey Cox tells of the efforts made by some city churches to organize apartment dwellers into some sort of togetherness; over and over again the efforts failed, for these people simply didn't want to meet their neighbors socially. This, says Cox, is a sort of survival technique. "Resistance against efforts to subject them to neighborliness and socialization is a skill apartment dwellers must develop if they are to maintain any human relationships at all."[17]

Furthermore, the plain fact of the matter is that you *have* to have impersonal relations with the majority of the people you encounter during the day. If you were to get deeply involved in the life of every clerk you deal with, or every customer, you would completely destroy yourself; there would be nothing left of time or energy to give to your friends. "In most of his relations," says Cox, "[the modern man] will be dealing with people he cannot afford to be interested in as individuals but must deal with in terms of the services they render to him and he to them. This is essential in urban life."[18]

Perhaps the epitome of the non-involvement of people in our day is seen in incidents like the murder of Kitty Genovese in New York City. All of us remember the horror with which we read of this episode. The man followed her from the parking lot toward her apartment building, set upon her and stabbed her. She cried out, "Oh my God, I've been stabbed! Please help me! Please help me!" Lights came on all through the apartment building, and one man opened the window, yelling out, "Let that girl alone." The assailant retreated, but very shortly he returned to the attack; finding her on the floor of the building, he stabbed her again and again. Later he reported that he heard an upstairs door open two or three times, but when he looked up, he saw nobody. Evidence gathered later indicates that at least 38 people witnessed at least part of the horror, but none went to her, nor did any of them even call the police until after she was dead. One would be tempted to conclude that the strands of community had pulled completely apart, and that in this situation, no one cared about his neighbor.

The Good Samaritan?

In contrast, look at the parable of the good Samaritan. Go back and read Luke 10:25–34. The Samaritan encounters a man he's never seen before, but he recognizes that this is nevertheless his neighbor, for whom he is responsible. The Samaritan believes that to be confronted by a neighbor in need is to be called to serve that neighbor.

We need to ask, however, if Jesus would tell that same story today. In the complexity of our society, do we find conditions somewhat different from the simplicity of Jesus' day? Would Jesus still say that whenever we encounter a person in need—like Kitty Genovese—we must go directly and personally to his aid? Consider some problems this might raise:

1. There are practical limitations to the Samaritan impulse. If a citizen were to react to *every* needy person he encountered, he couldn't take proper care of his own affairs.

2. In our complex society, how can you be sure what the need is? Some of the 38 in the Genovese case might have thought this was a drunken brawl, or a prank of some teen-agers—in which case it would do more harm than good to go rushing out to intervene.

3. Note the actual danger that sometimes comes with getting involved—even with just calling the police. Back in the 1950's a man named Arnold Schuster spotted an escaped criminal in the subway. He reported this to the police, the criminal was arrested, Schuster was acclaimed as a hero. Fine—but he was

dead within the month! He was murdered in reprisal, just for having done nothing more than phone the police. To be involved with the police often means being called as a witness and being subject to reprisals. Can most of us really afford to get involved?

4. Sometimes there is danger even in going to answer a knock at the door. In a world where there are more and more people, there will inevitably be more criminals, and a person has to take reasonable precautions. We all remember the story of the Boston Strangler, who murdered eleven women between June of 1962 and January of 1964. Evidence indicated that the criminal did not pick locks or break windows, and many of his crimes were committed in full daylight rather than at night. It was apparent to investigating officers that the victim in each case opened the door to admit him. An account in *Newsweek* during that time points out that all the victims were found by the criminal "safely" at home.

> There is something special about the terror that harrows Boston by night. It comes not in ill-lit wintry streets but in the snug of home, not from the menace in winding waterfront alleys but in the solid comfort of Beacon Hill.[19]

In the light of all these considerations, think through the following questions:

1. How would Jesus tell the parable of the Good Samaritan if he were telling it in late twentieth-century America?

2. What do you think about the following statement? "A calculated and strategic indifference is an unavoidable part of life in our cities, and it must be faced without sentimentality or rage."[20]

3. Christ's great commandment is that we love one another (John 13:34). Can you love people and yet refuse to be personally involved in their lives? If so, how would that love be expressed practically?

CHAPTER 17

Population,
Personhood, and Nature

Visitors travel hundreds, even thousands of miles, to escape
the big cities and enjoy the beauty of unmolested nature; they
find themselves in the erstwhile wilderness, breathing the
fumes of their neighbor's car, and falling over his tent pegs.[1]

People seem to feel the need to get away from the city, get
out to where they can be in contact with nature. (Witness the
bumper-to-bumper traffic in our parks, and the campers so thick
that they fall over each other's tent pegs!) They could not put it
into words, perhaps, but here are great hordes of Americans acting
on the assumption that to be whole they need nature. We have been
talking about personhood and the way in which we need both to
express our individuality and to find a relatedness with our neighbors. Some would say that there is more than this, that full personhood depends also on our being in tune with the created order; we
need—as human beings we *need*—to be able to get to the out-of-

doors. As William O. Douglas has put it, "Being in tune with the apartment or the community is part of the secret. Being in tune with the universe is the entire secret." And he goes on:

> . . . industrialization . . . does not produce wholeness in men. It produces the despair of our times, the monotony of life whose ultimate expression is communism, the diseases of tension, full bellies but sick minds, the ultimate ant hill.[2]

If this is true, we are in trouble, for with our burgeoning population there is less and less chance to get to untrammelled nature; when we try, we beathe the fumes of our neighbor's car and fall over his tent pegs. But do we really need contact with "unmolested nature"?

DO WE NEED NATURE?

People will disagree on the answer to that question. The novelist, Robert Wernick[3], believes that it is city life which is really human life (and we might note in passing that "civil-ized" means, really, "citified"!), and our human task is to *conquer* the wilderness, not to worry about preserving it. Why *shouldn't* we spoil the wilderness? he asks.

> Have these [wilderness lovers] ever stopped to think what the wilderness is? It is precisely what man has been fighting against since he began his painful, awkward climb to civilization. It is the dark, the formless, the terrible, the old chaos which our fathers pushed back, which surrounds us yet, which will engulf us all in the end. . . . Spoil it! Don't you wish we could?

The conservationists have a right to go out camping if they wish; that is their business. Let them suffer through their primitive living if they want to.

> We ought to recognize, however, that other people have equally strong and often equally legitimate urges to build roads, dig mines, plow up virgin land, erect cities. Such people

used to be called pioneers; now they are apt to be called louts. At all events, we are faced with sets of conflicting drives, and it is up to us to make a rational choice among them.[4]

Jimmy Breslin echoes this suspicion that we don't need nature; we need city life if we are to be human. He snorts at the suburban concern for grass and trees and gardens and elbow room[5], and exalts the fascination of life in the city.

> I live three blocks from an express on the subway. . . . At eight o'clock at night in the city, you can go out and in 20 minutes be at someplace like Sullivan Street, in Manhattan's Little Italy. Sullivan Street is closed for three blocks because it is the Feast of St. Anthony. Colored lights hang from tenements. Stands where they make *calzone* and *zeppoles* line the sidewalks. A Ferris wheel spins in a parking lot. Up at the end of the crowded street you can bet two dollars on dice or a roulette wheel. Out in the suburbs, if you ever go out of the house at night—and I don't think anybody does once they flick the beautiful television set on—the only thing you see is a neighbor inspecting his lawn.
>
> . . . Sure, there are things wrong with the cities. They can be ugly. But at least you can have a human life there. In a city you have to live more because you're not allowed to live less. There is this extra touch of alertness which comes from getting through a day.[6]

"But at least you can have a human life there." There are good theologians who will back up this judgment. Truman B. Douglass has observed that it is city life more than any other kind of life which reminds us human beings of our need for each other.

> The city declares the glory of God by its achievements of human acceptance. Not always do these achievements represent the highest form of fellowship and love, but they represent a degree of mutual recognition that is the necessary preliminary to fellowship and love. Before men can begin to

love one another they must learn to tolerate one another and
to practice a certain peaceful coexistence. In most of our
human relationships we have not come even this far.

In our cities, however, we have declared a truce in the
ancient warfare in which men set themselves against one
another because they are different. Now and again this truce
becomes a triumph. In our cities we have in the main won this
enormous victory over primitive hostilities between man and
man. After I have been a week or two in the South, with signs
"White" and "Colored" painted all over the place, it gives
me a kind of fierce joy to walk along Fourteenth Street or
Upper Broadway and to see there faces of all colors and
shapes, and to hear voices speaking in twenty different lan-
guages—everybody accepting everybody else's presence and
recognizing his right to be there. . . . In this atmosphere personal dignity and liberty become possible.[7]

All of this raises a question that needs to be asked. People go
out to the wilderness or move to the suburbs to escape the cities
and the crowds; but is this a good thing? If we go out seeking solitude, are we missing the human lessons of living with different
kinds of people, accepting them and acknowledging our dependence upon them? Are we settling for a life that is less than human?

Well, some would say that we will never know a really human
life unless we *do* have some solitude, that unless we manage to
maintain some contact with the wild and the natural, we will lose
any life that is worth the living. Wallace Stegner, poet and novelist, points out that our contemporary literature is sick and bitter
because it has lost faith in America. Our novelists are constantly
attacking our society, he says. "There has hardly been a serious or
important novel in this century that did not repudiate in part or in
whole American technological culture for its commercialism, its
vulgarity, and the way in which it has dirtied a clean continent and
a clean dream." Granted that preserving some wilderness would
not cure our condition; "but the mere example that we can as a
nation apply some other criteria than commercial and exploitative
considerations would be heartening to many Americans, novelists
or otherwise."[8]

Many agree with Stegner that for the good of our souls we need contact with wilderness. Some affirm that we need it because it brings release from tension.Wilderness veterans say that a man can arrive for a spell in the woods with his jaw clenched and his hands twitching. But when he has stayed for a while around the slow pulsing of nature, he begins to slow down and to find deep relaxation. A veteran guide in the Lake Superior region reports that he has watched men come from crowded city lives to spend a few days in the bush. They shucked off city patterns and settled down to primitive living, and as they did so, they began to laugh more, to take pleasure in all sorts of little things. "I once saw a business magnate engrossed for over an hour watching an ant hill, a man who until then had counted any moment lost that was not devoted to making money."[9] Great forests, says Wallace Stegner, can "give industrial man what he most needs; they hush the spirit."[10]

Others go beyond the psychological and practical to the theological as they make their case for the wilderness: we need the wilderness, they say, to give us a sense of perspective on life and man's place in it. The great mystic Evelyn Underhill wrote:

> I remember once in the Alps finding myself alone in a high pasture surrounded by the strange, almost unearthly mountain life. I was still then, with an absolute contentment and solemn happiness which hardly anything else can bring to those who have the mountain sense. I stood there getting smaller and smaller and happier and happier as I contemplated my real role in the world.[11]

Surrounded as we are by man-made things, it is easy for us to forget our "real role in the world," to get to thinking that we are our own creator and redeemer, dependent on no one but ourselves. We need the experience of being dwarfed, of getting "smaller and happier" as we see ourselves relative to a great mountain or waterfall or giant fir. We need to be deminded that God's creative power is at work in the world, independent of ourselves, and that we are not in charge of the whole show, only part of it.

Theologians push even deeper, however, to remind us of the

basic Biblical understanding that man and nature are one. Man is embedded in nature, says the Bible: when man fell, nature fell, too, and the two will be redeemed together. As Paul puts it, the whole creation "waits with eager longing for the revealing of the sons of God . . . [for] the creation itself will be set free from its bondage to decay and obtain the glorious liberty of the children of God." (Rom. 8:19, 21)

Man and nature belong together. Paul Tillich has said it this way: "Man reaches into nature, as nature reaches into man. They participate in each other and cannot be separated from each other."[12] Secular writers echo the same understanding. Stewart Udall observed that "little by little we are learning . . . that we are not outside nature, but in it; that it is not a commodity which we can exploit without restraint, but a community to which we belong."[13]

Joseph Wood Krutch points out that we share the earth with a vast number and variety of living things. We differ from them, but all of us share in aliveness. They are our only living companions "in an infinite and unsympathetic waste of electrons, planets, nebulae and stars," and to know companionship with them is to know "perennial joy and consolation."[14]

All of these people are saying that we are a part not only of the community of men but also of the larger community of nature. Not to know either is to fall short of full personhood.

Is man essentially an urban animal who no longer needs to worry about the consequences of being divorced from nature; or does he have a deep need for continued contact with nature? As Robert Wernick has told us, we will have to be making some rational choices—partly because if we do not choose now to preserve some parts of nature in their integrity, there will soon be nothing left to preserve.

What constitutes personhood? Do we need nature if we are to know fullness of humanity? It is worth pondering.

A CALL TO DECISION
Our Opportunities Are Fading

If we decide we *do* need nature—that to be fully human we need to be in tune not only with the human community but also with the natural community around us—then we need to be making some decisions very soon, for a crisis is upon us. At the rate we are going, there will soon be no nature left to fill our need. Sometimes we men act as though we were hell-bent to destroy this natural world which has been entrusted to us as stewards of God.

Look at the way we are polluting our natural environment. All of us know, for instance, what we in our industrial society are doing to our water. We see stories in our newspapers with headings like "Rappahannock Pollution Causing Fish to Die," or "Pollution Poisons a Beautiful Stream." In our magazines we see cartoons like this one:

"My dad says he used to swim here, but I think he's kidding."

Le Pelley in *The Christian Science Monitor* © TCSPS.

These point to the fact that we are dumping into our once clear streams the equivalent of the sewage of 165,000,000 persons and that by 1980 that figure will have risen to 183,000,000. Rivers which used to be gems of beauty, teeming with fish, are now open cesspools where only eels and a few slugs can live.

We know that we are doing the same kind of thing to the air we breathe. The newspaper stories are headlined "Ghost-like Cloud of Filth Hangs Heavy Over Cities," and "Kneeling Cow Becomes Florida Pollution Symbol" (the cow in question was not kneeling in prayer on our behalf; she was diseased from eating the grass fouled by gaseous fluorides from nearby phosphate plants!). Endless cartoons appear on this subject, too, like the one below.

We are aware that much of the pollution comes from the phosphate plants and the paper mills and the textile factories, but that

"The air pollution is so terrible
you can't see the billboards."

Le Pelley in *The Christian Science Monitor* © TCSPS.

often the chief offenders are our own private automobiles, along with the trucks that fill our highways. And these pollutants which can darken white housepaint, corrode metal, disintegrate masonry, and dissolve nylon stockings can reasonably be assumed to have some effect on the delicate tissues of the human lungs—so much that it is reported that breathing the air of a city like Birmingham exposes a person to a hazard of lung cancer equivalent to that of smoking two and a half packs of cigarettes a day!

Now, our governments at all levels have become alert to these dangers and are moving to amend the situation. Federal and state legislation is beginning to force industries to take care of their wastes, and automobiles to control their exhaust. Local communities are regulating factories and home furnaces and even backyard trash burners. But we are still confronted with decisions as individual citizens. Will we support governmental regulation of factories—to the extent of paying higher prices for the products that come from those factories? For the plain fact is that if plants are required to put in pollution controls, somebody has to pay the cost, and usually it is the consumer. Do we value clean air and clean water that much?

There is an even harder decision to make, and that is, What shall we do about air pollution from our automobiles? Pollutant control devices on our cars are helpful, but the growth in number of automobiles on our roads is more than double our population growth, and whatever controls we have (from which older cars are exempt, anyway) will not cleanse and improve our air; they will just enable us to stay where we are. Stringent smog control devices in Los Angeles are enabling that area simply to hold the line; even so, pollutant levels in 1975 will be three times the 1940 level.

There is one possible solution, but it is a difficult one to accept. Many experts believe that mass transportation is the only answer to the auto pollution problem in our cities, for the stop-and-go driving of rush-hour traffic spews out four times as much poison as normal driving. Is the day coming when we will have to give up the luxury of commuting to the city in the privacy of our own automobiles, and travel by bus or train or subway instead? John W. Gardner, while Secretary of Health, Education, and Welfare, observed:

We need to look into the electric car, the turbine car, and any other means of propulsion that is pollution free. Perhaps we also need to find other ways of moving people around. None of us would wish to sacrifice the convenience of passenger automobiles, but the day may come when we may have to trade convenience for survival.[15]

Would we be willing to give up our own convenience for the general welfare? "New occasions teach new duties"; is this a new occasion which confronts us with a new responsibility?

We seem to be well on our way to destroying our natural environment; one evidence of this is the pollution we pour into our streams and into our air. There is another evidence of the destructive impact of our civilization on the open country which we need as human beings: look at the way our road-building chews up endless square miles of countryside. Back in 1966 there were about 3.6 million miles of roads—a mile of road to every square mile in the country. And note that the interstate system involves not just road mileage, but rights-of-way ten times wider than the old 33-foot span, and every interchange devours acres of what was once open country. Moreover, once laid, a highway is *there* for a while. There is no reversing the process, for the highway quickly comes to be bordered with the necessary accompaniments of travel, including filling stations, motels, restaurants, and what have you.

The criteria for the placing of our highways are usually engineering criteria, not aesthetic ones: engineers are responsible for building the best road at the least cost so as to enable people to get from here to there. They cannot add miles and cost just to preserve a good trout stream or a lovely forest; they cannot, that is, unless the public *demands* that our routes be selected on more than just engineering criteria. And thereon hangs the kind of decision that we citizens have to make.

Now is the time to ask questions about our road-building programs. The interstate highway program is to end in 1972, and along with it the Highway Trust Fund program providing Federal funds for the construction of other major roads. But there will be tremendous pressures on the Federal government to continue with more and more highway construction. Road building is one of the biggest businesses in America. One out of every seven Americans has a job related to highway transportation; one out of every six businesses is somehow related; seven of the ten largest corporations in the world are based on it—three auto makers, four oil companies. Many pocketbooks have a vested interest in what William G. Wing has called "the Great American Assumption: That wherever you want to go, there you should be carried in an automobile." Since automobiles came on the scene, says Wing, "nothing has been too good for the family car and truck. Roads are going wherever Americans want to go. . . . Who *can* make the routes swerve to avoid valuable open space?"[16]

The question is, do we *want* to make the routes swerve? Do we care that much about the open space? That is one of the decisions with which we are faced in our day. How much really do we need nature?

The greatest threat to our countryside, however, lies not in our propensities to pollute the atmosphere or to build roads in every nook and cranny of the land, but in the sheer pressure of our expanding population. We were citing figures back in chapter 15: three thousand acres bulldozed under every day, over a million acres a year. We *have* to have homes for all our people to live in, but one of the problems is that we build them with very little thought for long-range values. The builders are free to develop any land they are able to buy, and county commissions are only too willing to rezone from agricultural to residential or industrial, for building means payrolls and progress.

Consider what has happened to some islands off the Florida coast. The Tierra Verde are a group of islands which, according to an editor of *Sports Illustrated,* are one of the few remaining great marine nursery grounds in the South, a breeding place for all sorts of marine animals. A real estate development company has already taken over 1120 acres of those nursery grounds for housing areas, and there were plans to dredge up 9,250,000 yards of the bay bottom to make more land area, thus destroying the basis of a whole chain of marine life. This is characteristic of the pattern our development has followed.[17]

Moreover, much of our development is of tasteless buildings, as all of us know from experience—highways lined with hot dog stands and dairy bars that are a poor substitute for the trees that fell to make way for them. And what is not covered with buildings is covered with litter, so much that Stewart Udall could call us Americans "the litter champions of the world."[18]

"The more I see," said Robert Boyle, a senior editor of *Sports Illustrated,* "the more I am forced to conclude that from New York to California, from Florida to Alaska, America the beautiful is becoming America the ugly, the home of the neon sign, the super-duper highway, the billboard, the monotonous housing tract."[19]

The consequence of it all? Suppose we do feel the need to get away from our crowded towns and cities, to get out to open space. Will the open space be there for our soul's refreshment? There is not much left, and what is there is less and less beautiful because of what we keep on doing to whatever we touch; we have "dirtied a clean continent and a clean dream." Do we care enough to begin to undo the damage?

Decisions that Confront Us

The basic problem is the problem we have been facing in the last three chapters: the problem of our expanding population. The primary question that confronts us here, then, is the question raised in chapter 15: will we set drastic limits for ourselves in the size of our families? If not, there is no need to talk about conservation of the nature around us; there will simply not be space for us and for the wilderness, too.

Even if we take steps to stabilize our birth rate, however, our population will not likely be going *down,* and already we are over-crowded. This means there are hard decisions which we will have to make. We have gotten to the place where there is intense competition for the remaining land areas: factories, mines, parks, dams, highways, wildlife—all of these claims for space will be colliding more and more. Many are saying that we will simply not be able to leave it to individuals to make absolute decisions about how the land will be used, that we will have to vest the decision-making in the hands of people responsive to the long-term public welfare rather than to momentary profit for the individual. But this means overall planning, done by public officials. Are we willing to see this happen? We will have to be deciding very soon.

Whatever is done to conserve the beauty of the out-of-doors, governmental bodies will take the lead. But we individuals are responsible for supporting the people in the state capitol or in Washington when they move in this direction, and for sticking pins in them when they do not. There are times when beavers and red-woods and marine life get short shrift in the councils of state, and citizens who care have to band together to get action. It has been done, and done effectively. In New Jersey, just thirty miles west of Times Square, is an amazing area of swampland which has re-mained untouched amid all the metropolitan expansion around it. In 1959 the New York Port Authority proposed to drain and fill the swamp and to build there a fourth jetport for the New York area. The people in the communities surrounding the swamp rose up in wrath to protect the place of beauty and peace in their midst. Organizing in the various communities, they raised 1.5 million dollars to buy 3,000 acres of swamp, which they turned over to the U.S. Fish and Wildlife Service to be made into the Great Swamp Wildlife Refuge. Those people believed, as Brooks Atkinson re-ported, that the swamp "is good for nothing except life, knowledge, peace and hope,"[20] and for those values they are ready to fight.

A group in suburban Westchester in New York banded to-gether to form the Cortlandt Conservation Association, to work for a farsighted use of the land in their area. They were able to stop the dumping of old automobiles in a lovely Hudson River marsh-land. They bought a piece of ravine that was auctioned off at a delinquent tax sale, bought it to be preserved as a little enclave of wildness in their midst. They have been buying bits and pieces of land in a river gorge and gradually putting them together in a park that will remain wild. "There is no use sitting by and mourning and allowing the ruin of our country, our waters and our heritage," observed their president. "We have to get out and do something to stop it. If we try, we may even succeed."[21]

Behind all these decisions lies the major question, Are we will-ing to demand that government and business get together in plan-ning for a use of our shrinking land which will take into account more than just economic factors? Stewart Udall reminds us, "Once we decide that our surroundings need not always be subordinated to payrolls and profits based on short term considerations, there is hope that we can both reap the bounty of the land and preserve an inspiring environment."[22]

Are we willing to sacrifice some economic progress in our county, to give up an occasional new factory; to pay a bit more in taxes? "New occasions" may be teaching us "new duties."

Will Something Go Out of Us?

Something will have gone out of us as a people if we ever let the remaining wilderness be destroyed; if we permit the last virgin forests to be turned into comic books and plastic cigarette cases; if we drive the few remaining members of the wild species into zoos or to extinction; if we pollute the last clean air and dirty the last clean streams and push our paved roads through the last of the silence, so that never again will Americans be free in their own country from the noise, the exhausts, the stinks of human and automotive waste. And so that never again can we have the chance to see ourselves single, separate, vertical and individual in the world, part of the environment of trees and rocks and soil, brother to the other animals, part of the natural world and competent to belong in it. Without any remaining wilderness we are committed wholly, without chance for even momentary reflection and rest, to a headlong drive into our technological termite-life, the Brave New World of a completely man-controlled environment.[23]

Is the writer there exaggerating? Do we need nature that desperately? If there *is* validity in what he says, then decisions must be made soon, for the work of the bulldozer is irreversible. "God speaks ever afresh to men by bringing them into new situations."[24] Here is a situation we have never before faced in our world; what is God saying to us through it?

SECTION III

JOINING
GOD IN
HIS WORK

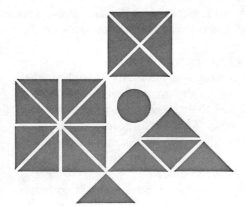

Throughout our study we have been seeing how limited our freedom is; our ability to respond to God is all fenced in. Our self-centeredness makes it hard for us to see beyond our own interest or that of our group. Social influences mold our attitudes and color the way we think. All of which makes us raise the question, How free *are* we, really, to respond to God?

In chapter 10 we were talking about young Julie, a teen-age girl who had no real family relationships, who felt *driven* to seek acceptance in the only way she knew—in sex. What else could we expect of her? We were talking about young David, cheating on an English paper. Here was a boy urged into dishonesty by parents who wanted to brag about his grades. What else could we expect of him? Can these youngsters really be held to account by God or by us for what they do? Their actions were shaped by the influence of their parents; were they free to do other than they did?

We will be concerned with this question in Section III of our study. We will also be concerned with the way in which joining God in his work makes us free. But before we get there, let us consider two preliminary observations on this matter of freedom.

Granted, in the first place, the forces around us condition what we do. They influence us, bend us in certain directions. But we must retain our faith in the fact that there is still a self to react to these environing influences; there is interaction here. There is the influence of parents, yes, and of teachers and friends and colleagues. There is also a *me* which responds, which takes the *given* of all these influences and makes out of them a life. Our actions are *conditioned,* not *determined,* and we are accountable for what we do with the givens.

Common sense tells us that we would not feel responsibility for what we did if we acted without real alternatives—unless when we acted, we believed that we might do otherwise. The fact of remorse points to our awareness that though we acted in one way, we might have acted in another. The whole gospel emphasis on *decision* would be utterly meaningless if we did not in fact make real choices. Our environment conditions our thinking and attitudes; it does not determine our decisions.

Secondly, it ought to be noted that accountability is corporate as well as individual. We tend to think of being held accountable only in the context of a final judgment, when each man's life will be judged individually. To hell, or to life with God, and that's the end of it. But we need to recognize that judgment upon sin and selfishness and irresponsibility comes also in the form of daily consequences, right on the human level. We all share in the consequences of sin, even when we don't share equally in the sin that has produced them. Julie's parents failed in their responsibility to their child; the guilt for what happened could be laid largely at their door. But Julie bore the brunt of the tragedy that followed. The child suffered the consequences of the parents' irresponsibility —a situation not unusual in human life! The iniquity of the fathers is visited upon the children; we have only to look around us to know that this is true.

Our freedom is limited; there is no question about that. But it is nevertheless real freedom. God has given us the opportunity to respond to him and to obey him voluntarily in love. By the same token, of course, he has given us the freedom to turn away from him in rebellion. The animals, says Jeremiah (8:7), obey God from instinct; only man has the freedom to rebel.

> Even the stork in the heavens
>   knows her times;
> and the turtledove, swallow, and crane
>   keep the time of their coming;
> but my people know not
>   the ordinance of the LORD.

The focus of our study has been the responsible self, called to respond to God by joining him in his work. In this last section we will see that our freedom is freedom to act within our limitations, to respond to God *where we are* and (in the power of his Spirit) to build an abundant life within the realities of our own situation.

In chapter 18 we will see that we are in fact *incarnate* creatures. We are embedded in nature and society; this is the reality of human life. It is here that we find a major source of our limita-

tions, of our un-freedom: there are certain givens and it is within
those givens that we have to work. Yet God will not let us rest
content with things as they are. We cannot remain complacently
at the animal level. He has implanted within us a restlessness, an
urge to shape the nature around us, to change ourselves, to influence the society out of which we have come. There are limitations
which hem us in, yes; but in the midst of those limitations is the
open door to freedom.

Chapter 19 speaks of what happens as we seek to carry out
this shaping and influencing: we experience the reality of suffering.
For if we are to respond to God, we must do it in the midst of a
"crooked and perverse generation," as Paul put it (Phil. 2:15),
in a society that is sinful. To love and serve one's neighbors in
that kind of world means that suffering is inevitable—not literal
crucifixions, of course, nor even spectacular martyrdoms, for the
most part, but daily crucifixions of the comfort and convenience of
the self, the daily suffering of sharing the hurt of others. Response
to a crucified God means sharing in his suffering.

In chapter 20 we will see how we move by way of crucifixion
and suffering to resurrection and new life. In the New Testament,
cross and resurrection are inseparable. Either is meaningless without the other; both constitute one single event. As we respond to
this God who raised Jesus Christ from the dead, we discover that
through suffering we come to newness of life. We know crucifixion
on this side of renewal and re-creation. We come to new life on the
other side of crucifixion.

"If any man would come after me," said Jesus, "let him deny
himself and take up his cross and follow me. For whoever would
save his life will lose it; and whoever loses his life for my sake and
the gospel's will save it." (Mark 8:34–35)

CHAPTER 18

Response to God Within the Givenness of Life

It is in this real world that we real men respond to God.
Ernest Gordon has told in *Through the Valley of the Kwai* the moving story of a group of British prisoners of war during World War II. Living in the midst of misery, despair, and death, they were forced by their Japanese captors to build a railroad through the valley of the Kwai River, at frightful cost in suffering and death. What was happening in their camp life, however, was worse than death: men were losing their very humanity. Gordon describes it:

> As conditions steadily worsened, as starvation, exhaustion, and disease took an ever-growing toll, the atmosphere in which we lived was increasingly poisoned by selfishness, hatred, and fear. We were slipping rapidly down the scale of degradation.[1]

The sick were left to suffer in their loneliness, the dying heard no word of mercy. "Everyone was his own keeper." No man trusted another; none helped another. And there were some who descended to the depths of sheer animality.

The minute roll call was over in the evening there would be a rush to the Japanese cookhouse. The cooks would bring out swill pails and set them on the ground. Then they would stand back, fold their arms, and look on with self-satisfied smiles while prisoners pushed, kicked, and shoved one another out of the way as they fought for scraps from the enemy table.

One evening this too familiar scene was taking place as I passed by. A wretch broke away and stumbled toward me. In his hand he clutched a soggy mess of rice and stew. Bits of gravy dripped through his fingers. He had turned his back on the others, lest they should see what he had and be tempted to rob him. A wolfish leer contorted his face as he craftily licked at his spoils. He considered himself lucky.

"Rather than do that," I thought to myself, "I'd die!" He passed me at a kind of trot, like an animal going to his lair, except that an animal would have had more dignity.[2]

Ernest Gordon's story gives us a beautifully clear picture of the incarnateness, the embodiedness, of man, and this we will be talking about in the present chapter. It ought to be noted as we begin, however, that we are using the word "incarnation" with a meaning slightly different from our use of it in chapter 3. There we were talking about a God who incarnates himself. We were saying that the God who was incarnate in Jesus Christ is *always* like that: he chooses to involve himself in the material and historical reality of this world. He works through the mundane, the particular, the concretely historical. Because he was incarnate in Christ, we know assuredly "that God will not remain apart from the world, for His heart is here."[3] And to respond to that God means to live in the midst of the world, to fully share its life, and to be concerned with the worldly realities of every day. This is an imperative laid upon us if we are to respond fittingly to an incarnate God.

In this chapter, however, we are talking about the incarnateness of ourselves, and here incarnation is not so much *imperative* as *indicative*. It is not that we *ought* to be but that we *are* incarnate creatures: this is a given in life. God freely chooses to incarnate himself; we have no choice.

Let us look at two aspects of our incarnateness. We are creatures of clay, embedded in nature, and we are social creatures, embedded in society. This is part of the given reality of life with which we have to come to terms. As we look at each of these, we will see that there is goodness here, and cause for rejoicing. We will also see that there is limitation here, and restriction on our freedom.

How shall we respond to God within these realities of human life?

TWO ASPECTS OF OUR INCARNATENESS

There is no question that, *in the first place, we are inescapably embedded in and part of nature*. The body simply cannot be ignored. No one who shares vicariously in the experience of that prison camp by the Kwai will be tempted to think that man's soul can operate independently of his body. "As conditions steadily worsened," Gordon tells us, "as starvation, exhaustion, and disease took an ever-growing toll," the imperious bodily needs of the men made them forget about caring for each other, made them forget the joys of human community, turned each one into a self-centered beast.

Physical need is a given in human life, a fact with which we simply have to come to terms. We are part of the natural world, subject to all its laws. The physicist can describe us human beings in terms of atoms, molecules, and physical forces; and the physicist is right. The chemist can describe us in terms of the chemical substances of which we are made, our very lives dependent upon the maintaining of fantastic chemical balances; and he is right. The biologist can describe us as he describes other animals, as creatures who need food and drink and sleep and activity; and he is right. We will not be responding to God as disembodied spirits but as those whose response is influenced by the pressure of bodily needs, whose attitude toward life and toward God will be conditioned by the state of our bodies.

The body is good, not evil. God made this everlastingly clear when he became incarnate in Jesus Christ. Jesus was a man like us, with human needs. He knew hunger and thirst; he knew weariness; he knew the need for sleep. And he affirmed the goodness and joy of satisfying these needs. "The Son of man has come eating and drinking," said Jesus, in contrast to the fasting of John the Baptist (Luke 7:33, 34). He fed the five thousand and rejoiced in the marriage feast at Cana. And in the greatest crisis of his life he shared himself to the very depths with his disciples—in a supper, in the Upper Room.

We can affirm the goodness of our bodies and at the same time recognize the extent to which they limit our freedom. We are not free to ignore the reality of our bodily needs. We *must* take care of our bodies, or there will be no self to respond to God. It is simply a fact "that we can, to take two concrete instances, neither philosophize clearly nor pray attentively if we are suffering from influenza or arthritis or from some disorder of the ductless glands."[4]

Moreover, we have to work within the givens of the created order around us, or suffer the consequences. Rachel Henderlite has pointed out that created things must be used as God intends them to be used, or we will suffer in the long run from the disharmonies we have caused. The carpenter must study the grain of the wood he is working with; if he goes against it, the wood will crack and break. If we strip the hillsides of trees erosion will take over, and ultimately streams and rivers will flood. When "our use of God's material is out of harmony with God's greater plan," she says, "destruction follows."[5]

Are we free, and therefore accountable for what we do? Well, certainly we are not completely free; we must work within the reality of the givens of nature. We ignore the reality of this at our peril.

There is no question, *secondly,* that *we are inescapably embedded in and part of society*. We are not free simply to go out and do those things which as individuals we believe we ought to do. The prisoners in the camp by the Kwai had to function within the realities of that prison camp; whatever they were able to do had to be within its confines. Ernest Gordon of the 93rd Highlanders may have felt called by God to continue his university studies, but he was not free to obey. He lived in a sinful world which had gotten itself embroiled in the insanity of war, and now he was a prisoner of the Japanese. This was the fact, and he had to face it.

Once again, the fact that we are social creatures is good, not evil. Back in chapter 9 we were rejoicing that we human beings are so built that we can help each other, can share in each other's lives. This is the joy of families—the comradeship of parents and children. This is the joy of friendship—the sharing of jokes and disappointments and ideas. This is the joy of the church—the sharing of life's greatest gift: faith in God.

We need to affirm the goodness of being social creatures but at the same time recognize how this limits our freedom. We said in chapter 9 that the groups of which we are part shape our thinking and mold us into what we are as persons. Family, business colleagues, fellow-teachers, fellow-churchmen—all these folks contribute to our attitudes and our affections, our biases and our prejudices. We never start from scratch, saying, "Go to now, I will form some attitudes." Our attitudes and reactions are formed for us and in us by the people around us.

Moreover, we must suffer the consequences of each other's sins; this is a reality of human life with which we have to come to terms. We are not free to opt out of this liability of community. Ernest Gordon had contributed little as an individual to the causes of World War II; yet there he lay in the death house of a Japanese prison camp. He was not free to escape the consequences of corporate sin. Leslie Weatherhead has pointed out that this is due to the fact that God has created human life according to a "family plan"; he has made us all members of one another, dependent upon each other as are members of a family. "Shall we, then," he asks, "receiving such untold benefit from our membership of the family, deem it unfair when we are asked to bear the consequences of the family ignorance, the family folly, the family sin?" And he goes on to affirm, "God cannot give me the benefits of the family life without its risks and liabilities."[6]

Most important of all, if we believe that obedience to God requires us to work for change in society, we have to reckon with the stubborn resistance to uncomfortable changes that is part of the givens of social living. Robert L. Calhoun, in his excellent little book *What is Man?*, says that "in all the contacts that membership in organized society entails, the accepted ways of doing things and their complex grounds are *there,* and have to be taken into consideration as fully as physical laws."[7] Social patterns can, of course, be changed (as physical laws cannot); but social change requires slow, broad, deep mass movements, beyond the control of any one individual.

Reinhold Niebuhr has helped us to understand why it is that changed attitudes come so slowly in society. Part of the problem, he says, is the fact of group egoism, which is tremendously difficult to do away with. A privileged group will in all honesty and sincerity identify their own group interest with the welfare of the whole of society, and will oppose those who seek change as subversives. Political issues, then, are not just matters which people debate in an unbiased way; they are rooted in economic interests, and a majority will not ordinarily give up its privileges just because it is persuaded that this is the right and just thing to do. Change comes when the power balance shifts.

This is to say that you don't change society by just willing it so; nor do you do it simply by education and by rational arguments. Niebuhr contends that to work for change you must organize power. "When collective power, whether in the form of imperialism or class domination, exploits weakness, it can never be dislodged unless power is raised against it."[8] Political parties, big corporations, and big unions bring most changes.

All of this is part of what is *there* in organized society, which has to be taken into consideration as fully as physical laws. Are we free, and therefore accountable for what we do? Well, certainly we are not completely free; we must work within the given realities of society and social forces. We ignore the reality of this at our peril.

AND YET . . .!

The prisoners in the camp by the river Kwai had to live and work within severely circumscribed limitations. The jungle effectively kept them within the bounds of the camp; they well knew that they would be freed only by death or by the ending of the war. Yet they were free to respond to the conditions of their life there in differing ways. They were not *compelled* to give up in defeat and to sink to the level of animals. The fact is that they did *not* finally give up their humanity. Ernest Gordon tells us that within the confines of their suffering and despair, they were able eventually to build a real community, a life of sharing and of concern for each other in which gradually they came to act not like animals but like human beings.

They began to do acts of kindness and love. The officers decided to use part of their pay for buying foodstuffs from the canteen to be given to the sick. Some amputees learned how to make artificial limbs, and soon volunteers were scrounging in camp and forest to find the materials that were needed. A jungle university was organized, the educated ones dredging back into their memories of Greek grammar or European history or whatever to teach those who had never studied. A new vitality was stirring in the camp. Where men had known only the despair of isolation, now they were finding the joy of sharing together in a human community.

The truth is that God simply will not let us rest content within these limitations we have been describing. We are embodied creatures, but God plants in us a restlessness within that embodiedness, a refusal to rest content with things as they are.

We are immersed in nature, yet we are called by God to transcend and to control nature in obedience to his purposes. We men are close kin to our fellow-creatures, yet also above them. We can study our environment, can even stand off from ourselves and work out the laws to which our own bodies are subject. More than that, we have the ability to see what exists now in contrast with what could be "better" than this—to conceive of a different state of affairs and to set out to achieve it. Though we are dependent on our natural environment for our very existence, we can yet modify that environment according to our needs and desires. So we bull-doze forests and bridge gorges and dam rivers, and all this we do in response to the Creator's imperative, "Be fruitful and multiply, and fill the earth and subdue it; and have dominion over the fish of the sea and over the birds of the air and over every living thing that moves upon the earth." (Gen. 1:28)

Man's freedom is not to escape from nature, but to mold it; and the realm of his responsibility is to care for the creation as stewards of God. God has called man to mold nature, but to do so in obedience to God's purposes. He expects man to have reverence for the goodness of nature and to use its resources for the welfare of all men, not just for the good of himself and his group. Rachel Henderlite comments pointedly: "In a world created and owned by a God of love and righteousness we cannot dump wheat into the sea while men are starving anywhere in the world without setting up retaliatory movements of hostility and fear and resentment."[9]

Likewise, *we are immersed in society, yet called by God to reshape it in obedience to his purposes.* As Dr. Henderlite puts it, man is "both creature and creator of community."[10]

We grow up and become selves in a world we did not choose and in a society whose standards we did not set, yet we have influence on the shaping of our community's life. An individual can be disturbed by the patterns of his community, can see what exists now in contrast with something better in the future, and set out to change the community toward the something better. Much of our moral progress has come from this kind of gap—the tension between what a community is and what individuals can see that it ought to be.

This is man's freedom—not to escape from society, but to exert influence upon it; and this is the realm of his responsibility—to exert that influence in line with the will and purpose of God. He has to work within the realities of the sinful social order, with all its stubbornness and its reluctance to change. But he is called to re-shape it in the light of God's purpose, knowing that God intends for men to live together in community, where each can be a person and grow toward responsible maturity. To ignore the realities of the social order is sentimental folly, but to rest content with its sinfulness is rebellion against God.

ONLY MEN CAN SIN

It is interesting to note that our language reflects the relationship between these two forms of our embodiedness. We talk about the physical body of man as his *corporeal* nature. When we talk about his sociality—about how men live together—we use a word from the same Latin root and we call it his *corporate* nature.[11] The language here suggests that we human beings recognize that society is an extension of—indeed a form of—our incarnateness; both are different dimensions of the same human reality: we are incarnate beings.

In our incarnateness lie all manner of limitations upon our freedom, but the fact remains that we are not just embodied; we are in some sense "amphibian"; we are both in the body and capable of transcending it. "We find in ourselves," says Rachel Henderlite, "a strange and unaccountable quality that keeps us forever unsatisfied to be merely a part of nature and a part of society, dependent upon nature and society for our being." There are times when we accept it all complacently, "yet at other times we find ourselves yearning to be different from the clod and from the crowd."[12]

In this yearning for what is not lies the freedom of man. We can accept the possibility of transcending present reality, to work with God in the molding of nature and the reshaping of society; or we can reject this possibility and turn against the intention and purpose of God. We can sink to the animal level and live like a wolf, grabbing garbage and exulting over getting things that others do not have. We can turn inward upon ourselves, living for our own welfare and denying the need to build a community which affirms the welfare of all men.

To speak of man as a sinner, said a college professor of philosophy to his class, is the greatest compliment you can pay him, for it indicates that he is a being with a capacity unlike that of all other created beings. It indicates the capacity

to become something other than he is, the capacity to build
and create and dream and hope, the capacity to dwell with
God. And what the professor said is true. No other being can
sin. Man is the only being on earth who can reject God. Nothing else but ourselves has the capacity for fidelity which makes
infidelity possible.[13]

Are we free? Not completely. Our freedom is severely limited;
we cannot escape our embodiedness. But we are free to make of
our incarnate life what God wants—or to shut him out. For our
response God rightly holds us accountable.

CHAPTER 19

Sharing in God's Sacrifice

"It seemed aeons since I had heard anyone volunteer to help a sick man."[1] The spirit in that camp by the Kwai was each for himself and the devil take the hindmost. But there lay Ernest Gordon, just back from the death house and not far from death himself, and here was a total stranger appearing at his door offering to nurse him.

" 'Dusty, are you quite sure you want to help me?' I asked the question not knowing what to expect. His offer surprised me, for it was so different from the attitude we had come to accept as normal."[2] It was unbelievable that in that camp where men lived like animals, scrounging for their very existence, Dusty Miller, himself still recovering from diphtheria, should volunteer to bathe and tend a man helpless with dysentery, to wash his ulcerous legs, to try to make him comfortable with pitifully few resources.

Dusty was a symptom, however, of a new spirit stirring in that camp by the river. Ernest Gordon tells us that there was "a move-ment, a stirring in our midst, a presence."[3] Stories about self-sacrifice and love had begun to circulate. There was the story of Angus McGillivray who had literally given his own health to save the life of a sick buddy. A great strapping man, Angus determined that his dying friend should *not* die. He gave up his own blanket to replace one stolen from his friend. He gave up his rations so that his buddy could be nourished. He gave all his spending money to buy duck eggs or medicine which his friend needed. Gradually, the soldier began to recover his health; but Angus, exhausted, col-lapsed and died. The cause, starvation, said the doctors, compli-cated by exhaustion. He had given all he had—even his life.[4]

The story of Angus spread like wildfire through the camp, firing the imaginations of the men. Soon there were others inspired by his example to acts of sacrificial love. One Scot gave his life for his fellows in a work detail. Their Japanese captors accused them of stealing a shovel, threatening to shoot the whole group in retaliation. This Scot stepped forward and said quietly, "I did it." The infuriated guard beat and kicked him to the ground, finally leaving his lifeless body lying there. Later, the tools were counted again—and no shovel was missing![5]

There were less spectacular but no less important incidents in which this sacrificial spirit showed up. The British officers met to consider using part of their allowance to buy food for the sick. There was grumbling and argument, but the group agreed. "We sink or swim together," they said, and the decision was made. This spirit of generosity proved contagious, and soon men throughout the camp were buying duck eggs for the sick or giving gifts of food to newly-arrived prisoners.[6]

"It was dawning on us all . . . that the law of the jungle is not the law for men. We had seen for ourselves how quickly it could strip us of our humanity and reduce us to levels lower than the beasts."[7] Through sacrifice, the men in the camp by the Kwai were beginning to turn from death to life.

SUFFERING IS INEVITABLE

We are incarnate creatures. We live and move and act in a society that is sinful. If we seek to respond to God in that world, there will be suffering; there is no escaping it. It was not pleasant for Dusty, or comfortable, to clean Ernest Gordon's festering ulcers. Angus was not eager to give up his own health for the health of his buddy. But a war not of their own making had trapped these men in a Japanese prison camp; given that sinful situation, to love was to suffer. And so it is in our sinful world—a world full of sin not all of our making: the person who really loves his neighbor in obedience to God will know physical and mental anguish in his life.

For one thing, our efforts to obey God will meet with frustration and disappointment. Because we live and work in a sinful society, we will not be able to carry out God's will as we discern it, and often we will be oppressed by a sense of failure. There may be times when we are working for justice in society, and people will misunderstand our motives. They will accuse us of self-seeking, or they will call us Communists, and refuse to listen to what we have to say. There will be other times when in obedience to God we are seeking changes in our community, and we so rub against vested interests that we arouse ferocious opposition—opposition that sets out in retaliation to hurt us and those we love. Sometimes obedience to God will mean the suffering of personal rejection, even by people we had thought loved us. As H. Wheeler Robinson expresses it, "In proportion as [the Christian] rises above the average decency of others, he condemns himself to spiritual loneliness."[8]

More than that if we love others, if we identify ourselves with them, then we will suffer with them; we will share in the hurts that come to *them* in a sinful society. For love makes us feel what they feel, be frustrated as they are frustrated, be despairing as they despair. Eugene Debs once said:

> Years ago I recognized my kinship with all human beings, and I made up my mind that I was not one whit better than the meanest of the earth. I said then, and I say now, that while there is a lower class I am of it, while there is a criminal class I am of it, while there is a soul in prison I am not free.[9]

This sensitivity is the price we pay for being human; indeed, it is part of what makes us human. The lower creatures have little sensitivity and little capacity for emotional suffering, for they cannot love as human beings love. It is in man that sensitivity appears clear and full, and the more fully developed a person is, the wider is his range of affection and the greater is his capacity for suffering.

This is what Christ-on-the-cross is all about. The purer the love, the more poignant is its suffering with others. When we come to God's infinitely holy love, we find sensitiveness and therefore suffering lifted to an infinite degree; the cross is the manifestation of God's suffering for us. "The Cross," says Stanley Jones, "is God sensitive to human sin and sorrow—so sensitive that it becomes His very own."[10]

The cross, then, is the outward and historical event which expresses the inward cross in God's life. This means that the atonement is not just a mechanical transaction on some record books somewhere; it is, rather, God's glad willingness to suffer for and with us in our sin. God is love, and he will not refuse the burdens of love.

This God of love calls us to be willing to share with him in his suffering. "If any man would come after me," says Jesus, "let him deny himself and take up his cross and follow me." (Mark 8:34) To be his disciple means to join in his ministry of love, with the suffering that inevitably accompanies it. In chapter 3 of this textbook we were quoting Paul's assertion (Col. 1:24) that "in my flesh I complete what is lacking in Christ's afflictions for the sake of his body. . . ." Paul is saying there that we are incorporated (note: in-*corp*-orated—embodied, made a part of a body) into Christ's life by faith so that he can work through us. We become his body, we are enabled to love with his love, we suffer as he suffers. There is a sense in which Christ's life is really present in our lives, and we share in his ministry of suffering for others.

To serve a God of love in a sinful world is to take upon ourselves a cross of suffering.

BUT WHAT KIND OF SUFFERING?

What do we mean by sharing in the crucifixion of Christ? When we talk about suffering for others, we tend to think of great

big martyrdoms—Stephen being stoned to death, praying radiantly
for the forgiveness of his enemies; Cranmer and Ridley being
burned at the stake in England, standing firm in the faith to the
very end; Madeleine Barot in our own day, going to live in a prison
camp and risking death by disease or even by execution in order to
minister to despairing prisoners of war. Most of us are not the
Joan of Arc type and we do not expect to face the challenge of
that kind of suffering.

To be crucified with Christ, however, does not always mean
spectacular suffering. Jesus said, "Let him deny himself and take
up his cross," but this need not be the Scot who gave his life for
his work group. Let us see what Jesus *does* mean here. For one
thing, says Halford Luccock, he is talking about crucifixion as
denial of self.

> The word "deny" is not a vague, foggy word, easy to evade.
> It is appallingly sharp and clear. It is the same word used of
> Peter's denial of Jesus, and means "Let him make himself a
> stranger" to himself. Not a pampered favorite whose insistent
> desires are law, but a complete stranger, to whom he can and
> does say "No!" Denying ourselves means far more than re-
> fusing to give things to ourselves. . . . It is subordinating the
> clamoring ego, with its shrill claim for priority, its preoccupa-
> tion with "I," "me," and "mine," its concern for self-assertion
> . . . not for the sake of denial as a sort of moral athletics, but
> for Christ's sake, for the sake of putting the self into his
> cause.[11]

Jesus means also, undeniably, says Luccock, that to be a Christian is to be in danger of a cross—"the danger that life will be upset,
that it will be loaded with the burdens of others, that it will be
thrown into deadly combat with strong powers of evil."[12]

The point is that cross-bearing can manifest itself in the
plain things, the routine things of every day. It can mean *the
sacrifice of comfort and convenience*—"the danger that life will be
upset." A housewife, cumbered with much serving (and much
chauffeuring) gives up a morning every week to help in patterning

a child with brain injuries, or makes careful plans to have the car so that she can transport college students to the settlement house for a recreation program. A businessman, carrying the tensions of competition, foregoes the poker evening with the boys to sit with a troubled friend, or gives up the Sunday afternoon football game to take the family out for a hike in the autumn woods. A teacher, worn out with grading papers, gives up the evening at the movies to help a desperate student. Even so simple a thing as giving up *our* TV program so that the other folks in the family can watch *their* favorite might mean sacrifice or loss of comfort.

There is nothing spectacular in these things. We wouldn't ordinarily call them "suffering." Yet, in the routines of every day, these mean denying the self as the pampered favorite, subordinating the ego's claims to priority. They are undramatic ways in which crucifixion can express itself in the lives of us plain folks.

There is more to cross-bearing, though: it can also mean *bearing vicariously the burdens of others*. There is always the danger, says Luccock, that life will be "loaded with the burdens of others." To love is to take the risk of being hurt with the loved one, for love makes one sensitive. H. Wheeler Robinson tells of the father whose small son had to undergo a minor but painful operation for which the surgeons could not use anaesthesia. The father agonized as he heard the boy cry to him for help, and he never forgot the suffering of those few minutes (while the boy had completely forgotten the incident by the time he reached adulthood!).[13] Parents who love suffer when their children suffer.

Love not only makes us share with those in physical pain, however; it also makes for sensitivity to spiritual pain, which is worse. Crucifixion involves exposing ourselves to and sharing in the anxieties of the troubled. A physican spends endless time listening to the man whose marriage is breaking up, and does what he can to help. A mother drinks countless cups of kitchen coffee with another woman, anxious for her errant son. A commuter is sensitive to what people are going through as they lose their homes to the new downtown expressway, and works to find better homes for them.

There is nothing spectacular about these things. None of these things we do involves risking life as Madeleine Barot risked hers to share in the suffering of the prisoners. But these are nonetheless crucifixions—love being hurt because others are hurt; love sharing itself in the hurt. These are undramatic ways in which crucifixion can express itself in the lives of us plain folks.

To serve a God of love in a sinful world is to take upon ourselves a cross of suffering. Large sacrifices? Yes, on occasion. But life is largely made of the fabric of little things. It is woven out of the way we act in the routines of life, the way we treat people in ordinary situations—the fellows in the bowling club, the people we play bridge with, the guy at the next desk in the office (even the folks in the CLC study group!). And the habit of daily denying self as the pampered favorite prepares us for the great sacrifice if ever it comes.

God's call to us through Christ is to "complete what is lacking in Christ's afflictions" in our own lives, where we are, in the large and the small of life. Perhaps this will never mean any great, spectacular sacrifice; but it is sure to mean the willingness to undergo the little denials of the clamoring ego, the willingness to be hurt by the things that are hurting other people (and the willingness to bear the anger of our colleagues and friends, perhaps, when we try to help some of those folks who hurt!).

We are comfortable Christians, most of us; and part of the reason we have not suffered is that we have not been deeply obedient; we have loved our comfort too well. But to really join God in his work is to be willing to share in his sacrifice.

> "God—let me be aware," pleads a poet.
> Let me not stumble blindly down the ways . . .
> Stab my soul fiercely with others' pain . . .
> Let my hands, groping, find other hands.
> Give me the heart that devines, understands. . . .
> God, let me be aware.[14]

To share Christ's sufferings—that is the Christian's response to a suffering God.

THROUGH SUFFERING TO NEW LIFE

Ernest Gordon tells us that when the men began to sacrifice for each other, a new spirit began to move in that camp by the Kwai. "There was a movement," he said, "a stirring in our midst, a presence."[15] They were turning away from life at the animal level—mere existence, the struggle for survival, and turning to real life—human living, living in community. They were beginning to realize that "the law of the jungle is not the law for men." The whole atmosphere of the camp was changing. "There was a general reawakening. Men began to smile—even to laugh—and to sing."[16] It was as if they were wholly different men; and indeed, they were *new men*. Through suffering for each other had come new life to them all.

The New Testament writers knew about this; they knew that crucifixion and resurrection are inseparable. The story of Passion Week is one continuous story, almost one single event. As one poet interprets it:

> Lift up your heads, ye sorrowing ones,
>   And be ye glad of heart,
> For Calvary and Easter Day
>   Were just three days apart![17]

There need be no despair, for Calvary leads to Easter; but at the same time, there can be no Easter without Calvary.

Jesus himself made this quite explicit, especially in that incident where, during the last week, the Greeks came seeking him. Let us look at that passage to discover what Jesus means to say about the relation of suffering to new and abundant and fruitful life.

Read John 12:20–33.

1. First, look at the context of this passage in the whole of John 12:

    1–8—one of the disciples pays homage to Jesus: the anointing at Bethany (note that Jesus uses this act of love to point to his death and burial).

9–19—the Jewish crowd pays homage to Jesus: the triumphal entry.

20–33—Gentiles pay homage to Jesus: the Greeks seek him out.

2. The coming of the Greeks:

Who do you think they are? (You might want to check a commentary on this.)

What significance does Jesus see in their coming?

Why does their coming inspire Jesus to say, "The hour has come for the Son of man to be glorified"? (vs. 23)

(Recall how many times Jesus has said, "My hour has not yet come." See John 2:4; 7:6, 30; 8:20.)

3. When Jesus speaks of being glorified, what does he mean?

What are his disciples likely to think he meant? (Note that Jesus goes on immediately to speak of death as the avenue to life.)

4. What are the implications of Jesus' parable of the seed (vs. 24)?

What happens if the seed remains intact as a seed—safe and secure?

What is the necessary condition if the seed is to produce a rich harvest of grain?

Does the actual life of the seed perish when it is "buried" in the ground? What *does* perish?

Jesus is obviously talking about his own death and resurrection. What evidence is there here that he intends this as a "law of life" for disciples, too?

5. The paradox of losing and finding (vss. 25, 26):

How does this relate to what Jesus has just said?

Matthew Henry comments, "Many a man hugs himself to death, and loses his life by over-loving it."[18]

In what ways do we hug ourselves to death? Note Marcus Dod's comment on this:

It is a law we cannot evade. He that consumes his life now,
spending it on himself—he who cannot bear to let his life out
of his own hand, but cherishes and pampers it and gathers all
good around it, and will have the fullest present enjoyment
out of it,—this man is losing his life; it comes to an end as
certainly as the seed that is eaten. But he who devotes his life
to other uses than his own gratification, who does not so prize
self that everything must minister to its comfort and advance-
ment, but who can truly yield himself to God and put himself
at God's disposal for the general good—this man, though he
may often seem to lose his life, and often does lose it so far as
present advantage goes, keeps it to life everlasting. . . . The
law of the seed is the law of human life.[19]

6. Jesus' reaction to the prospect of suffering (vss. 27, 28): Note
   Jesus' reaction to the suffering he faces; what is he feeling?
   Jesus does not say "Why must I suffer?" but "What shall I
   say?" What is the difference between the two questions?
   Does he ask to be spared the suffering?
   John does not recount the story of Jesus' agony in Gethsemane.
   Is this present story somewhat similar to the Gethsemane
   story in the other Gospels?

It All Makes Sense

Ernest Gordon and his friend Dusty were talking together
about Angus McGillivray's sacrifice for his buddy. "Greater love
hath no man than this . . ." they were quoting to each other.

Dusty stood without moving. Then he said,
    "That's for Angus, all right."
    "By some ways of reckoning," I said, "what he did might
seem foolish."
    "But in other ways," Dusty returned, "it makes an awful
lot of sense."
    He bent over my legs and went on cleansing my ulcers.[20]

CHAPTER 20

New Life with a Risen Christ

"What I had experienced—namely, the turning to life away from death—was happening to the camp in general. We were coming through the valley. There was a movement, a stirring in our midst, a presence."[1]

It was a surge of life—new life—that was sweeping the camp by the River Kwai, and it expressed itself in many ways.

I was hobbling back to my shack after a rather late discussion session. Passing one of the huts, I stopped. I thought I heard the sound of men singing. They were singing—singing "Jerusalem the Golden." Someone was beating time on a piece of tin with a stick.

The words of the grand old hymn seemed symbolic to me as I listened. Maybe Jerusalem, the Kingdom of God, is here

after all, "with milk and honey blest." Maybe man "shall not
live by bread alone" (or "rice alone," as we were literally
doing). Maybe there is the milk and honey of the spirit that
puts hope into a man's eyes and a song on his lips.

They went on as I stood there, singing the hymn once
more. The song made the darkness seem friendly. In the difference between this joyful sound and the joyless stillness of
months past was the difference between life and death.

This hymn had the sound of victory.[2]

It was true; they were coming through the valley, the valley
of the shadow. These men had moved from the joyless stillness of
the past, where each thought only of himself and there were no joys
to share because there was no sharing, through painful learning to
sacrifice for each other, to the recovery of abundant life expressed
in hymns of faith and hope. "The resurgence of life increased. It
grew and leavened the whole camp, expressing itself in men's concern for their neighbors."[3]

There were the amputees who learned how to make artificial
limbs so that other amputees could walk. There was the spontaneous hunger for education and the willing sharing of knowledge
with each other. There was even an orchestra: the men fell to and
improvised instruments, a musician compiled scores from memory,
and off they went; working together in great excitement, they gave
a concert that thrilled the whole camp. Gradually these prisoners
of war, who had once stolen from each other and lived like animals,
were rebuilding a human community. Through sacrifice, they were
moving from the death of isolation to the warmth and life of sharing in community.

THROUGH SUFFERING—NEW LIFE

It is an inescapable truth about human life: "There will be
suffering; beyond it there will be a new quality of experience, a
new measure of power, a new awareness of our partnership in
God's purpose, and a new consciousness of the splendor which
surrounds even the daily lives of those who are 'risen with
Christ.' "[4]

Jesus made it quite clear. The grain of wheat must sacrifice itself if there is to be fruitfulness of life. In losing life, a man finds it. Not in hugging himself to himself, but in sacrificing the things of self; in that way lies renewal of life. But why should this be? Well, there is mystery about it, but we can understand in part.

What happens here is a change in priorities, indeed, a change in deities. Who is really the god in my life? *Myself* and my comfort? Or God, with myself seen in proper perspective? If I build my life around God, then I can get both other people and myself into the right focus; I can love us all properly in obedience to God.

But if that is to be, something has to happen to my preoccupation with myself, and that is what crucifixion is all about. Back in chapter 19 we were talking about denial of self. We quoted Halford Luccock's description of our problem: ". . . the clamoring ego, with its shrill claim for priority, its preoccupation with 'I,' 'me,' and 'mine,' its concern for self-assertion, its insistence on comfort and prestige."[5]

When that ego has priority, then I'm not living a genuinely *human* life; I'm really in the jungle. Strip off the mask of civilization and politeness—as hardship did in that prison camp—and you see what Ernest Gordon saw, the man licking his spoils with a wolfish leer. Like "an animal going to his lair," said Gordon, "except that an animal would have had more dignity."[6] It is animal self-concern, seeking its own welfare regardless of what happens to others. We cover it up, of course, with culture and with social graces, but the impulse is the same—to give priority to the clamoring ego. To turn my back on fellow human beings, however graciously, is to know the isolated existence of an animal; it is not *life* as God intended us to live it.

To turn toward God, then, and to his intention for my life, I have to be willing to see the clamoring ego get slapped down. I have to give up my preoccupation with "I" and "me" and "mine," to begin to look at life from God's viewpoint, to discover that other people's welfare is as equally important as my own. When I do this, then I have found *life,* human life—life as God intended it to be, a life of love and responsible sharing.

It is only through crucifixion of the self as god that we can come to resurrection. It is through the death of the clamoring ego that we can come to new life, human life, the life for which God has created us.

Paul—Through Crucifixion to Resurrection

No one knows this more richly nor speaks it more eloquently than the apostle Paul. Again and again in his letters he affirms the inseparable connection between crucifixion and resurrection. His whole purpose in life, he says to the Philippians, is "that I may know [Christ] and the power of his resurrection, and may share his sufferings . . . that if possible I may attain the resurrection from the dead." (Phil. 3:10, 11) Paul knows that to share the triumph of Christ's risen life he must first share in Christ's sufferings. He reminds the Corinthians quite clearly that the old (self-centered) self must die so that the new self can be raised to real life. "For the love of Christ controls us," he says, "because we are convinced that one has died for all; therefore all have died. And he died for all, that those who live might live no longer for themselves but for him who for their sake died and was raised." (2 Cor. 5:14–15)

Paul's clearest and most detailed discussion of crucifixion and resurrection, however, comes in Romans 6 and 8. Let us look now at the first few verses of Romans 6; later we will come back to chapter 8. Study this passage for yourself, and be prepared to discuss it with your class.

Romans 6:1–14

1. Note the context of this chapter.
   Vss. 1–4: what it means to come into relationship with God by faith.
   Vss. 5–8: the new life of those who have become related to God.

2. What is the significance of Paul's talking about *baptism* here?

3. Vss. 6, 7: "Our old self was crucified with him."
   What had to be crucified in the lives of the men in the valley of the Kwai? How would you identify the "sin" in their lives which had enslaved them?

What is there about *us* that needs to be put to death? What attitudes toward our family? What habits at work? What omissions? What kinds of indifference? To what and whom? Do we ever "pass by on the other side" because it's easier that way?

4. Vs. 4: "We too might walk in newness of life."
In what sense might life be re-*new*ed for us if we changed those attitudes and habits? If we moved out of that indifference?

5. Vss. 11, 12–14: Note that word "therefore."
What are the ethical consequences of being "dead to sin and alive to God in Christ Jesus"?

From Sacrifice to Sacrament

In chapter 3 we were saying that to respond to a re-creating God—the God who raised Jesus Christ from the dead—is to be caught up in the great tide of his creative power so that he can make us into new people. Has this resurrection power been withdrawn, asks James Stewart?

Surely we are sent to proclaim that in Christ it is available still. And to the man who objects—"This power you talk of is not for me! I am not the stuff out of which God's Easter victories are made. Don't mock me with the mirage of Christ-likeness. I know myself too well: my thwarting frailties are too baffling, the contradiction of my nature too inexòrable, the chains of defeat too firmly shackled on my soul"—the real New Testament answer is to say: "You surely do not imagine that the power which took Christ out of the grave is going to be baffled by you? That the God who did that colossal, prodigious act of might is going to find your problem too hard for His resources? That He who on that great day broke the last darkness of the universe may have to confess Himself impotent on the scale of your life and say, 'I can achieve nothing here: this is too intractable for Me'? But that does not make sense," these men of the New Testament

protest, "that doubt is utterly irrational! He who brought
again from the dead the Lord Jesus, shall He not—to-day if
you will ask Him—revive and quicken you?"[7]

Oftentimes we fail to lay hold of the possibility or resurrection,
partly because we view it all in such a limited way: we think only
of Jesus Christ in Jerusalem, or of our own personal resurrection
after physical death. But when Paul talks about being raised with
Christ, he is talking about *this* life. We "walk in newness of life,"
he says—*walk,* with steady pace, from day to day. How, then, does
it work? Well, look back to chapter 19, to the examples of crucifixion in the routine of everyday life. Let us ask how God works
to transform those people, how he works in greater or lesser degree
to bring newness into their lives.

Consider the housewife. She is repelled by the thought of giving up a morning a week for patterning a child; she has no mornings to spare. The very day they need her is the day she usually
meets the girls downtown for shopping and for lunch at the cafeteria. Why should she give up her only chance for an outing to help
some child she's never seen? Anyway, everybody's been nagging
at her to give time lately—the church, the PTA, now this thing.
Why can't they leave her some time for herself?

But somehow, she does it; she is willing to make the sacrifice.
And as the weeks go by, by some alchemy it ceases to be a sacrifice. It becomes, rather, a regular part of her week, and she discovers that those weeks when the child goes back to the hospital
for therapy—well, somehow *those* weeks have something missing.
What has happened? God has taken the sacrifice and turned it into
joy. A woman who had been reluctant to give up her time for someone else now is discovering that she *wants* to do this, that she finds
deep satisfaction in it, and that the shopping tour is not quite as
crucial in her life as she had thought!

This is no spectacular overnight transformation of a person;
there are no visible signs of re-creation that anyone would be aware
of. But God is using her sacrifice to move her gently one step away
from preoccupation with her own conveniences and pleasures. God
is enabling her to say No to her clamoring ego, and the process of
resurrection is under way.

Or consider the young father. He had planned to spend Sunday afternoon enjoying the pro football game, and he grumbles to himself about his thoughtless family putting him on the spot by asking him to go out to the woods. They'd make him feel guilty and selfish if he said No. And doggone it, it's the Colts who're playing today. Anyway, the kids have been getting on his nerves lately—always wanting something when he's reading or watching TV. When a man works hard all day, why can't people let him enjoy his evening in peace?

But somehow, he goes, quite aware of this fatherly sacrifice of his own pleasure for his family's pleasure. They get out into the autumn woods, and—well, it *is* pretty. They leave the car and go splashing through the leaves. The six-year-old discovers a hairy caterpillar enjoying the sunshine and squats there entranced. The other two play tag with their parents as base. The afternoon has a warm glow, and the father discovers he's feeling a contentment he hadn't expected to feel. It's good to be with the kids; maybe they could do this kind of thing more often!

This had started out as a sacrifice, but God turned it into a blessing and a joy. The father who had been resenting his family's intrusions on his convenience now discovered that he *wanted* to do this with his family. And suddenly, they were a greater joy to him than ever before.

This is no spectacular overnight transformation of a person; there are no visible signs of re-creation that anyone would be aware of. But God is using his sacrifice to move this man one step away from preoccupation with his pleasure. God is enabling him to say No to his clamoring ego, and the process of resurrection is under way. The sacrifice of self becomes the sacrament of God's presence and renewing power.

Now, in that prison camp by the Kwai, the change in the men was dramatic: from mere existence, at the animal level, to real living, to abundant life. Men who had snarled at each other and scrapped for garbage now were smiling, laughing, singing. As they began to make sacrifices for each other, small and large, they began to discover that this is what makes life worth living—makes it really *life*.

With us, though, it is not so dramatic. We never sink that low, so the change in us is not so drastic; ours is a matter of growing response. But change can assuredly come. The God who is great enough to raise Christ from the dead will not be baffled by us. He will not raise us, however, if we are so enamored with our own comfort that we shut out the needs of other people. Our part is to be willing to deny the clamoring ego; God then can take the sacrifice and turn it into a sacrament.

NEW LIFE, ABUNDANT

Paul's eighth chapter of Romans is one of the most triumphant chapters in the whole Bible, and rightly so, for he is talking about the glory of the risen life in Christ. Chapter 7 is covered with a pall of gloom and despair. "I can will what is right," Paul says there, "but I cannot do it. . . . Wretched man that I am! Who will deliver me from this body·of death?" Then chapter 8 breaks out in radiance and assurance, in thanksgiving and victory: we who have been crucified with Christ are now raised up with him, to new life in the Spirit. There is the assurance of freedom from guilt (8:1, 2); anxiety about the past need not shackle our service in the present. There is the assurance that we are God's children (8:14–16); we can rest secure in the knowledge that whatever happens to us, we are still at home with God. Provided, that is—"provided we suffer with him!" Always that proviso: new life is ours on the other side of the sacrifice of ourselves. There is the assurance of God's Spirit in our lives, enabling us to turn all things into good (8:28). We are incarnate creatures and we cannot escape our limitations, but if we choose to obey God within our situation—whatever suffering that obedience may bring—then his Spirit enables us to transform that suffering into victorious new life. Finally, there is the assurance of God's love (8:37–39). "For I am sure that neither death, nor life, nor angels, nor principalities, nor things present, nor things to come, nor powers, nor height, nor depth, nor anything else in all creation, will be able to separate us from the love of God in Christ Jesus our Lord." What more could any of us ask?

Over and over again, people have found this kind of victory in their own lives. Charles Dickens tells movingly of what happened to Sydney Carton in that great story of the French Revolution, *A*

Tale of Two Cities. Dissolute, profligate, Carton was a man who had lived only for himself; life had no meaning for him beyond pleasure. Only one noble quality lighted this man's life: his love for Lucie Manette—and she had married another. A man who had turned his back on his fellow human beings, Carton knew with full cynicism that his life was meaningless; it was not really *life* at all.

But Sydney Carton came to know real life for the first time as he gave his life for another. In one of the most moving episodes in English literature, Carton made the decision to put himself in the place of Lucie's husband Charles Darnay, waiting in a prison cell for his trip to the guillotine. When Carton had made up his mind and set his plans in motion, he walked home at midnight. There was nothing more to be done, he said to himself, and sleep was impossible.

> It was not a reckless manner, the manner in which he said these words aloud under the fast-sailing clouds, nor was it more expressive of negligence than defiance. It was the settled manner of a tired man, who had wandered and struggled and got lost, but who at length struck into his road and saw its end.[8]

As he walked along, he stopped to pick up a child and carry her across a muddy street—this man who had lived a selfish and useless life—and kissed her as he put her down. Carton had joined the human race. And the words that throbbed in his brain were the words he had heard at his father's funeral:

> "I am the resurrection and the life, saith the Lord: he that believeth in me, though he were dead, yet shall he live: and whosoever liveth and believeth in me, shall never die."
>
> Now, that the streets were quiet, and the night wore on, the words were in the echoes of his feet, and were in the air. Perfectly calm and steady, he sometimes repeated them to himself as he walked; but, he heard them always.[9]

Sydney Carton had given his life away, and now for the first time had found it. He went to the guillotine hearing still those words, "I am the resurrection and the life. . ." "They said of him, about the city that night, that it was the peacefullest man's face ever beheld there. Many added that he looked sublime and prophetic."[10] Carton had come home, to life abundant.

Most of us, however, have not turned our backs so completely on our fellows. For us, new life is a matter of degree; it is finding new richness in being part of the human community as we allow God to turn suffering into triumph. A Southern Presbyterian elder and his family found this kind of renewal on the other side of suffering. Through anguish and pain they came to know in a new and deeper way the meaning of community in Jesus Christ and the Easter message of resurrection.

One Christmas their college-age son was severely injured in an automobile accident, suffering extensive brain damage. There followed more than two long, anguished years of efforts at therapy —patterning by local people, long trips to see the neurologist, treatments of all kinds. The family hoped against hope for some recovery, however partial. But in Easter week, 1967, Bill gave up his arduous struggle, dying quietly from cardiac arrest.

The boy's parents sent out an Easter letter to friends, a moving testimony to faith in the God who in everything works for good with those who love him. "The loss of Bill," they said, "whom we loved so intently, enjoyed so heartily, and admired so strongly is difficult to take, but we all have jobs to do and we shall get on with the doing of them." And then they told of how God had used the long anguish to teach them to know more deeply the meaning of Christian community.

> Many, many of our friends at Bill's Memorial Service, had been involved in one way or another in helping with Bill's recovery. We certainly do not feel their actions over these twenty-seven months were in vain. We realize more than ever that no one person and no family can be independent or self-sufficient very long—though by comparison it seemed that way several years ago. We found it difficult at first to accept help which we could not return. Now it has been so clearly

demonstrated that Christian Fellowship is not offered for its return but because it is a living conviction. God's gift of love is expressed through individual people and their personal relationships. We cannot accept God's gift of love without being concerned and responsive to the needs of those about us. Perhaps this is a part of the EASTER story.

. . . Your expressions of understanding and love have sustained us in far more ways than you might know or imagine. A Happy Easter.

May God bless you abundantly,

"A Happy Easter." For this family these were no empty words, for they had come through long suffering to the victorious knowledge of *two* kinds of resurrection.

"For I am sure that neither death, nor life, nor angels, nor principalities, nor things present, nor things to come, nor powers, nor height, nor depth, nor anything else in all creation, will be able to separate us from the love of God in Christ Jesus our Lord."

incarnation

God is a seeking God
who comes where men are.

God is not too holy or too good to
involve himself in human affairs.

If we would discern what God is doing
we must look for him in the world
wherever men are being made human

---

incarn

God is with us—Immanuel,
a God who gives himself in close,
warm relationship to man.

love

in

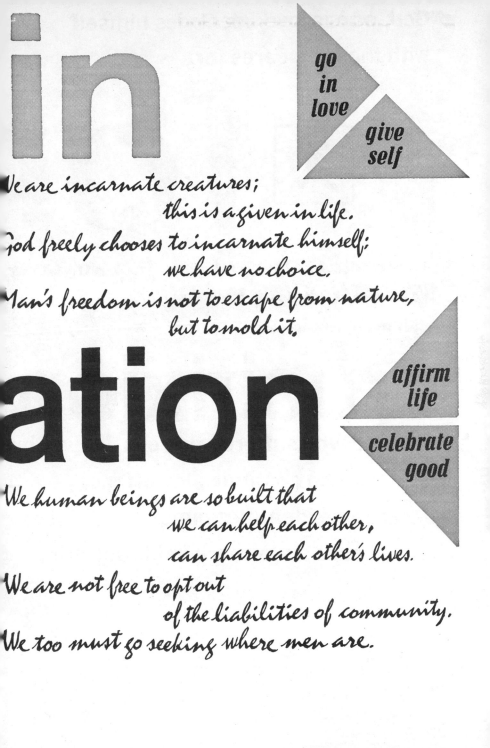

go
in
love

give
self

We are incarnate creatures;
                  this is a given in life.
God freely chooses to incarnate himself;
                  we have no choice.
Man's freedom is not to escape from nature,
                  but to mold it.

ation

affirm
life

celebrate
good

We human beings are so built that
                  we can help each other,
                  can share each other's lives.
We are not free to opt out
                  of the liabilities of community.
We too must go seeking where men are.

God, who is love, identifies himself with those he cares for.

We are called to love and care for people in need. We must be willing to share fully in the lives of other men, whatever suffering this may bring with it

crucifixion

The God who suffered there in Jesus Christ is a God who continues to suffer because he identifies himself with men; and he calls us to share in his suffering.

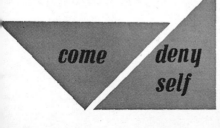

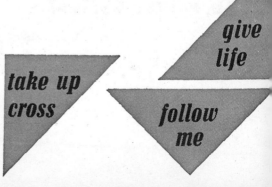

come deny self take up cross give life follow me

To serve a God of love in a sinful world is to take upon ourselves a cross of suffering.

crucifixion

It is costly love because God takes upon himself and bears with and for us the consequences of our sin.

At any time, on any issue, even when we act with the very best of motives, we may be dead wrong — and in our wrongness, help to crucify the sons of men.

This God of costly love is a God who both judges and forgives.

repent

accept forgiveness

accept yourself

Only through the crucifixion of the self as god can we come to resurrection.

resurrectior

The God who gave life anew to Jesus Christ can give life anew to the Christian who shares Christ's life.

live power

alive

Christ is alive and present in our midst today.

To come to know Christ—to be closely related to him, to be "in Christ"—is to be caught up in the great tide of God's creating power.

Through the death of the clamoring ego we can come to new life, human life, the life for which

live in hope

live

resurrection

The giving of life is an act of creation; only the Creator, God, can do this.

be renewed

become a man

be human

The sacrifice of self becomes the sacrament of God's presence and renewing power.

God, who raised Christ from the dead, calls us to share in Christ's risen power.

There is power in the presence of Christ, not to remove the daily problems that are ours but to enable us to face them and live with them and genuinely care for the people who cause them.

EPILOGUE

CHAPTER 21

This Is
the Beginning

In a book on the nature of the church, R. Benjamin Garrison
makes this comment:

> Recently, I read a book which concludes with a preface. The
> author, with genuine modesty, offers his thinking to the
> Church in the knowledge that whatever validity it possesses
> will be as a diving board and not as a finish line. He engages
> in this clever little literary device for a deeper reason, how-
> ever. The very nature of the Christian faith requires it. Its
> conclusions are preliminaries. This does not mean that they
> are uncertain, but that they are unfinished. If there is such
> a thing as a "Christian" punctuation mark, it is a colon, not a
> period.[1]

What Garrison says about the Christian faith in general can most surely be said about Christian ethics in particular. Any study of ethics must end not with a period but with a colon, for what is important is what lies ahead. Robert E. Fitch has entitled his brief book on Christian ethics *Preface to Ethical Living.*[2] What he is saying is that we cannot go on studying and reflecting and discussing forever; all this is simply the prelude to the action—the preface to the ethical living to which God calls us.

What lies ahead is decision and action, in faith. We have certainly seen in our study that we will find no final, infallible answers to the ethical problems we've been considering. We Christians have not been handed some precise calendar of events, telling us what God will do on March 12, 1970. Nor have we been given a precise rule book, telling us what *we* must do on March 12, 1970. We have seen that whatever Jane and Ed Johnson decide to do, there will be hurt for someone involved. Whatever Tompkins decides to do, or Jamison, or Jean Frazier, or Kendrick, there will be no finally satisfactory answers to their dilemmas. And so it is with us; in few of our decisions will we know beyond the least shadow of doubt that we have decided rightly. We will be continually aware that equally conscientious Christians disagree with us on what is right and what is wrong.

We go ahead and act, anyway, recognizing that in the last analysis an ethical decision is an act of faith. J. H. Oldham has put it nicely: "It is a living response in a new situation to the call of a personal God. To respond to an unconditional demand is always to reach beyond the security of experience and to put life to the hazard, to engage in a wager in which the stake is ourselves."[3]

There is risk here, and we know it; but we Christians nevertheless can make decisions in that relaxation of spirit which Reinhold Niebuhr has called "the nonchalance of faith."[4] We can be relaxed in our ethical living because we know we serve a forgiving God. This is the meaning of "justification by faith" in ethics—that God accepts us in our sins and errors and treats us as his children. We know that our vision is not perfect, that we can discern only dimly what God is doing in our world and what the fitting response to his action will be; we will often make errors in judgment. We know further that even when we know God's will, sin and self-centeredness dog our footsteps and make it difficult for us to respond. And we know that even when we are drawn to some extent out of ourselves in concern for others, still we cannot perfectly fulfill God's will, for we must function in a sinful society.

In all this we can know, however, that God has forgiven, at cost of a cross, and that we remain his children, at home.

Moreover, we can be relaxed in our decision-making because we serve a God who governs; he is the sovereign ruler of creation. God has limited himself by giving us freedom, and he has taken heartbreak upon himself because of it. Through it all, however, he is working his purposes out, and in that confidence our hearts can rest.

This is the Biblical testimony from beginning to end. From Joseph, who could say to his brothers, "As for you, you meant evil against me; but God meant it for good . . ." to Paul, who could say to *his* brothers, "We know that in everything God works for good with those who love him . . ." the Biblical writers agree that God can take even our sins and our blunders and weave them into his own overarching purposes.

This kind of faith frees us from the illusion of false expectations, since it sees clearly the sin of man; but it also frees us from despair, for it is an indestructible hope in the sovereignty of God.

We cannot escape the burden of decision in each situation; we cannot prepare our decisions in advance. God is at work in the changes that are taking place in human society, and we Christians must be alert to participate with him in his continuous work of reconciliation. Never absolutely sure that we have correctly discerned God's will, we must nevertheless act, and we can act in the "nonchalance of faith," knowing that we can leave the outcome in the hands of God.

APPENDIX

Speaking Out—"Let's Quit the Suburbs"

by Jimmy Breslin

Move, everybody says. Move out of the cities and into the suburbs and get room for your children. Give yourself a life too. Get away from these cities that are falling apart. In the cities the buildings climb out of the hot sidewalks and shut out the sky. Cars and trucks burn the streets into barely moving rivers of metal. The few trees wither in the exhaust fumes. The parks are unsafe at night, the schools are falling behind. And there are these people who have colored skin. Their women hang out the windows and the men crowd street corners. Lazy, you know. There is poverty and dope and crime, and a race riot can happen on any hot night.

The people move. From 1950 to 1960, the New York City Board of Education figures show 1,238,738 whites left the city. At the same time, a total of 381,752 nonwhites came into the city. These figures show us very conclusively that it takes 3.08 nonwhite people to make 10 white people jump on the tailgate of the moving van and hang onto the couch while they go out of town. And this ratio works in other cities.

These people who move spill out of buildings in the cities at 5:00 p.m. and they head out, until the tall buildings dissolve into these flat seas of shingled roofs that are the suburbs. Now the people are at home. They are on 60-by-100 foot lots with Merion-bluegrass lawns and stained redwood basket-weave fences. The houses have these wonderful model names, the Salem, the Manor, the Mediterranean Court. There are family rooms and patios and reception hallways. "The Meadow School is right behind the houses here," the real-estate salesman says. "The church is just down at the bottom of the hill—and look right over there, right up there is a new supermarket!"

The suburbs offer the things that count to people today. Like barbecue pits and awnings over the patio and these cars with great action names. There is no place in the world like the suburbs, which is why anybody who lives in a suburb when he has a chance to be in the city ought to reach for the razor blades.

For these big, crowded, dirty, creaking cities of ours are the only places in the world where people can live and work and, over the generations, show some kind of improvement as human beings. They are expensive and sometimes violent. They also are the last weapon left to fight against the incredible pasteurization of people and ideas that is going on today. Say what you will about a city like New York. But don't ever say that New York would produce a Ronald Reagan on an election ballot. . . .

I tried living both ways. I was raised in a couple of sections of New York City, none of them too classy. When I got married and had a couple of kids, this fellow I know, Manny Goldberg, a cap manufacturer, told me, "How could you do it to your family? You can't raise kids in the city." . . . I listened to him and moved out to Baldwin, Long Island. . . .

For some reason, I began not to get along with the people on the block. Once they wanted to build a community basket-weave fence along the backyard. I said I wouldn't go in with them unless we put ladders on the fence so we could get up and shoot over the fence at the people on the block behind us. Then a woman rang the bell and said one of my kids had done a terrible thing. He had dropped the stick from his ice cream right on their lawn. The next day I went to my friend Walter, from the Dazzle Sign Company, and had him make a big sign, painted in blue and orange and red, which said, PEOPLE I'M NOT TALKING TO THIS YEAR. Under that, I had Walter list the name of everybody on the block. I put the sign up on the front lawn. My wife phoned the real-estate agents. Back we came, inside the city limits.

For me it couldn't have been any better. I live three blocks from an express on the subway, which is the world's best transportation. At eight o'clock at night in the city, you can go out and in twenty minutes be at some place like Sullivan Street, in Manhattan's Little Italy. Sullivan Street is closed for three blocks because it is the Feast of St. Anthony. Colored lights hang from tenements. Stands where they make *calzone* and *zeppoles* line the sidewalks. A Ferris wheel spins in a parking lot. Up at the end of the crowded street you can bet two dollars on dice or a roulette wheel. Out in the suburbs, if you ever go out of the house at night—and I don't think anybody does once they flick the beautiful television set on— the only thing you see is a neighbor inspecting his lawn.

Then, on a hot afternoon, just in case you don't feel like sitting at the beach, you can get the kids and go to someplace like the Museum of Natural History. They have these exhibits of how the Iroquois tribes used to live. Kids drink it up. Upstairs is my favorite, the mounted white bones of the great racehorse Sysonby. For every bit of air pollution and every overcrowded street, and for every dingy apartment, there is a place that gives you more than deodorant commercials. What do you have in the suburbs when the walls close in? I'll tell you what you have. You have a plywood head.

Suburban living is designed for sitting and going nowhere and worrying about possessions and how they look. And out of these atmospheres come the votes for George Murphys and Ronald Reagans. . . .

But the main reason for living anywhere is the kids. And those kids you have home in the split level, growing up tall and strong are exposed to a way of judging values that would corrupt anybody. It all centers around what a man has in his garage. Collins, who lived down the street, came home with a new Jaguar. It was an event. Everybody says hello to Collins. Breslin has a 1959 heap. The muffler makes a sound like a gangland killing. Everybody, of course, is embarrassed by Breslin. Big car, big man. Good lawn, good people. This is what you let a kid grow up around?

Of course, kids go to school. These stories about suburban schools being academically ahead of many city schools are true. The public grammar school my two boys go to in New York is an older building, and the schoolwork is not as advanced as it was in Baldwin. This new custom called integration has put a lot of colored kids into this particular public school. Some of them haven't been prodded to learn and they slow the schoolwork pace down.

But then you have this strange thing that apparently can happen in an integrated school. For months my twin boys kept telling me of the speed and prowess of classmate Marcus Feldman. One night they brought the great Marcus Feldman around for dinner and terrible embarrassment, he was not white. Apparently my kids, at age 11, didn't know that it was important for Marcus to be identified as colored right from the start.

Now before everybody throws up, please be advised this is not the start of a passage on Brotherhood. . . . But it does seem to me that right now, today, if a boy can go to school and learn something about living with people, then I would say the boy is getting the only education worth discussing. . . .

In the city, the pressure of living with so many varieties of people produces a sensible recognition of worth. In one neighborhood in a city, you can have a grocery-store owner, a professor in a college, a doorman who takes policy numbers play, an artist who doesn't shave and wears sandals and lives with a funny-looking girl, a young guy who dresses immaculately, and a thousand other people who do different things. You might find out, by living in the neighborhood, that while the college professor is affable and brilliant, he has a habit about stealing newspapers from the stand in front of the candy store. The doorman is really a sports buff—a nice nut, and very honest. The artist and the girl have absolutely nothing—they're boring. And the young guy who dresses well doesn't work and is a thief of some kind, and they took him away and he got a year in jail, and you can see that he was a sucker with an ego. Then there are all those people who go to work, obey the law, mind their manners, and sometimes are extremely interesting; they worry about Vietnam, their kids, other people's kids—and, somehow, they can talk about these things so that they become worth thinking about in ways you never imagined. And if you don't happen to like any of the people, you can go some place else. You do not have to do what everybody else does. There are too many others to choose from. In the suburbs you have to fit in.

*   *   *

Sure there are things wrong with the cities. They can be ugly. But at least you can have a human life there. In a city you have to

live more because you're not allowed to live less. There is this extra
touch of alertness which comes from getting through a day. There
are ideas flowing and people are more ready to accept them. The
city is old, and it changes. The suburbs are new, and they are
stodgy. Commuting may look leisurely, but it takes pieces out of
your life and drops them on the floor of the train. On the bar car
of the commuter trains they sell Martinis and take up your time
and also make you pay for the ride. Insanity. Two Martinis before
dinner when a man gets home from work? If I have to ride a railroad train to get home, I want to have a whole bottle of gin when
I get into the house.

From *Saturday Evening Post,* 239:10, September 24, 1966

The Shortchanged Children of Suburbia

by Alice Miel with Edwin Kiester, Jr.

The child of suburbia is likely to be a materialist and somewhat of a hypocrite. He tends to be a striver in school, a conform-
ist, and above all a believer in being "nice," polite, clean and tidy.
He divides humanity into the black and the white, the Jew and the
Christian, the rich and the poor, the "smart" and the "dumb." He
is often conspicuously self-centered. In all these respects the suburban child patterns his attitudes after those of his parents.

These were findings of a four-year study, conducted by teachers, sociologists and researchers from Teachers College, of New
Village, the cover name given to a shoreline suburb of New York
City. Our study concentrated chiefly on the elementary schools as
the chief training ground for American children today. We sought
to discover how suburban youngsters are taught (or not taught)
about human difference, and how their attitudes toward it are
shaped. Our study as well as other inquiries indicates clearly that
to grow up in an American suburb today is not a wholly enviable
lot.

At first glance, New Village, not far from New York City, seems an idyllic place to grow up in. The homes are mostly ranged along quiet, winding streets. There are open spaces, greenery, woods to explore. The churches and community centers run dances, teen programs and other youth activities. The schools are new and modern, with well-kept lawns and the latest in playground facilities: the curriculum is tailored to students headed for college.

Yet children miss something in New Village. You do not recognize it at first, but as you drive along the streets, you suddenly realize that all the homes are pretty much of a stripe. None are very lavish, none are very poor. The people are of a stripe, too—almost all of them are white and young or fairly young. New Village has many things to offer, but diversity is not one of them. . . .

In one aspect of their education, suburban children are underprivileged. Though other races, other nationalities, other generations have a great deal to teach them, there is little in their education, formal or otherwise, to familiarize them with the rich diversity of American life. In this sense, the children of suburbia are being shortchanged.

The average elementary school child in New Village does not know and has never known a Negro child his own age. The school population includes several hundred "non-whites," most of them Negroes, but they are concentrated in one school in the least desirable section. . . . The full scope of racial prejudice in New Village is difficult to measure. . . .

Once their teachers faced up to the fact that prejudice did exist among their students, they recollected previous incidents. One recalled a girl in kindergarten who had looked at a picture of a pretty little Negro girl and said, "I wouldn't play with her because she's black people. I hate black people." Another remembered that her students had once had a discussion in which the words "spics," "niggers," and "Japs" had been thrown out.

Most of the teachers admitted that they were not sure how to handle such situations in the classroom. Some felt that it was their duty to smooth over prejudice if it cropped up, but not to raise the question. Where teachers tried to deal with the matter at all they did it deviously and vaguely. . . .

"Goodness, they really don't know much about poor white children, do they? They don't see many, I guess." This teacher's comment points up one of the most surprising—and appalling—gaps in suburban children's knowledge. The children of New Village knew almost nothing about persons less well off than themselves. Moreover, their attitude toward the less fortunate was almost insufferably patronizing. For any New Village child to know a person from an underprivileged class would be highly unusual, for the simple reason that there are few such persons in New Village. Some parents wished their children could come to know improverished families—because they would make the youngsters more appreciative of what they had at home.

The consensus of teachers was that the children, like the adults, rated their peers in terms of economics. Differences were noted openly. "In Show and Tell it comes out that 'He doesn't have as much money as we do,' or 'They don't have as many cars as we do,'" a teacher reported. "They are greatly concerned with material gain—lots of getting and little giving on their part," another wrote.

Our talks with students revealed an early and widespread concern with such material matters as zoning, preserving neighborhoods, keeping out "undesirables"—all of which, of course, preoccupied their parents. One child said, "People should cooperate about doing something to stop crowding because all the people from the city are moving in."

In the face of disquieting attitudes like these, what are the schools of suburbia doing to teach children about economic difference, its causes and consequences? Very little. Although poverty was often touched upon in discussing other nations, the issue was carefully sidestepped in studying American society. Why was not more done? . . .

To understand the attitudes of suburban youngsters toward human difference, one needs to know something about their values and their family milieu. This sort of influence has as much bearing on how they regard human diversity as do their more precisely measureable feelings about Negroes, Jews, the poor or foreigners.

One of the foremost yardsticks children use to measure difference is academic achievement. The suburban child is quite aware of who gets good grades and who does not. He judges his peers accordingly.

This should come as no surprise. When the sociologist on our team asked parents why they had moved to New Village, the largest single bloc said: "To have better schools."

"Competition here is keen and strong; the push from the home is hard in some cases," one teacher wrote. "We have kids here who are making 90 and 95 and still there is a terrific push." Not all the pressure came from home. Teachers constantly urged the children into academic striving. At a fall orientation meeting, school administrators told the teachers that while they must take an interest in children's moral and spiritual and social values, acquiring adademic concepts was more important than any other accomplishment.

Passion for conformity seems to be another trait which affects the suburban child's feeling toward "different" people. Our studies show clearly that he takes a dim view of anyone who deviates from the norm, and that he places a premium on being exactly what adults want him to be. . . .

There can be little doubt that, at least in suburbia, the school is second only to the family in shaping a child's feeling toward other people. . . . Here are some of the changes in thinking and curriculum that we recommend:

1. Develop higher thought processes. . . . Children should be encouraged and helped to plumb controversial subjects, to see that in many aspects of a democracy there are no "right" answers.

2. Help children attain some insight into their own values and those of others. . . . Yet the child has a right to understand the values which influence him. He needs to recognize that others' values stand as highly in the scheme of things as his own.

3. The issue of race is the one where improved teaching is most urgently needed. Children must be taught to recognize that the white society surrounding them is very different from the rest of the globe, where the majority is nonwhite. Stereotypes can be combatted through personal contacts with Negroes (students or adult visitors), and through films and other media. . . .

4. Teach comparative religion, even at early ages....Help students understand the common elements of various faiths, as well as the kinds and sources of differences between them.

The composition of New Village and other suburban communities is not likely to change greatly in the near future. Neither are the world's problems of human difference going to disappear overnight. Children must be educated to deal fairly and realistically with questions of social justice, civil rights, national unity and international peace. Teachers, supervisors and parents will have to come together to bring this innovation about. There is no more urgent business in the schools of America today.

The New York Times Magazine, April 16, 1967, pp. 99, ff. "The Short-changed Children of Suburbia," the pamphlet on which this article is based, is available from the American Jewish Committee, 165 East 56th Street, New York, N. Y. 10022, for 75 cents.

Teen-Age Drinking May Reflect Home

by William J. Moll

It seems to me that enlightening emphasis was put upon the alcohol problems of youth during the workshop lectures given this week at Roslyn Conference Center at the meeting of the Middle Atlantic Institute of Alcohol Studies, sponsored by six interfaith bodies.

The lectures were led by nationally known figures in the field of alcohol studies and dealt with the problems of counseling and ministering to teen-age drinking problems, the teen-ager and the parent, enabling the clergymen and interested church-related laymen to enlarge their ministry to include this most vital area of human concern. Here are some of the things I learned.

In a great many cases, the drinking patterns of teen-agers begin early. They are thrown into a society that is drinking. Most young people do not have to be told the potential of alcohol. They seem to know the distinction between drinking, drunkenness and alcoholism.

But youth is a commentary on adults. They live in a milieu which creates adolescents and forces the young to play at becoming adult in installment periods. We cannot understand teen-age and adolescent drinking until we understand the teen-ager and the adolescent.

The young move from a nonsexual culture to a sexual one, and it is not easy. They move from irresponsibility to responsibility. They move from dependence to independence.

And the key problem of the young person is to discover who he or she is. We cannot relate to young people unless we appreciate the difficulties they face. We must like them; we must not sit in judgment.

Live in Subculture

The drinking patterns of the young reflect those of their parents. They look upon adults as "the establishment," and they are often sad at the way "the establishment," with youth living on the fringes, is working things out.

They cannot reconcile the ethics and moralities they are taught at church and school with the behavior in their home. As adults we say we believe in one way, but behave in another. So the young think that parents are "phonys."

The teen-ager and adolescent live in a subculture, fostered by glamorous advertising. Due to our affluent society, they stress the values of fun, leisure, and material possessions, and do not have much of a sense of responsibility.

So the young go through a period of adjusting to psychophysical changes, trying to get free of parents, but still needing the approval of adults. Drinking can be and often is, a declaration of independence.

It is not easy for teen-agers to find a sense of integration, and they may drink to combat loneliness and isolation. There is a tendency of young people to move more and more into habits of adults in the use of alcohol. . . .

———————————

Richmond Times-Dispatch, October 22, 1966

"The Open Generation"

Conversations parents never hear . . . . . No. 7.
"Sometimes, I get awfully lonely."
"My father is not the type who sits and listens. He sits and tells you."
"I haven't talked seriously with anyone around here in ten years."
Jerry, Warren, Christopher, Josh and Charlie are "model"

teen-agers, articulate, intelligent members of respected families. Each is a youth leader in their common community, a Boston suburb. All are "A" or "B" students in high school. Their guidance counselor calls them "ideal, untroubled." Promised anonymity, these five talked out about their fathers. Their words voice the feelings of more than three-fourths of the 55 boys interviewed.

    Jerry K. is 17, handsome and laconic—about most things. My father works 100 hours a day. He brings work home every evening. He goes into his office on Sunday. A month ago, he went into the backyard and shot some baskets with me. He thought he was a hero because he spent 15 minutes there. I couldn't wait until he left. I literally have no idea who he is. How could I? We have rarely discussed anything meaningful. We used to talk at dinner at least. Then, he bought a small television set and put it in the kitchen. We were forbidden—*forbidden*—to talk. I tried once or twice and quit. I got sore. I wanted to talk. I got a job as stockboy in a department store. It keeps me out until after dinner is finished at home. Now, I go three-four days without seeing my father. I tell him he works too hard. He says he has to work hard to build a business for us. By the time the business is paying for itself, who'll need it anyway? I used to wonder why he was hiding from me. Now, I don't care.

    Warren C., 18, plans to join the Navy upon graduation. His family can afford only a local college, which means living at home. Warren wants to get out of the house.
I haven't talked seriously with anyone around here in ten years. My father is not the type who sits and listens. He sits and tells you. When he bothers. I sit down to talk to my father, and he falls asleep. If I take a problem to him, he immediately jumps into a stand and tells me what to do. That does me no good. I'm old enough for a discussion, not an ultimatum. One day, I came home to tell my folks I had just gotten an "A" in Advanced Placement physics. My father and I got involved in something the minute I walked in the door, and it ended with him telling me I'm not old enough to have a serious opinion about anything. I walked out of

the house. I never did tell him about the "A." I can't win an argument with my father. So I duck him or become indifferent when he's around. My mother says I must respect him. I want to. But he has to have some respect for me too. With the Navy next year and then college, if I'm lucky, this will be my last year at home.

Christopher H., 18, is bright, outwardly poised. He says he wants to be an engineer, seems hesitant about his choice.
I have few problems with my parents because I don't have that much to do with them. Why should I? What do they know about me? They know I go to school, and I come home. When I was trying to select a college, they never said a word. They said they would send me, and that was all. No opinion about where to go, how much money there was to spend or anything. They never even asked me which ones I was applying to.

My father said I was old enough to decide for myself. I have freedom. Boy, do I have freedom! I wish someone would tell me what to do sometimes. Members of a family should be genuinely interested in each other and be straight-forward about it, without detours. I haven't had this much interest [the *Look* interview] shown in me since I was in elementary school. Sometimes, I get awfully lonely. Why don't they try to get closer to me?

Josh W., 17, husky, a football halfback as well as an excellent student, wonders about the importance of grades.
Every now and then, I feel like escaping. Everybody pressures me for grades. My father and I have only two topics of conversation, cars and marks. If I come home with a "C" on a test, he reminds me that he was a *magna cum* from Harvard. My mother and I frankly deceive him now. She signs anything unfavorable from school that requires a signature and doesn't tell him. My grades generally are very good. Maybe I'll get into Harvard. But what happens if I don't? College is a starting, not an ending, point. It won't be the biggest thing in my life. Why the pushing? How much of it is phony panic? There are so many real things to worry about, why should we invent problems? And if I realize this, why doesn't my father?

Charlie B., 17, is one of the most popular boys in the senior class. A smile rarely leaves his face. It leaves when he talks about his father.

My father has his own problems, and I don't expect him to devote all his spare time to me or to understand all of what I want to do. But I ought to get a few credits from him. I volunteered last summer to tutor some poor kids in reading in a town near here. My father laughed when I told him, and said if I were smart, I'd earn some money. We don't need the money, and he didn't want any of what I would have earned. But I wasn't getting paid for tutoring, so it was no good. Two years ago, a group of us went to a school basketball game. It was a rough game with a lot of heckling. On the way home, two guys from the other school jumped my best friend. They really began pounding him. The other two in my group just watched. I couldn't stand there and let my friend watch me watch him getting hurt. So I jumped in to help him. I was cut up pretty badly. When I got home, my parents were sore. They couldn't understand why I had to interfere. About six years ago, I ran away. We were driving home from my grandfather's funeral— my mother's father—and my father criticized my grandfather. On the way home from the man's funeral. I didn't say anything, but I left that night and stayed away three days.

From *Look* magazine, September 20, 1966. Copyright 1966 by Cowles Communications, Inc.

A Statement on Business Ethics
and a Call for Action

The ethical standards of American businessmen, like those of the American people, are founded upon our religious heritage and our traditions of social, political, and economic freedom. They impose upon each man high obligations in his dealings with his fellowmen, and make all men stewards of the common good. Immutable, well-understood guides to performance generally are effective, but new ethical problems are created constantly by the ever-increasing complexity of society. In business, as in every other activity, therefore, men must continually seek to identify new and appropriate standards.

Over the years, American businessmen in the main have continually endeavored to demonstrate their responsiveness to their ethical obligations in our free society. They have themselves initiated and welcomed from others calls for the improvement of their ethical performance, regarding each as a challenge to establish and meet ever higher ethical goals. In consequence, the ethical standards that should guide business enterprise in this country have steadily risen over the years, and this has had a profound influence on the performance of the business community.

As the ethical standards and conduct of American private enterprise have improved, so also has there developed a public demand for proper performance and a keen sensitivity to lapses from those standards. The full realization by the business community of its future opportunities and, indeed, the maintenance of public confidence require a continuing pursuit of the highest standards of ethical conduct.

Attainment of this objective is not without difficulty. Business enterprises, large and small, have relationships in many directions —with stockholders and other owners, employees, customers, suppliers, government, and the public in general. The traditional emphasis on freedom, competition, and progress in our economic system often brings the varying interests of these groups into conflict, so that many difficult and complex ethical problems can arise in any enterprise. While all relationships of an enterprise to these groups are regulated in some degree by law, compliance with law can only provide a minimum standard of conduct. Beyond legal obligations, the policies and actions of businessmen must be based upon a regard for the proper claims of all affected groups.

Moreover, in many business situations, the decision that must be made is not the simple choice between absolute right and absolute wrong. The decisions of business frequently must be made in highly complex and ever-changing circumstances, and at times involve either adhering to earlier standards or developing new ones. Such decisions affect profoundly not only the business enterprise, but our society as a whole. Indeed, the responsible position of American business—both large and small—obligates each participant to lead rather than follow.

A weighty responsibility therefore rests upon all those who manage business enterprises, as well as upon all others who influence the environment in which business operates. In the final analysis, however, the primary moral duty to establish high ethical standards and adequate procedures for their enforcement in each enterprise must rest with its policy-making body—its board of directors and its top management.

We, therefore, now propose that current efforts be expanded and intensified and that new efforts now be undertaken by the American business community to hasten its attainment of those high ethical standards that derive from our heritage and traditions. We urge all enterprises, business groups, and associations to accept responsibility—each for itself and in its own most appropriate way —to develop methods and programs for encouraging and sustaining these efforts on a continuous basis. We believe in this goal, we accept it, and we encourage all to pursue its attainment.

Some Questions for Businessmen

The following questions are designed to facilitate the examination by American businessmen of their ethical standards and performance. They are intended to illustrate the kinds of questions that must be identified and considered by each business enterprise if it is to achieve compliance with those high ethical standards that derive from our heritage and traditions. Each reader will think of others. No single list can possibly encompass all of the demands for ethical judgments that must be met by men in business.

1. *General understanding:*

Do we have in our organization current, well-considered statements of the ethical principles that should guide our officers and employees in specific situations that arise in our business activities, both domestic and foreign? Do we revise these statements periodically to cover new situations and changing laws and social patterns?

Have those statements been the fruit of discussion in which all members of policy-determining management have had an opportunity to participate?

Have we given to our officers and employees at all levels sufficient motivation to search out ethical factors in business problems and apply high ethical standards in their solution? What have we done to eliminate opposing pressures?

Have we provided officers and employees with an easily accessible means of obtaining counsel on and resolution of ethical problems that may rise in their activities? Do they use it?

Do we know whether our officers and employees apply in their daily activities the ethical standards we have promulgated? Do we reward those who do so and penalize those who do not?

2. *Compliance with law:*

Having in mind the complexities and ever-changing patterns of modern law and government regulation:

What are we doing to make sure that our officers and employees are informed about and comply with laws and regulations affecting their activities?

Have we made clear that it is our policy to obey even those laws which we may think unwise and seek to have changed?

Do we have adequate internal checks on our compliance with law?

Have we established a simple and readily available procedure for our officers and employees to seek legal guidance in their activities? Do they use it?

3. *Conflicts of interest:*

Do we have a current, well-considered statement of policy regarding potential conflict of interest problems of our directors, officers, and employees? If so, does it cover conflicts which may arise' in connection with such activities as: transactions with or involving our company; acquiring interests in or performing services for our customers, distributors, suppliers, and competitors; buying and selling our company's securities; or the personal undertaking of what might be called company opportunities?

What mechanism do we have for enabling our directors, officers, and employees to make ethical judgments when conflicts of interest do arise?

Do we require regular reports, or do we leave it to our directors, officers, and employees to disclose such activities voluntarily?

4. *Entertainment, gifts, and expenses:*

Have we defined our company policy on accepting and making expenditures for gifts and entertainment? Are the criteria as to occasion and amount clearly stated or are they left merely to the judgment of the officer or employee?

Do we disseminate information about our company policy to the organizations with which we deal?

Do we require adequate reports of both the giving and receiving of gifts and entertainment; are they supported in sufficient detail; are they subject to review by appropriate authority; and could the payment or receipt be justified to our stockholders, the government, and the public?

5. *Customers and suppliers:*

Have we taken appropriate steps to keep our advertising and sales representations truthful and fair? Are these steps effective?

How often do we review our advertising, literature, labels, and packaging? Do they give our customers a fair understanding of the true quality, quantity, price, and function of our products? Does our service as well as our product measure up to our basic obligations and our representations?

Do we fairly make good on flaws and defects? Is this a matter of stated policy? Do we know that our employees, distributors, dealers, and agents follow it?

Do we avoid favoritism and discrimination and otherwise treat our customers and suppliers fairly and equitably in all our dealings with them?

6. *Social responsibilities:*

Every business enterprise has manifold responsibilities to the society of which it is a part. The prime legal and social obligation of the managers of a business is to operate it for the long-term profit of its owners. Concurrent social responsibilities pertain to a company's treatment of its past, present, and prospective employees and to its various relationships with customers, suppliers, government, the community, and the public at large. These responsibilities may often be, or appear to be, in conflict, and at times a management's recognition of its broad responsibilities may affect the amount of an enterprise's immediate profits and the means of attaining them.

The problems that businessmen must solve in this area are often exceedingly perplexing. One may begin his reflections on this subject by asking—

Have we reviewed our company policies in the light of our responsibilities to society? Are our employees aware of the interaction between our business policies and our social responsibilities?

Do we have a clearly understood concept of our obligation to assess our responsibilities to stockholders, employees, customers, suppliers, our community and the public?

Do we recognize and impress upon all our officers and employees the fact that our free-enterprise system and our individual business enterprises can thrive and grow only to the extent that they contribute to the welfare of our country and its people?

From *The Annals of the American Academy of Political and Social Science,* September 1962, Vol. 343 (Philadelphia: The Ethics of Business Enterprise), pp. 137–140. Special editor of this volume—Arthur S. Miller.

Service of Ordination

Minister: While Moses was tending sheep on a mountainside, the Lord appeared to him in a burning bush and called out to him, saying, "Put off your shoes from your feet, for the place on which you are standing is holy ground." Jesus embodied this idea fully, teaching that all ground is holy. All of life for our Master was hallowed, to be dedicated fully to God; all of life was a sacrament. The new "holy of holies," the new inner sanctuary, is in each of us, for each of us is a temple of the Holy Spirit. A Christian is on holy ground wherever he is.

Today, __(name)__ has come to acknowledge to God and to us that the work he does each day takes place on holy ground. He comes to ask God's blessing on his work and for guidance in making each act he performs pleasing in God's sight. He comes to give back to God the work which God has given him to do. In turn, we in the Christian community come to offer __(name)__ the strength and love and encouragement which our being together in Christ makes possible.

(*Participant moves forward, facing the altar*)

Minister to Participant: Your work and your worship are intimately interwoven. In fact, they are not separate at all: Your work grows out of your worship and your worship grows out of your work. __(name)__ , do you come today to acknowledge that the place where you work is as holy as the place where you worship?

Participant: I do. (*Kneels and speaks as follows, or in words of his own*): Enabled by Christ's love for me, I shall endeavor to make each day's work a sacrament. I pray that my work will be cleansed of all spiritual or material selfishness, of all impatience or criticism, of all secret desire for consolation, recognition or reward. Turn, O God, my seeing into loving, that I may witness to the redeeming love of Jesus Christ for all men. In His name I make my prayer.   Amen.

    (Participant remains kneeling, and sponsor moves forward, placing his hand on shoulder of participant)

Minister: It is fitting that the dedication of your work to God be sealed with the strengthening devotion of your Christian community.

  (Sponsor) , by placing his hand on your shoulder, offers ourselves to you as channels of the empowering grace of the Body of Christ, pledging our love, interest, and encouragement in the work you have dedicated to God's care and guidance. Let us pray:

O Master Workman, Christ, how thankful we are that Thou has called out (name) to work with Thee. As he goes out to do Thy will; wilt Thou forgive him, train him, use him, to Thine own glory. Cause him, we pray, to recall again and again that the ground on which he works is holy ground. Light a burning bush of Thy love within his spirit as he takes his particular place in the world to do Thy work. In the name of the Father, and of the Son, and of the Holy Spirit. Amen.

From *Call to Commitment* by Elizabeth O'Connor, pages 105–106. Harper & Row, Publishers. New York, Evanston, and London, 1963.

Lines to a Rickshaw Puller

I pass you every morning
on my way to the station.
The light is raw and the wind is keen.
All around you the city is stretching its limbs
and wiping the sleep from its eyes.
The raucous voice of the crow is everywhere.
But you hear nothing, you see nothing.
You lie curled up in your rickshaw
with sprawling limbs and inert body
like some tired animal.
Some mother must have cradled you
pressing you against the soft comfort
of her warm breasts.
But now you shape your body
to fit the wooden embrace
of the hard sides of your rickshaw
for its walls are your home, your rented home.
Your intimacy with it is very great.
Your worldly possessions are in the box
under the seat with its torn fibre cushion
keeping company with your oil lamps,
the battered old *topee*
you wear on rainy days,
and a few *beedis*.
The shafts are worn smooth
by the contact of your forearms.
The rickshaw and you—
you belong together.
I have passed you by at other times—

when you were not asleep
and something of your life
has trailed after me.
I remember the laughter of your fellows
as you twitted the grain seller
who sits by the rickshaw stand
until the old hag exposed her gums
in a toothless grin. . . .
I have watched you fight with your creditors
with the ferocity of a trapped beast
over pitiful sums, the price of a packet of fags.
I have heard you whine for a fare
when the day's earnings were poor.
I have seen you resentful and bitter
when you spat on the ground
and talked unconscious communism.
I pass you by like a hundred others
who also pass you by—
and the road may be the road
from Jerusalem to Jerico for all we know.
I would like to put my hand on your shoulder
and say to you, "Comrade,
there is One who died for us
and dying made us blood brothers."
But I am filled with the cowardice of the well-dressed—
for clothes are by no means flimsy
when it comes to erecting barriers
between man and man.
I am afraid you will wake with a start
and betray resentment in your eyes
as you see in me what I really am—
your well-dressed enemy.
And then you will acknowledge defeat
and put on your mask of patient stupidity.
You will jump up and dust the seat
and grin and point to it with a flourish of your hand.
You will want us to sell our brotherhood
for eight *annas*.

Day after day I pass you by,
you the man by the roadside
and I the priest and the Levite rolled in one,
passing you by.

From *The Cross Is Lifted,* by Chandran Devanesen. Friendship Press, N. Y. Copyright 1954.

topee: hat, *beedis:* cheap Indian cigar, *annas:* coin worth about twenty cents in American currency.

From *The Secular City*

Urban man has a wider variety of "contacts" than rural counterpart; he can choose only a limited number for friends. He must have more or less impersonal relationships with most of the people with whom he comes in contact precisely in order to choose certain friendships to nourish and cultivate. This selectivity can best be symbolized perhaps by the unplugged telephone or the unlisted number. A person does not request an unlisted number to cut down on the depth of his relationships. Quite the opposite; he does so to guard and deepen the worthwhile relationships he has against being dissolved in the deluge of messages that would come if one were open on principle and on an equal basis to anyone who tried to get through, including the increasing army of telephone salesmen who violate one's privacy so arrogantly. Those we want to know have our number; others do not. . . . (p. 41)

*   *   *

Urban man must distinguish carefully between his private life and his public relationships. Since he depends on such a complex net of services to maintain himself in existence in a modern city, the majority of his transactions will have to be public and will be what sociologists call functional or secondary. In most of his relationships he will be dealing with people he cannot afford to be interested in as individuals but must deal with in terms of the services they render to him and he to them. This is essential in urban life. Supermarket checkers or gas-meter readers who became enmeshed in the lives of the people they were serving would be a menace. They would soon cause a total breakdown in the essential systems of which they are integral parts. Urban life demands that we treat most of the people we meet as persons—not as things, but not as intimates either. (pp. 41–42)

*   *   *

Urban anonymity need not be heartless. Village sociability can mask a murderous hostility. Loneliness is undoubtedly a serious problem in the city, but it cannot be met by dragooning urban people into relationships which decimate their privacy and reduce their capacity to live responsibly with increasing numbers of neighbors. . . . [Urban man] had stumbled upon an essential protective device, the polite refusal to be chummy, without which urban existence could not be human. . . . [He] *must* cultivate and guard his privacy. He must restrict the number of people who have his number or know his name.

*   *   *

Urban man . . . wants to maintain a clear distinction between private and public. Otherwise public life would overwhelm and dehumanize him. His life represents a point touched by dozens of systems and hundreds of people. His capacity to know some of them better necessitates his minimizing the depths of his relationships to many others. Listening to the postman gossip becomes for urban man an act of sheer graciousness, since he probably has no interest in the people the postman wants to talk about. Unlike my parents, who suspected all strangers, he tends to be wary not of the functionaries he doesn't know but of those he does. (pp. 45–46)

The Secular City (paperback) by Harvey Cox. New York: The Macmillan Co., 1965.

Requiem for a Woodland

by Kenneth D. Morrison

A small woodland in Central Florida died the other day. There was no notice in the morning paper, no recognition anywhere that something of value had been lost.

A few days ago the woodland looked much as it must have when the Seminole Indians pursued game in its shadows. Statuesque longleaf pines towered high above the second story of oaks and wild cherries. Below were clumps of palmetto and lantana. The wildlife community was bustling. No unemployment was visible.

Red-bellied woodpeckers hammered on the pines, a Carolina wren scolded from a palmetto frond, a red-tailed hawk watched from a high snag for a careless mouse or rabbit. The tracks of foxes, raccoons and opossums were clearly discernible in the sandy soil. The lazy drone of insects provided a background counterpoint for the life-and-death dramas unfolding on nature's woodland stage.

Suddenly a hush spread through the woods. An intruder roared its warning—a monstrous species of bulldozer, guided by a dour master who seemed oblivious to the destruction left in his wake. Large and small trees were toppled as though they were papier-maché. The form and character of each tree was crumbled into a blurred mass of exposed roots and rumpled foliage.

Then the crushed and torn remains of what had been a vibrant woodland a few hours earlier were pushed into neat piles to await the oblivion of fire.

By a peculiar distortion of meaning, this and other assaults on our native landscape are widely referred to as "progress." Progress toward what? Obviously we are rushing ahead full throttle toward obliterating the end products of two billion years of evolution. Nature's intricate handiwork commands little respect. What is important, we are urged to conclude, is man's blueprint for change.

Perhaps this is inevitable, but is our technology so rapacious that it cannot spare a few more outstanding samples of the living landscape as God and time have fashioned it? Must every wild acre—no matter how exceptional its biological attributes—yield its quota of oranges or bungalows?

I pondered these things while viewing the desecration of a woodland that I had regarded as a close friend. I fancied that the cardinals and towhees were chanting a funeral dirge as they inspected the fallen branches of trees where, the previous morning, they had sought insects and berries. A gopher tortoise appeared to be searching for the entrance to its burrow, now covered by debris. Every living thing had been evicted, and no notice had been served.

Where will the wildlife go when the ground is spick-and-span and small orange trees have been planted? Move they must, for most of their food will be killed by pesticides. The only remaining woodland in the vicinity, however, already is crowded with refugees from the bulldozer and probably can support no more. Thus chances are that when we evict wildlife from its land, we also condemn it to death.

Oddly, a few spindly native palms were left standing in the woodland, perhaps a sop to the owner's conscience. But at their sides were the fallen trunks of magnificent old longleaf pines that were 150 to 200 years old. They had been monarchs of the countryside since the days when Central Florida was a place of pristine beauty, of clear lakes and streams, sprawling forests, abundant wildlife. The pines had seen the relentless surge of "progress"—polluted water and air, burned and bulldozed wilderness, the shameful slaughter of wildlife. Yet even in recent months, bald eagles had alighted in their top branches.

Nevermore. Perhaps the majestic old birds can rest on utility poles nearby. But don't call me to look at them. I remember seeing them perched atop those stately pines, with the arching lakeshore in the background and wispy clouds drifting by.

That's the way I want to remember the eagles—and the woodland that died.

Audubon Magazine, May/June, 1966, p. 185.

Let's Spoil the Wilderness

by Robert Wernick

A rancher in the hills north of San Francisco saw two bald eagles, one day last spring, killing his lambs. He did what King Agamemnon, or King David, or any other sheepman mentioned favorably in our history books would have done. He killed the eagles. But this is 20th-century America, and there is a law against harming any feather on a bald eagle. The rancher was arrested, and for days he was subjected to vile abuse in the press. Right-thinking people rained down such vituperation that you would have thought he had been caught molesting little girls or sending parcels to the Viet Cong. For right-thinking people he was guilty of a gruesome crime. What crime? He was spoiling the wilderness.

The trumpeting voice of the wilderness lover is heard at great distances these days. He is apt to be a perfectly decent person, if hysterical. And the causes which excite him so are generally worthy. Who can really find a harsh word for him as he strives to save Lake Erie from the sewers of Cleveland, save the redwoods from the California highway engineers, save the giant rhinoceros from the Somali tribesmen who kill those noble beasts to powder their horns into what they fondly imagine is a wonder-working aphrodisiac?

Worthy causes, indeed, but why do those who espouse them have to be so shrill and intolerant and sanctimonious? What right do they have to insinuate that anyone who does not share their passion for the whooping crane is a Philistine and a slob? From the gibberish they talk, you would think the only way to save the bald eagle is to dethrone human reason.

I would like to ask what seems to me an eminently reasonable question: *Why shouldn't we spoil the wilderness?*

Have these people ever stopped to think what the wilderness is? It is precisely what man has been fighting against since he began his painful, awkward climb to civilization. It is the dark, the formless, the terrible, the old chaos which our fathers pushed back, which surrounds us yet, which will engulf us all in the end. It is held at bay by constant vigilance, and when the vigilance slackens it swoops down for a melodramatic revenge, as when the jungle took over Chichen Itza in Yucatan or lizards took over Jamshid's courtyard in Persia. It lurks in our own hearts, where it breeds wars and oppressions and crimes. Spoil it! Don't you wish we could?

Of course, when the propagandists talk about unspoiled wilderness, they don't mean anything of that sort. What they mean by wilderness is a kind of grandiose picnic ground, in the Temperate Zone, where the going is rough enough to be challenging but not literally murderous, where hearty folk like Supreme Court Justice Douglas and Interior Secretary Udall can hike and hobble through spectacular scenery, with a helicopter hovering in the dirty old civilized background in case a real emergency comes up.

Well, the judge and the Secretary and their compeers are all estimable people, and there is no reason why they should not be able to satisfy their urge for primitive living. We ought to recognize, however, that other people have equally strong and often equally legitimate urges to build roads, dig mines, plow up virgin land, erect cities. Such people used to be called pioneers; now they are apt to be called louts. At all events, we are faced with sets of conflicting drives, and it is up to us to make a rational choice among them.

The trouble is, it is difficult to make a rational choice when one of the parties insists on wrapping all its discourse in a vile metaphysical fog.

One cannot talk of eagles, for instance, without being told by the wilderness folk that man, vile man, has no right to destroy one of God's beautiful creatures; that the bald eagle, besides being the symbol of the United States of America, represents all the will to be free and wide-ranging quest which made life worth living for our forefathers; and finally, that killing eagles upsets the balance of nature.

These aren't arguments; they are 100 percent nonsense. The most savage nature lover thinks nothing of vindictively squashing one of God's beautiful creatures when the creature happens to be an anopheles mosquito. And yet the mosquito in every respect but size is just as awe-inspiring, just as beautiful, just as free as any eagle. The individual eagle you see stretching his great wings as he searches for a fish or a lamb to eat is quite unaware that he is a symbol of anything. And quite rightly too: The eagle on our Great Seal is a perfectly mythical creature, and could go on being a symbol even if all eagles in the land were exterminated. The British, after all, have got on quite well without Acts of Parliament to protect lions and unicorns.

As for the balance of nature, this is simply an arty phrase to denote the status quo, whatever exists in a certain place at a certain time. In truth, the status quo is always changing. On our Great Plains, for example, the balance of nature consisted for centuries of immense herds of bison browsing thunderously on buffalo grass. In the late 18th century the balance consisted of Indians, who had acquired Spanish horses, slaughtering bison. Nowadays it consists of strip-farming, beauty shops, filling stations, beer cans, etc.

Naturally some balances are more desirable for interested parties than others. From the point of view of the bison, the balance of 1750 was infinitely preferable to any balance afterward; the Indians might have preferred the balance of 1800. From the point of view of Mother Nature, it doesn't seem to make the slightest difference. In her bloody, blundering way, she has been lurching along for millions of years, wiping out whole species, drowning whole continents, burning, ravaging, destroying. Our rifles and DDT are puny compared to the forces that annihilated dinosaurs and the multi-colored world of the trilobites.

The most we can do, it seems to me, is to look after our own interests as best we can, and no more consider the feelings of the eagle and the rhinoceros than they consider ours. . . .

There is actually one legitimate reason for saving the wilderness, and that is that some people enjoy it and feel thrilled and ennobled by it. They have a taste for desolate landscapes and lonely nights under the stars. There is nothing wrong with such a taste. Everyone, everywhere, in whatever culture or society, needs something to help transcend the daily round of work and grief and boredom. Some find such transcendence by driving at illegal speeds on freeways, some by chomping on sacred mushrooms. An exultant thrashing through the wilderness may be a rich human experience —not quite so rich perhaps as reading the book of Isaiah or visiting the Parthenon, but certainly more varied, and more deeply satisfying than sniffing glue. . . .

Wilderness lovers are a phenomenon of modern time; they are not tolerated in primitive cultures; the Bible doesn't have a good word to say for Ishmael. They breed in highly developed civilizations, where men have become bored with excessive cultivation and refinement. They affect old rumpled clothes, unshaved jaws, salty language; they spit and sweat and boast of their friendship with aborigines. But this is all veneer: Underneath, they are decadents, aristocrats, snobs. . . .

But I urge them to avoid the great vice of their kind, which is megalomania. A man who has been infected with the wilderness lust is not satisfied with one stretch of forest, or one uncluttered mountainside. He wants hundreds of square miles of thicket and coulee and beaver dam and white water; and he wants them all for himself.

In the full euphoria which attends this fever, all ordinary human connections are apt to be broken. You struggle, slipping angrily through chalky rock and prickly pear, to the top of a ridge, and before you are miles of sagebrush flats, with white streaks of alkali, dry lakes, purple rocks, an immensity of desolation. Your heart fills with delight and then you catch sight of a rickety service station at a forsaken crossroads, and all the beauty drains out of the scene. A single beer can will spoil a square mile of woods; and as for the lovers' initials and fraternity Greek letters painted on rocks, it takes but one such pitiful imprint of humanity to spoil a mountain. . . .

The population of California, as of the world, is growing; this population is becoming more affluent and more mobile, and as it expands and covers the land with its detritus of motels and soda bottles, there are just not enough square miles left to satisfy the wilderness lovers.

I suggest to these worthy people that they bow gracefully to the inevitable and model their conduct on that of the kings of England. William the Conqueror and his descendants were great wilderness lovers, and they turned half of England into royal forests where, through the brambles and under giant oaks, they could ride for giddy days chasing the red stag and the wild boar; and any Saxon hind who came sneaking in looking for firewood or a rabbit had his ears, or worse, chopped off.

Grudgingly over the centuries the kings gave up this demi-paradise to the uncouth people of England, who insisted on parceling it out into grubby farms and grimy factories. The loss was irreparable, but the royal huntsmen prudently swallowed their grief, and sought a replica of their old pleasures on safaris in East Africa.

Just so our modern wilderness lovers may soon have to abandon the whole North American continent to the suburbanite hordes. Barring a nuclear war, which would bring back the wilderness with a vengeance, they will have to spread their wings a little, and indulge their special tastes in Spitzbergen and the mountains of New Guinea. And if the tides of civilization lap eventually over these too, there will soon be available excursion rockets to Mars and Alpha Centauri. And there should be enough unspoiled wilderness out there for anybody's taste.

Saturday Evening Post, November 6, 1965, 238:12ff.

Why Not Rapid Transit?

A survey of 5,000 Chicagoans who commute to work by automobile revealed that most of them would not use public transit *even if they were paid to do so.*

If rides were made free, only 13 per cent of the commuters would give up their travel by car and use elevated trains. Only 18 per cent would patronize free buses.

A few more—24 per cent—would ride buses if they (the riders) were *paid* 10 cents per trip. Half the motorists would ride the subway to work if they received 45 cents a trip.

In an article in *Harper's* magazine, C. W. Griffin, Jr., an engi-

neer specializing in building and city planning, wrote that he had
"heard grown men boast that no snowstorm ever forced them into
the humiliation of taking the bus or subway."

'Captive' Riders

Surveys were made in numerous cities to determine how many
of the people using public transit were "captive" riders—that is,
riders who, because they had no automobiles available or couldn't
drive, had no choice but to use public transit.

The number of "captive" riders ranged from 50 per cent of
the total in one city up to 91 per cent in another. In other words,
most people using public transit had no alternative.

Editorial Research Reports, in a report titled "Mass Transit
vs. Private Cars," says:

> Americans appear willing to put up with no end of in-
> convenience rather than give up driving their cars into the
> center of the city. Despite the physical and nervous strain of
> rushhour driving, the automobile offers portal-to-portal trans-
> portation, privacy, comfort and, to many motorists, a sense of
> social distinction.
>
> Another consideration is that the motorist, unlike the
> transit patron, is free from schedule worries. Other factors
> being equal, the car owner is not likely to use a public carrier
> unless it takes him within a block or so of his destination.

What does all this mean?

*Simply that no form or forms of public transit could possibly
solve Richmond's traffic congestion problems.*

Some of the reasons many people don't use public transit may
be capricious. Many perhaps could save money by riding public
carriers and suffer little, if any, inconvenience.

But public transit, even the best system possible, has disadvantages. The commuter has to go to the place where he can get
on the public carrier, he has to travel according to the carrier's
time schedule, and the carrier may not take him close enough to
his intended destination.

Rail Limitations

These disadvantages are much greater in the case of rail carriers than in the case of buses. A moment's reflection will reveal the considerable inconvenience that would be involved on the part of most commuters if they traveled to downtown Richmond by rail and faced the problem of getting to and from the stations at each end of each trip.

Railroad commuter service is feasible only in very large metropolitan centers. A commuter who lives, say, thirty or thirty-five miles or more from New York or some other great urban center may be willing to ride a train to town, because the problems of driving and parking are more than he is willing to cope with. But people living five or ten miles from a smaller city, such as Richmond, would not use a railroad in sufficient numbers to make such service financially feasible.

For the foreseeable future, Richmond needs a system of expressways, along with greater emphasis on, and encouragement of, local bus transit. The expressways will help make better bus service possible, because buses, as well as private vehicles, will use the fast, limited-access roadways.

Richmond Times-Dispatch, November 18, 1966, page 18-A.

I. Our contemporary culture fails to realize the power, extent and persistence of group egoism in human relations. It may be possible, though it is never easy, to establish just relations between individuals within a group purely by moral and rational suasion and accommodation. In inter-group relations this is practically an impossibility. The relations between groups must therefore always be predominantly political rather than ethical, that is, they will be determined by the proportion of power which each group possesses at least as much as by any rational and moral appraisal of the comparative needs and claims of each group.[1]

*   *   *

II. There are, no doubt, rational and ethical factors in the democratic process. Contending social forces presumably use the forum rather than the battleground to arbitrate their differences in the democratic method, and thus differences are resolved by moral suasion and a rational adjustment of rights to rights. If political issues were really abstract questions of social policy upon which unbiased citizens were asked to commit themselves, the business of voting and the debate which precedes the election might actually be regarded as an educational programme in which a social group discovers its common mind. But the fact is that political opinions are inevitably rooted in economic interests of some kind or other, and only comparatively few citizens can view a problem of social policy without regard to their interest. Conflicting interest therefore can never be completely resolved; and minorities will yield only because the majority has come into control of the police power of the state and may, if the occasion arises, augment that power by its own military strength.[2]

*   *   *

III. The individual or the group which organizes any society, however social its intentions or pretensions, arrogates an inordinate portion of social privilege to itself. . . . If superior abilities and services to society deserve special rewards it may be regarded as axiomatic that the rewards are always higher than the services warrant. No impartial society determines the rewards. The men of power who control society grant these prerequisites to themselves. . . . Most rational and social justifications of unequal privilege are clearly afterthoughts. The facts are created by the disproportion of power which exists in a given social system. . . . As individuals, men believe that they ought to love and serve each other and establish justice between each other. As racial, economic and national groups they take for themselves, whatever their power can command.[3]

A Brief Bibliography

If you would like to do some additional study of Christian ethics here are some books which you might find particularly valuable. They represent differing approaches to the subject, so of course my listing them here does not mean that I agree with the point of view in all of them. Most are paperbacks.

Fletcher, Joseph. *Situation Ethics*. Philadelphia: The Westminster Press, 1965. Paperback $1.95. Reflection of one particular approach to ethics namely, that there are no valid ethical principles; the situation determines the decision. Should perhaps be read in conjunction with Paul Ramsey's volume, below.

Henderlite, Rachel. *A Call to Faith*. Richmond: John Knox Press, 1955. Paperback, $1.25. Section III deals with man's response to what God has done for man and in man. Very helpful.

Kee, Howard Clark. *Making Ethical Decisions*. Philadelphia: The Westminster Press, 1957. Paperback, $1.00.

Niebuhr, H. Richard. *The Responsible Self*. New York: Harper & Row, 1963. Niebuhr's is the viewpoint which pervades *In Response to God*.

Pike, James A. *Doing the Truth: A Summary of Christian Ethics*. New York: The Macmillan Co., 1965. Paperback, $1.45. Ethical analysis on the Trinitarian pattern.

Ramsey, Paul. *Deeds and Rules in Christian Ethics*. Chicago: Alec R. Allenson, Inc., 1965. Paperback, $2.50. Claims that there *are* valid principles in ethics and that we flounder, morally, without them. This book is hard reading, but it is a good balance to Fletcher's book, above.

Of course one previous book in the Covenant Life Curriculum for adults is of special importance in this course:

Waldo Beach, *The Christian Life*. Richmond: CLC Press.

Three youth books in the Covenant Life Curriculum will be of interest, too:

William J. Fogleman, *I Live in the World*.
Donald W. Shriver, Jr., *How Do You Do—And Why?*
Albert C. Winn, *The Worry and Wonder of Being Human*.

An Index of Scripture Citations and Quotations in This Book

Acknowledgments

CHAPTER 2

1. H. Richard Niebuhr, *The Responsible Self* (New York: Harper & Row, 1963), p. 166.
2. You may want to study for yourself *The Responsible Self* (see note above), the book in which Niebuhr clearly states this kind of pattern for making ethical decisions. Much of what is said in this present book is an interpretation of the thinking of Niebuhr.
3. *Ibid.,* p. 126.

CHAPTER 3

1. Shirley C. Guthrie, *Christian Doctrine* (Richmond: CLC Press, 1968), p. 239.
2. *Ibid.,* p. 240.
3. Rachel Henderlite, *A Call To Faith* (Richmond: John Knox Press, 1955), p. 82.
4. George MacLeod, *We Shall Re-Build* (Glasgow: McCorquodale & Co., Ltd., 1962), p. 93.
5. George Webber, "Renewal Through Witness," *Princeton Seminary Bulletin* LVI, 1, October, 1962, p. 47.
6. Guthrie, *op. cit.,* p. 254.
7. E. L. Allen, *Divine and Human* (London: Epworth Press, 1952), p. 49.
8. Robert Merrill Bartlett, *They Dare to Believe* (New York: Association Press, 1952), pp. 112–118.
9. "The Bomb That Fell on America" (Santa Barbara: Pacific Coast Publishing Company, 1946), p. 43.
10. Webber, *op. cit.,* p. 47.
11. Vincent Taylor, *The Cross of Christ* (London: Macmillan and Co., Ltd., 1956), p. 42.
12. Georgia Harkness, "The Agony of God," *Masterpieces of Religious Verse,* ed., James Dalton Morrison (New York: Harper & Row, 1948), p. 474.
13. Henderlite, *op. cit.,* p. 109.
14. From *The New Testament in Modern English* © J. B. Phillips, 1958. Used by permission of The Macmillan Company.
15. From *A Pattern for Life,* by Archibald M. Hunter. Published in the United States by The Westminster Press, 1953. Used by permission. P. 115.
16. Webber, *op. cit.,* p. 47.
17. John R. Mumaw, *The Resurrected Life* (Scottdale, Pa.: Herald Press, 1965), p. 84.

CHAPTER 4

1. Albert C. Winn, *Concerning Year Three of the Covenant Life Curriculum* (printed and distributed by action of the 106th General Assembly, Presbyterian Church in the United States, 1966), p. 51.

2. *The Interpreter's Bible* (Nashville: Abingdon Press, 1953), X, p. 124. Used by permission.
3. From *The First Epistle of Paul to the Corinthians,* by Charles R. Erdman. The Westminster Press. Copyright 1928 by Charles R. Erdman. Renewed, 1956, by Charles R. Erdman. Used by permission. P. 97.
4. John Bright, *Biblical Authority and Biblical Theology* (Crozer Theological Seminary Reprint), p. 11.

CHAPTER 5

1. Joseph Fletcher, *Situation Ethics* (Philadelphia: The Westminster Press, 1966), p. 30.
2. *Ibid.,* p. 26.
3. Elton Trueblood, *Foundations for Reconstruction* (New York: Harper & Row, 1946), p. 95.
4. A. D. Lindsay, *The Moral Teaching of Jesus* (London: Hodder & Stoughton, 1937), p. 114.
5. Trueblood, *op. cit.,* p. 95.
6. From *A Pattern for Life,* by Archibald M. Hunter. Published in the United States by The Westminster Press, 1953. Used by permission. P. 113.
7. *Ibid.,* p. 115.
8. Martin F. Dibelius, "The Message of the New Testament and the Orders of Human Society," *Christian Faith and the Common Life* [Vol. IV of "The Church, Community and State" Series] (London: George Allen and Unwin, 1938), p. 34.

CHAPTER 6

1. "The Rock," Part I (New York: Harcourt, Brace & World, Inc., 1934), p. 21.
2. Langdon Gilkey, *How the Church Can Minister to the World Without Losing Itself* (New York: Harper & Row, 1964), p. 111.
3. A. Leonard Griffith, *God and His People* (London: Lutterworth Press, 1960), p. 75.
4. Samuel H. Miller, *The Life of the Church* (New York: Harper & Row, 1953), p. 118.
5. Gilkey, *op. cit.,* p. 108.
6. Rachel Henderlite, *A Call to Faith* (Richmond: John Knox Press, 1955), p. 121.

CHAPTER 7

1. Harvey Cox, *God's Revolution and Man's Responsibility* (Valley Forge: The Judson Press, 1965), p. 71. Used by permission.
2. Paul S. Minear, *Eyes of Faith* (Philadelphia: The Westminster Press, 1946), p. 131.
3. "A Theological Analysis of Race Relations," *Faith and Ethics,* Paul Ramsey, ed. (New York: Harper & Row, 1957), p. 219.
4. Stanley Sanders, "The Language of Watts," *The Nation,* 201: 491, December 20, 1965.
5. *Life,* 59:33, August 27, 1965.

6. Martin Luther King, "Next Stop: The North," *Saturday Review*, 48:34, November 13, 1965.
7. *Loc. cit.*
8. Jerry Cohen and William S. Murphy, "Burn, Baby, Burn!" *Life*, 61:51, July 15, 1966.
9. *The Nation*, 201:90, August 30, 1965.
10. Thomas Pynchon, "A Journey Into the Mind of Watts," *The New York Times Magazine*, June 12, 1966, p. 84.
11. Cohen and Murphy, *op. cit.*, p. 46.
12. "Watts Today," *Life*, 61:57, July 15, 1966.
13. *Time*, 88:53–54, July 22, 1966.
14. "Watts Today," *loc. cit.*, pp. 58–59.
15. See, for instance, *The New York Times*, September 3, 1965, 33:1; November 28, 1965, 67:1; January 7, 1966, 9:2; April 10, 1966, 61:8.
16. Cox, *op. cit.*, pp. 15–16.
17. *Ibid.*, p. 18.
18. Lorena A. Hickok, *The Touch of Magic* (New York: Dodd, Mead & Co., 1961), pp. 1–54.
19. From *Teacher: Anne Sullivan Macy*, by Helen Keller. Copyright © 1955 by Helen Keller. Reprinted by permission of Doubleday & Company, Inc.
20. *Ibid.*, p. 51.
21. *Ibid.*, p. 61.
22. *Ibid.*, p. 44.
23. *Ibid.*, p. 41.
24. *Ibid.*, p. 228.

CHAPTER 8

1. Daniel Jenkins, *Prayer and the Service of God* (London: Faber and Faber, 1944), p. 66.
2. Guy Bowden, *The Dazzling Darkness* (London: S.P.C.K., 1963), p. 116.
3. George S. Stewart, *The Lower Levels of Prayer* (London: SCM Press, 1939), p. 169.
4. *Peer Gynt*, Act IV, Scene VIII. Tr., R. Farquarson Sharp (New York: E. P. Dutton and Co., 1950).
5. Jenkins, *op. cit.*, p. 102.
6. Quoted in N. G. D. MacLennan, *Christian Obedience* (New York: Thomas Nelson and Sons, Ltd., 1948), p. 133.
7. H. H. Farmer, *The World and God* (London: Nisbet and Co., 1939, p. 274.

CHAPTER 9

1. Will Herberg, *Protestant-Catholic-Jew* (Garden City: Doubleday and Co., Inc., 1960), p. 75.
2. *The Nation*, 201:90, August 30, 1965. Cf. Thomas Pynchon, "A Journey Into the Mind of Watts," *The New York Times Magazine*, June 12, 1966, pp. 34–35ff.

CHAPTER 10

1. Bill Davidson, "Teen-Age Drinking," *Saturday Evening Post*, April 10, 1965, p. 25.

2. *Richmond Times-Dispatch,* Sunday, March 12, 1966, p. 12.
3. *Ibid.*
4. *Ibid.*
5. "Conversations Parents Never Hear," No. 7, *Look,* September 20, 1966, p. 101.
6. *Ibid.*
7. *Richmond Times-Dispatch,* March 12, 1966, p. 12.

CHAPTER 11

1. Paul Tournier, *The Meaning of Persons* (New York: Harper & Row, 1957), p. 125.
2. Reuel L. Howe, *Herein Is Love* (Valley Forge: The Judson Press, 1961), pp. 70, 71. Used by permission. See also Howe, *Man's Need and God's Action* (Greenwich: Seabury Press, 1953), pp. 51–52.
3. Martin Buber, *I and Thou,* tr., Ronald Gregor Smith (New York: Charles Scribner's Sons, 1958), p. 28.
4. *Ibid.,* p. 11.
5. Martin Buber, *Between Man and Man,* tr., Ronald Gregor Smith (Boston: The Beacon Press, 1959), pp. 97, 101.
6. Reprinted from *The Feminine Mystique* by Betty Friedan. With the permission of the publisher, W. W. Norton & Company, Inc., New York, N.Y.
7. Phyllis McGinley, *Sixpence in Her Shoe* (New York: The Macmillan Company, 1964), p. 30.
8. Friedan, *op. cit.,* p. 186.
9. *Ibid.,* p. 187.

CHAPTER 12

1. *The Presbyterian Journal,* February 16, 1966, p. 13.
2. Gayraud S. Wilmore, "Report of the Lay Committee of the National Council of Churches," 1954. (Philadelphia: The Westminster Press, 1962), p. 22.
3. Harvey Cox, *God's Revolution and Man's Responsibility* (Valley Forge: The Judson Press, 1965), p. 24.
4. Robert Strong, "Christ the King," *The Presbyterian Journal,* October 26, 1966, p. 8. Used with permission.
5. Mike Engleman, "Reform Society or Individual Men?" *The Presbyterian Journal,* November 2, 1966, p. 11. Used with permission.
6. Donald W. Shriver, Jr., "Now We Know Our Neighbor," *The Presbyterian Outlook,* September 26, 1966, p. 6.
7. Don M. Wardlaw, "Pew, Creed and Social Concern," *The Presbyterian Outlook,* September 19, 1966, p. 5.
8. William Barclay, *The Gospel of John* (Philadelphia: The Westminster Press, 1955), II, p. 250.
9. Peter Green, *Our Great High Priest* (London: Longmans, Green and Company, 1939), p. 88.
10. "What NCC Membership Involves," *The Presbyterian Outlook,* July 25, 1966, p. 5.
11. *Ibid.,* pp. 5–6.

12. Dietrich Bonhoeffer, *Life Together,* tr., John W. Doberstein (New York: Harper & Row, 1954), p. 93.
13. Dietrich Bonhoeffer, *Sanctorum Communio,* tr., R. Gregor Smith (New York: Harper & Row, 1963), p. 137.
14. John H. Law, "Poems," *Presbyterian Survey,* 57:20, February 1967. Quoted with permission from *Presbyterian Survey.*

CHAPTER 13

1. Cameron P. Hall, ed., *On-the-Job Ethics* (New York: The National Council of The Churches of Christ, 1963), p. 7.
2. For a good discussion of this, see *On-the-Job Ethics,* pp. 39ff.
3. Hans-Ruedi Weber, *Salty Christians* (New York: The Seabury Press, 1963), p. 59.
4. From *God's Frozen People,* by Mark Gibbs and T. Ralph Morton. The Westminster Press. © 1964 by Mark Gibbs and T. Ralph Morton. © 1965 by W. L. Jenkins. Used by permission. P. 71ff.
5. Hall, *op. cit.,* p. 19.
6. *Ibid.,* p. 13.
7. From *A Theology of the Laity,* by Hendrik Kraemer. Published in the U.S.A. by The Westminster Press, 1959. Copyright © 1958, Hendrik Kraemer. Used by permission.
8. See Hans-Ruedi Weber's book by that title, note 3, above.

CHAPTER 14

1. Hans-Ruedi Weber, *Salty Christians* (New York: The Seabury Press, 1963).
2. *Ibid.,* p. 15.
3. From *God's Frozen People,* by Mark Gibbs and T. Ralph Morton. The Westminster Press. © 1964 by Mark Gibbs and T. Ralph Morton. © 1965 by W. L. Jenkins. Used by permission. P. 182.
4. *Ibid.,* p. 121.
5. George W. Webber, *The Congregation in Mission* (New York: Abingdon Press, Copyright ©, 1964), p. 127; Elizabeth O'Connor, *Call to Commitment* (New York: Harper & Row, 1968), p. 106.
6. O'Connor, *op. cit.,* p. 104.
7. *Ibid.,* p. 106.
8. Webber, *op. cit.,* p. 146.
9. O'Connor, *op. cit.,* p. 106.
10. Gibbs and Morton, *op. cit.,* p. 147.
11. O'Connor, *op. cit.,* p. 105.

CHAPTER 15

1. *The Population Bomb* (New York: Hugh Moore Fund, n.d.), p. 4.
2. David E. Lilienthal, "300,000,000 Americans Would Be Wrong," *The New York Times Magazine,* January 9, 1966, p. 88.
3. Martin F. Dibelius, "The Message of the New Testament and the Orders of Society," *Christian Faith and the Common Life* [Vol. IV of "The Church, Community and State" Series] (London: George Allen and Unwin, 1938), p. 34.

4. *The Population Bomb*, p. 16.
5. Conrad Taeuber, "Population and Food Supply," *Annals of the American Academy*, January 1967, p. 79.
6. Paul Simon, *The Christian Encounters a Hungry World*, "The Christian Encounters Series" (St. Louis: Concordia Press, 1966), p. 42.
7. J. S. Mill, *Principles of Political Economy*, quoted in Lincoln H. and Alice T. Day, *Too Many Americans* (Boston: Houghton Mifflin Company, 1964), pp. 73–74.
8. Day, *op. cit.*, pp. 67–71.
9. Lilienthal, *op. cit.*, p. 25.
10. See note 3.
11. Simon, *op. cit.*, p. 49.
12. *Ibid.*, p. 89.
13. *Ibid.*, pp. 77–78.
14. *Ibid.*, p. 78.
15. Jere Neussman, "Perspective on National Affairs," *Presbyterian Survey*, November 1967, p. 30. Quoted with permission from *Presbyterian Survey*.
16. *Ibid.*, pp. 30, 32.
17. Margaret Mead, "Why Americans Must Limit Their Families," *Redbook*, 121:32, August 1963.
18. Lincoln Day, "Middle-Class Litters," *The Nation*, 200:687, June 28, 1965.
19. John Fischer, "What Women Can Do for Peace," *Harpers*, 226:24, April 1963.

CHAPTER 16

1. *Nineteen Eighty-Four* by George Orwell. Copyright, 1949, by Harcourt, Brace & World, Inc. Reprinted by permission of Brandt & Brandt.
2. Vance Packard, *The Naked Society* (New York: David McKay Company, 1964), p. 16.
3. *Newsweek*, 63:81–82, March 9, 1964.
4. *Ibid.*, p. 81.
5. Packard, *op. cit.*, p. 11.
6. Orwell, *op. cit.*, p. 4.
7. See, for instance, Myron Brenton, *The Privacy Invaders* (New York: Coward-McCann, 1964); Vance Packard, *The Naked Society*, previously cited.
8. Packard, *op. cit.*, p. 229.
9. "Let Me Alone," *The Christian Century*, 83:1135, September 21, 1966.
10. "When Noise Annoys," *Time*, 88:25, August 19, 1966.
11. *Ibid.*, p. 25.
12. Packard, *op. cit.*, p. 209.
13. J. D. Ratcliff, "Quiet, Please," *Reader's Digest*, 79:126, December 1961.
14. "Assault on the Ear," *Newsweek*, 67:70, April 4, 1966.
15. *City Noise* (Noise Abatement Commission, Department of Health, City of New York, 1930), p. 89.
16. Norman Cousins, "The Noise Level Is Rising," *Saturday Review*, 45:20, December 8, 1962.
17. Harvey Cox, *The Secular City* (New York: The Macmillan Company, 1965), p. 44.
18. *Ibid.*, p. 41.

19. Copyright *Newsweek*, Inc., February 24, 1964.
20. Stanley Milgram and Paul Hollander, "The Murder They Heard," *The Nation*, 198:604, June 15, 1964.

CHAPTER 17

1. "Parkscape, USA," *Audubon Magazine*, 68:416, November/December 1966.
2. William O. Douglas, "Wilderness and Human Rights," in David Brower, ed., *Wilderness: America's Living Heritage* (San Francisco: Sierra Club, 1961), p. 14.
3. See article by Robert Wernick in the Appendix, chapter 17.
4. Robert Wernick, "Let's Spoil the Wilderness," *Saturday Evening Post*, 238:12, November 6, 1965.
5. See article by Jimmy Breslin in the Appendix, chapter 9.
6. Jimmy Breslin, "Let's Quit the Suburbs," *Saturday Evening Post*, 239:10, September 24, 1966.
7. Truman B. Douglass and Constantinos A. Doxiadis, *The New World of Urban Man* (Philadelphia: United Church Press, 1965), pp. 83–84. Used by permission.
8. Wallace Stegner, letter quoted by Stewart L. Udall, "Conservation in the 1960s: Action or Stalemate?" in David Brower, *op. cit.*, p. 99.
9. Sigurd F. Olson, "The Spiritual Aspects of Wilderness," in David Brower, *op. cit.*, p. 19.
10. Wallace Stegner, Editorial, *Saturday Review*, 47:50, September 19, 1964.
11. Quoted by David R. Forbes in David Brower, *op. cit.*, p. 34.
12. Paul Tillich, *Systematic Theology* (Chicago: University of Chicago Press, 1957), Vol. II, p. 43.
13. Stewart Udall, "To Save the Wonder of the Wilderness," *The New York Times Magazine*, May 27, 1962, p. 40.
14. Joseph Wood Krutch, "Man, Nature and the Universe," *Audubon Magazine*, 64:130–132, May 1962.
15. *Time*, 89:52, January 27, 1967.
16. William G. Wing, "The Concrete Juggernaut," *Audubon Magazine*, July/August 1966, pp. 272, 268.
17. Robert H. Boyle, "America Down the Drain?" condensed from *Sports Illustrated*, © 1964 Time, Inc., *Reader's Digest*, 86:241, April 1965.
18. Stewart Udall, "The Quiet Crisis," *Saturday Review*, 46:22ff., November 23, 1963.
19. Boyle, *op. cit.*, p. 235.
20. Brooks Atkinson, "Great Swamp Is Good for Nothing," *The New York Times Magazine*, February 12, 1967, p. 42.
21. Boyle, *op. cit.*, p. 244.
22. Udall, "The Quiet Crisis," p. 52.
23. Wallace Stegner, letter quoted by Stewart Udall in David Brower, *op. cit.*, p. 97.
24. See note 3, chapter 15.

CHAPTER 18

1. Ernest Gordon, *Through the Valley of the Kwai* (New York: Harper & Row, 1962), p. 74.

2. *Ibid.*, p. 76.
3. Rachel Henderlite, *A Call to Faith* (Richmond: John Knox Press, 1955), p. 81.
4. E. L. Mascall, *The Importance of Being Human* (New York: Columbia University Press, 1958), p. 34.
5. Henderlite, *op. cit.*, p. 158.
6. Leslie D. Weatherhead, *Why Do Men Suffer?* (London: SCM Press, 1935, and Nashville: Abingdon Press, 1936), pp. 80, 81.
7. Robert L. Calhoun, *What Is Man?* (New York: Association Press, 1939), p. 13.
8. Reinhold Niebuhr, *Moral Man and Immoral Society* (New York: Charles Scribner's Sons, 1960), p. xii.
9. Henderlite, *op. cit.*, p. 158.
10. *Ibid.*, p. 65.
11. W. Norman Pittenger, *The Christian Understanding of Human Nature* (Philadelphia: The Westminster Press, 1964), pp. 42–43.
12. Henderlite, *op. cit.*, p. 67.
13. *Ibid.*, p. 70.

CHAPTER 19

1. Ernest Gordon, *Through the Valley of the Kwai* (New York: Harper & Row, 1962), p. 93.
2. *Ibid.*, p. 93.
3. *Ibid.*, p. 101.
4. *Ibid.*, pp. 101–104.
5. *Ibid.*, pp. 104–105.
6. *Ibid.*, p. 108.
7. *Ibid.*, p. 108.
8. H. Wheeler Robinson, *Suffering Human and Divine* (New York: The Macmillan Company, 1939; London: SCM Press, 1940), p. 149.
9. E. Stanley Jones, *Christ and Human Suffering* (Hodder and Stoughton, 1933), p. 180.
10. *Ibid.*, pp. 75–76.
11. Halford E. Luccock, "Exposition of Mark," *The Interpreter's Bible* (New York: Abingdon Press, 1951), VII, p. 770.
12. *Ibid.*, p. 771.
13. Robinson, *op. cit.*, p. 22.
14. Miriam Teichner, "Awareness," *Masterpieces of Religious Verse,* James Dalton Morrison, ed. (New York: Harper & Row, 1948), p. 128.
15. Gordon, *op. cit.*, p. 101.
16. *Ibid.*, p. 145.
17. Author unknown, "Calvary and Easter," *Quotable Poems,* ed., Thomas C. Clark and Esther A. Gillespie (New York: Willett, Clark & Colby, 1928), p. 243.
18. Matthew Henry, *Matthew Henry's Commentary* (New York: Fleming H. Revell Company, n.d.), V, p. 1076.
19. Marcus Dods, "The Expositor's Bible," *The Gospel of St. John* (New York: A. C. Armstrong and Son, 1898), II, pp. 35–36.
20. Gordon, *op. cit.*, p. 104.

CHAPTER 20

1. Ernest Gordon, *Through the Valley of the Kwai* (New York: Harper & Row, 1962), p. 101.
2. *Ibid.,* pp. 145–146.
3. *Ibid.,* p. 146.
4. Gerald R. Cragg, "Exposition on Romans," *The Interpreter's Bible* (New York: Abingdon Press, 1954), IX, p. 518.
5. Halford Luccock, "Exposition on Mark," *The Interpreter's Bible* (New York: Abingdon Press, 1951), VII, p. 770.
6. Gordon, *op. cit.,* p. 76.
7. Reprinted with the permission of Charles Scribner's Sons from *A Faith to Proclaim,* p. 128, by James S. Stewart. Copyright 1953, Charles Scribner's Sons.
8. Charles Dickens, *A Tale of Two Cities* (New York: Dodd, Mead & Co., 1942), p. 294.
9. *Ibid.,* p. 295.
10. *Ibid.,* p. 351.

CHAPTER 21

1. R. B. Garrison, *Portrait of the Church, Warts and All* (New York: Abingdon Press, 1964), p. 142.
2. Robert E. Fitch, *Preface to Ethical Living* (New York: Association Press, 1947).
3. J. H. Oldham, *The Church and Its Function in Society* (London: George Allen and Unwin, Ltd., 1937), p. 249.
4. Gordon Harland, *The Thought of Reinhold Niebuhr* (New York: Oxford University Press, 1960), p. 148.

APPENDIX—CHAPTER 18

1. Reinhold Niebuhr, *Moral Man and Immoral Society* (New York: Charles Scribner's Sons, 1960–Scribner Paperbacks), pp. xxii-xxiii.
2. *Ibid.,* p. 5.
3. *Ibid.,* pp. 6–7, 8, 9.

ISABEL ROGERS, born in 1924, attended Florida State University, graduating in 1945 with a B.A. in English and a Phi Beta Kappa key. She earned a Master's degree in Political Science at the University of Virginia in 1947 and an M.R.E at the Presbyterian School of Christian Education in Richmond in 1949.

After graduation from PSCE, she began work in campus ministry at Georgia State College for Women, Milledgeville, Georgia. While serving as chaplain at GSCW (now Georgia College at Milledgeville), Miss Rogers began her studies toward a Ph.D. at Duke University. She received the degree in 1961, having chosen the area of the history of Christian thought as her main emphasis.

Since 1961 Dr. Rogers has been a member of the faculty of PSCE, teaching courses in Christian ethics and historical theology. She has also written a Covenant Life Curriculum study booklet, *The Christian and World Affairs*. In 1957 she attended the Faith and Order Conference of the World Council of Churches, and in 1964 she represented the Presbyterian Church, U.S., at the World Presbyterian Alliance in Frankfurt, Germany.

Her concern for the impact of the church in society and the responsibility of churchmen for working toward social justice has led her to participation in such groups as the League of Women Voters and the Richmond Council on Human Relations.

ROBERT A. STRATTON, art director for the Covenant Life Curriculum, designed the visual pages preceding the Prologue and the Epilogue.

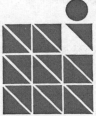

The first group of pages contains sentences selected from the first two chapters, eighteen photographs by Bruce Roberts (see below), and eighteen shapes. The seventeen triangles are isosceles right triangles, the simplest straight-sided shape. The seventeen may be construed as seven-plus-ten; seven is considered "perfect" from reference to Creation, ten as the number of human completeness. There is only one round, perfect, shape.

Just as life presents each of us with many possible choices, so this combination of shapes offers many possible arrangements. None is the "only solution." The blossoming pattern on the cover places the circle in the center, surrounded by triangles in series; three (God), six (man), eight (regeneration). All point outward.

The second group of art pages precedes the Epilogue. They are intended to recall issues and discussions of the course; they are not intended to be pondered before that point. The excerpts come from chapters 3, 18, 19, and 20 on the themes of incarnation, crucifixion, and resurrection. They are the artist's personal reflections; they are not meant to summarize the book. Other thoughts and insights should come to you, which may be more valid. The artist is looking at the subject from many angles, not one fixed-position perspective.

BRUCE ROBERTS' photographs appear frequently in national magazines. Some of the pictures used here have appeared in books published by the John Knox Press; *David,* by Nancy Roberts, the touching story of the birth and early years of their mentally retarded son; *You Can't Kill the Dream,* a gripping photo story, accompanied by essays by Malcolm Boyd and Eric Sevarid on the 1960's in America; *The Sense of Discovery; the Mountain,* by Nancy Roberts, a pictorial adventure opening the wonder of nature.